A High School Plan for Students with College-Bound Dreams

A High School Plan for Students with College-Bound Dreams

MYCHAL WYNN

Publisher's Cataloging-In-Publication Data

Wynn, Mychal.
  A high school plan for students with college-bound dreams / Mychal Wynn.

  p. : ill. ; cm.

  To be used in conjunction with A high school plan for students with college-bound dreams: workbook.
  An overview of the concepts covered in this book are given in College planning for high school students: a quick guide.
  Includes bibliographical references and index.
  ISBN-13: 978-1-880463-06-2
  ISBN-10: 1-880463-06-7

  1. Academic achievement--United States. 2. High school students--United States--Life skills guides. 3. College applications--United States--Handbooks, manuals, etc. 4. College choice--Handbooks, manuals, etc. 5. Universities and colleges--United States--Admission--Handbooks, manuals, etc. I. Title. II. Title: High school plan for students with college-bound dreams. Workbook. III. Title: College planning for high school students.

LB2350 .W961 2009
378.18/0973   2009908162

Disclaimers: The author, Mychal Wynn, or any of the content contained in this book should not in any way be construed as a representation or warranty that the reader will achieve this result. This book is designed to provide accurate and authoritative information in regard to the subject matter covered. The author and the publisher, however, make no representation or warranties of any kind with regard to the completeness or accuracy of the contents herein and accept no liability of any kind.

Credits:
Cover design by Mychal Wynn.
Student Photographs taken by Mychal Wynn.
Illustrations by Mychal-David Wynn.
Stock Photographs by Fotosearch.

Reference sources for style and usage: *The New York Public Library Writer's Guide to Style and Usage* and the *AP Stylebook, 2004.* The poem, *Be The Captain of Your Shi*p is reprinted from the book, ***Don't Quit – Inspirational Poetry*** copyright 1990 by Mychal Wynn.

RISING SUN
PUBLISHING

P.O. Box 70906
Marietta, GA 30007-0906
770.518.0369/800.524.2813
FAX 770.587.0862
E-mail: info@rspublishing.com
Web site: http://www.rspublishing.com

Printed in the United States of America.

Acknowledgments

I would like to acknowledge my wife, Nina, who, as a wife, mother, confidant, and business partner has greatly contributed to the ideas contained within this book. She has put into practice the strategies as she has successfully guided our older son's oftentimes complex and frequently frustrating journey from preschool through high school, into his acceptance via Early Decision into Amherst College. She has also inspired, enlightened, and encouraged other children and their families along their parallel journeys from preschool into college.

I would also like to thank and acknowledge the contributions of Dr. Melvyn Bassett and Dr. Glenn Bascome for their insight, ideas, and editorial review. Charles and Donna McCord, Karen McCord, Dee Blassie, Monica Obey, Dawn Small, Diane Young, and the many parents, teachers, counselors, and administrators who have shared the information, ideas, insight, and inspiration reflected in this book.

A special thanks to Pastor Raymond LeBanc, Pastor RC Hall, Yusef Harris, Toni Douglas, Barbara Mabary, Frannie Benner, Jessica Appleyard, Madge Marie Marks, Jo-Ann Duvall, Dr. Jeanelle Brown, Nancy Paule, Oscar Robinson, Pat Archibald, Greg Potts, Ms. Rosaro, Pat Craven, Kinnan Johnston, Joyce Gist, Richard Kooken, Cher Walters, Cathy Robinson, Nancy Therrien, Julie Smith, Linda Santiago, Kelly Hoban, Johnetta Haugabrook, Mr. Miller, Bruce Green, Irene Seybold, Mike Bailey, Carole Bronzino, Michaelle Labranche, Bonnie Lee, Willie Vincent, Claudia Yvette Greene, Leovan Vera, Jan Gaylord, Megan Gloede, Debra Mosley, Dr. Vicki Ferguson, Barbara Dillas, Sushila Bassett, Earl Hart, Dale Butler, Suzanne Freed, Alphonso Carreker, Greg Jones, Duane Smith, Jim King, Wayne Miller, Ako Kambon, Eric Cork, Jean Polyne, Sharon Taylor, Tony Carpenter, Theresa Dean, Duane McDonald, Tommy Cho, the coaching staff of North Springs High School, and to all of our friends and relatives. My wife and I appreciate the contribution of each of you to the growth, development, and maturation of our older son as he has navigated the oftentimes difficult road of early adolescence and emergence into manhood.

I would like to express my gratitude and appreciation to preschool, elementary, and middle school teachers who give children the social and academic foundation that nurtures their hopes and dreams. And, Reverend Kenneth Edward Marcus, Reverend Cassandra Young Marcus, Reverend Don Ezell, the Education Ministry, and the staff and members of Turner Chapel AME in Marietta, Georgia, who encourage, support, develop, inspire, and celebrate young people and their dreams.

Lastly, I would like to thank my mother and father who encouraged, sacrificed, and inspired me to become the first college graduate in our family.

Dedication

This book is dedicated to my sons, Mychal-David and Jalani, the thousands of students and parents I meet each year who have college-bound hopes and aspirations, and to those who sacrifice each day on behalf of students and their dreams.

Table of Contents

About the author . . . . *vii*

Introduction . . . . *viii*

Foreword . . . . *ix*

Overview: Who This Book is For 1

Section I: **Academics**

    Chapter 1:   Academics 30

    Chapter 2:   High School Graduation Requirements 47

    Chapter 3:   Course Work 54

    Chapter 4:   Academic Support 83

    Chapter 5:   Academic Honors. 89

    Chapter 6:   Plan Your Schedule 104

    Chapter 7:   Standardized Testing/Exit Exams 118

Section II: **Extracurricular Activities**

    Chapter 8:   Extracurricular Activities 129

Section III: **Personal Qualities**

    Chapter 9:   Personal Qualities. 150

Section IV: **Intangibles**

    Chapter 10: Intangibles 158

    Chapter 11: Your Essay 175

Section V: **Application & Financial Aid**

    Chapter 12: Financial Aid/Scholarships 188

    Chapter 13: Your Application Package. 199

    Chapter 14: Senior Year 223

Glossary 231

References 251

College-related Web Sites 255

Appendix: College Literacy Quiz Answer Key. 261

Index. 267

About the author

Mychal Wynn was an unlikely college-bound student, having been expelled from Chicago's De La Salle Catholic High School and barely earning enough credits to graduate from Chicago's Du Sable High School. Even more miraculous was his being accepted into Northeastern University, at that time, the largest private university in the United States and the only college to which he applied. Without a mentor to advise him or the benefit of the type of college planning outlined in this book, he had not taken the required courses to be admitted directly from high school into college. He received a *conditional acceptance*—conditional upon his taking and passing classes in Physics and Calculus (courses which were not offered at his high school). As a result of his not having the opportunity to take the necessary classes in high school, his college dreams were deferred as he was required to enroll in Chicago's Kennedy-King Junior College for one semester in the fall of 1974. While working the night shift at the U.S. Post Office from 10:30 p.m. until 2:30 a.m., he took classes in Physics and Calculus during the day, receiving an 'A' in Physics and a 'B' in Calculus.

In January 1975, he boarded his first airplane as he flew from Chicago, Illinois to Boston, Massachusetts, where he entered into the Northeastern University College of Engineering. In June 1979, Mychal Wynn became his family's first college graduate, receiving his Bachelor of Science degree. This once unlikely college-bound student was a highly-recruited college graduate and has worked for such multinational companies as IBM and the Transamerica Corporation. In 1985, he and his wife, Nina, founded Rising Sun Publishing, where his wife serves as the Publisher and Chief Executive Officer and he serves as the principal trainer and Chief Financial Officer.

Mr. Wynn is living his dreams as a husband, father, entrepreneur, and author of over 25 books. He, his wife, Nina, and their two sons, Mychal-David and Jalani, reside in Georgia.

Introduction

When our older son was in the first grade we were called in for a parent-teacher conference. His teacher was concerned with his lack of concentration and his continual failure to complete his class work. As an example, she showed my wife and me worksheets that were completely blank, with the exception of stick people running up the right side of the page, stick airplanes flying across the page, and stick people parachuting down the left side of the page. My wife and I, in collaboration with his classroom teacher, developed a series of strategies to not only get our son to complete more of his class work, but to provide greater opportunities to nurture his passion for "stick people."

Over the ensuing years, my wife and I developed the type of comprehensive plan contained in this book to help nurture our son's passion for drawing while ensuring that he had a well-rounded and rigorous academic schedule that provided a broad range of college opportunities. Subsequently, he not only had a choice of some of the country's top-ranked art schools like the Savannah College of Art and Design and the Art Center College of Design in Pasadena, California, he was a candidate for such Ivy League schools as Yale and Dartmouth, and was admitted into his first-choice, Amherst College.

Our younger son is now in high school and well into his college-bound plan. As a fourth-grader he visited several colleges and proclaimed, "I want to go to Yale" after listening to an admissions officer describe Yale's residential philosophy of creating a family environment where the same students live together for their entire four years.

I have written this book because I believe that every student deserves to be nurtured in the pursuit of his or her dreams and if those dreams include college, then every student needs a plan. Those who need to quickly scan through the book or focus on important points should look for the hand symbol.

Foreword

Students and families may question, "Is 9th grade too early to begin planning for college? Is that something you do during your junior year [of high school]?" It is never too late to begin developing your college plan; however, it is also never too early! In some school districts your high school plan has already been greatly influenced by your elementary and middle school academic record or performance on standardized testing. For example, in one school district, a student must earn A's and B's in 4th and 5th grade to be placed into the AT (Academically Talented) middle school classes; in another school district, students' 4th-grade CTBS (Comprehensive Tests of Basic Skills) scores determine middle school math and science placement; and, in another school district, placement into the Talented and Gifted program is determined by students' 3rd-grade ITBS (Iowa Tests of Basic Skills) scores.

Your 6th-grade math placement may have already determined the highest level of math you will be able to take in high school! As you enter into the 9th grade, the scope of the colleges and the majors to which you will be able to apply may have already been determined. A student interested in studying engineering in college may have had the opportunity to take Pre-Algebra (6th grade), Algebra I (7th grade), Geometry (8th grade), and four years of high school math that may include Algebra II, Pre-Calculus, AP Calculus, and AP Statistics. Good grades in such classes will put a student on track to apply to a broad range of colleges and universities, whereas the student who does not enroll into advanced math until the 9th grade will have very different course selections (e.g., Algebra I, Geometry, Algebra II, and Algebra III/Trigonometry), which may not meet some colleges' admissions requirements.

In addition to the academic schedule available to students based on their performance in elementary school, many families find that to ensure they have enough money set aside to contribute to a student's college tuition, room, and board (which may amount to tens of thousands of dollars each year of college) they have to begin saving for college BEFORE their children enter preschool or before their children are even born!

Some may ask, "Why all of this fuss about college planning? I know people who did not graduate from college and they have good jobs?" In today's competitive workplace the quality of your education will enhance your ability to follow your dreams and enter into the type of career that you really want. As a young person growing up in the 21st century, you have much to encourage you. There are more jobs and career opportunities for college graduates than there are people to fill them. Every year, companies and organizations throughout the world have to recruit teachers, doctors, lawyers, nurses, policemen, business managers, hotel workers, computer technicians, and bankers. Opportunities are everywhere and you must consider yourself more than just a resident of your local community, town, city, state, or country. An education opens up the gateway to the world— to opportunities that will be yours—if you are qualified to pursue them! The opportunities for college graduates are virtually endless!

There are many books and resources that can help you to make a decision on choosing a college. There are, for example, reviews and rankings of colleges and universities by *Newsweek, U.S. News and World Reports, The Princeton Review, The Kaplan College Guide,* international publications, and Internet web sites. You also have your parents, middle school and high school counselors, and many private agencies to assist you in making your college choice based on your interests and career aspirations.

This book, the second in the College Planning series, provides guidance through the high school years to assist you, the student, or parents, teachers, counselors, coaches, and mentors in developing a high school plan that will make you a strong candidate for admissions into a top college and prepared to succeed once you get there. Following the advice and strategies outlined will help to ensure that a student's dreams of attending college will not be delayed, deferred, or destroyed, as a result of not knowing how to maximize his or her opportunities by taking advantage of the wide range of programs and opportunities available during the high school years.

As this book was being written, the author's older son played varsity football and ran the 400 Meter on his high school varsity track and field team. Not many high school track and field athletes choose to run the 400 Meter. It is a tough race that requires sprinting ability and endurance. A successful race requires a good game plan, i.e., a strong start during the first 20 meters, sprinting while pacing yourself through the next 80 meters, breaking into a steady stride through the 200-meter mark, using your momentum to carry you around the curve through the 300-meter mark, and conserving enough energy to carry you into a full sprint during the final 100 meters.

Pursuing your dreams of attending college is going to require sprinting, steadying your pace, endurance, and a strong finish. If you are diligent at following the steps outlined in each chapter, completing the high school-planning worksheets in the *workbook*, responsibly doing your schoolwork, and making a notable contribution to your high school and local community, you will be on your way to a successful high school experience. In addition, you will develop a strong foundation that will prepare you for college success.

Remember that part of your planning must include financing the cost of college tuition, room, and board. You and your parents must begin this aspect of college preparation as soon as possible, if you have not already done so. There are thousands of scholarships, fellowships, grants, and low-interest loans available to assist young people in the pursuit of their college-bound dreams.

If you have a passion or talent in areas such as academics, sports, art, music, writing, public speaking, dance, drama, or automotive mechanics you must continue to explore every opportunity to showcase and develop your talent. Today's passion may become tomorrow's career or it may be the means of paying your way through college—the route taken by many students who have received scholarships to college because of their academic attainments, sporting abilities, creative or artistic talent, or their noteworthy contribution to their school or community.

There is an enormous amount of information, as well as many opportunities and support programs to pave the way for any student to attend college. In essence, there are no excuses!

Mychal Wynn
Author
Educational Consultant

Glenn Bascome, Ed.D.
Director/Dame Marjorie Bean Education Center
Sandys Secondary Middle School
Somerset, Bermuda

A High School Plan for Students with College-Bound Dreams

Overview

American higher education offers more colleges than any other system in the world, with more variety in disciplines and professional training, but a student who doesn't like the school she chose for her first year can, assuming she keeps her grades up, can easily transfer. High school students who bite their tongues and actually listen to what college counselors say on this matter will learn that being crowned by Ivy has little, if any, bearing on whether they will fulfill their dreams of love, power and wealth. Character traits–such as persistence, optimism and honesty– established long before anyone takes the SAT or the ACT–are far more crucial.

— *[Newsweek: How to Get into College, 2001 Edition]*

Who This Book is For

First and foremost, as the title implies, this book has been written for students with college-bound dreams. While thousands of students affirm college-bound dreams, far too many are not aware of the importance of using their four years of high school to prepare for college, make themselves a competitive candidate in the admissions process, or do what is necessary to acquire enough financial aid to pay the huge cost of college tuition, room, and board.

Within this group of students are highly-motivated young people who are enrolled in all honors and AP classes and yet have no extracurricular activities or community service to supplement their stellar academic credentials; students who are involved in sports and extracurricular activities, but who are taking the easiest possible academic schedule (and still putting forth only enough effort to be 'C' students); and students who are saying they plan to go to college, but who

Notes:

do not have any idea as to what is needed, how much work is involved, or how to prepare themselves to succeed should they successfully navigate the many hurdles of meeting their high school graduation requirements and admission criteria to a major college or university.

No matter which group of students you fall into, where you want to go to college, where your parent(s) want you to go to college, or where your counselors, coaches, aunts, uncles, mentors, or best friends are encouraging you to go to college, this book has been written to assist you or those who are supporting and encouraging you in the pursuit of your college-bound dreams.

What This Book is Going To Do

This book is designed to work hand-in-hand with the *workbook*. Together, they will outline what you need to do and allow you to track your progress during your four years of high school. They will also assist you in developing your plan by outlining what information you should ask for at your high school, gather from other books, and research on the Internet. Parents or mentors who are supporting you will better understand the type of questions they should ask and discussions they should have with your high school guidance counselor, who is perhaps the most important source of information in developing your high school schedule and college-bound plan.

This, the first chapter, is an overview of what follows. The remaining chapters are designed to help you develop or fine-tune your college-bound plans. While this book will provide an ongoing reference, the *workbook* provides the worksheets to set goals, track progress, gather important information, and organize yourself for the big day when you prepare your college application packages.

If you are a ninth-grader, you are probably more concerned with making friends, finding your way around, finding your niche (the group of people with whom you will begin identifying), and your clique (the group of people with whom you socialize) than you are with putting together your college plan. However, you must do both—enjoy your high school experience while at the same time remain focused on your college-bound plan.

The three primary areas of focus for a college-bound student are:

1. Meeting your high school graduation requirements.

2. Becoming a strong candidate for admissions to your first-choice colleges and being prepared to succeed academically once you get there.

3. Meeting your EFC (Expected Family Contribution) for college tuition, room, and board.

There will be two additional areas of focus for the recruited college-bound athlete:

4. Registering with the NCAA Clearinghouse and meeting the NCAA qualifications for a student-athlete.

5. Developing an athletic profile/portfolio specific to your sport.

The primary purpose of this book is number two, *Becoming a strong candidate for admissions to your first-choice college and being prepared to succeed academically once you get there*. There are four broad categories, that will ultimately, determine how successful you are in developing your college-bound plan.

Notes:

Section I: Academics

- Meeting high school graduation requirements
- Meeting college admission standards
- Course work
- Grades
- Class rank
- High School Profile
- SAT, SAT Subject Tests, ACT, and AP exam scores
- Awards, honors, noteworthy academic achievements and recognition

Section II: Extracurricular Activities

- Sports
- Clubs
- Student organizations
- Community service
- Volunteer hours
- Work experience

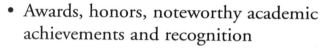

Section III: Personal Qualities

- Essay
- Interview
- Recommendations
- Contribution to your school community
- Unique artistic, musical, athletic, mathematical, or public speaking talent
- Personal achievements, e.g., overcoming adversity, resiliency, integrity, worthy ideals, or innovation

Section IV: Intangibles

- Ethnicity
- Gender
- Family background

- Geographical area
- Involvement in a club or activity for which the college has a unique need, e.g., genius-level I.Q., classical pianist, point guard, martial arts instructor, swimmer, or 400-meter sprinter

The chapters that follow are organized into these four sections followed by a fifth and final section outlining the all-important process of preparing your admissions package.

Section V: Application & Financial Aid

Parents who already have children in college and students with older siblings or relatives who have gone to college will have a clear advantage over students who are the first in their family to attend college. Students from private schools, where counselors have smaller student-counselor ratios, will have an advantage over public school students where counselors are responsible for working with several hundred students. Despite such advantages or disadvantages, every student will benefit from a plan and every parent will benefit from developing college preparations to reduce the stress and increase the joy of a student's four years of high school.

Developing your high school plan will require that you make a favorable impression in as many areas of the admissions criteria as possible. In essence, your application package must provide an admissions officer, whom you do not know, enough information about your academic potential, character, and ability to contribute to his or her

school community that he or she is willing to recommend to an admissions committee that you be accepted into the

Notes:

college's freshman class. At some colleges, that would mean that your application is placed ahead of 5,000, 10,000, or even 15,000 other applications.

This book is about giving the admissions officer enough information so that he or she will be inspired to make a case for you to be admitted into his or her college. However, before you can expect someone whom you do not know to believe in you, you have to believe in yourself. You have to believe that if you apply yourself, as best as you can toward the strategies and ideas that follow, you will be deserving of admission into college so that you may continue the pursuit of your dreams.

Test your knowledge of the college admissions process. On the following pages is a College Literacy Quiz pertaining to some of the terms and topics to be covered in subsequent chapters. The answers to the quiz can be found in the Appendix.

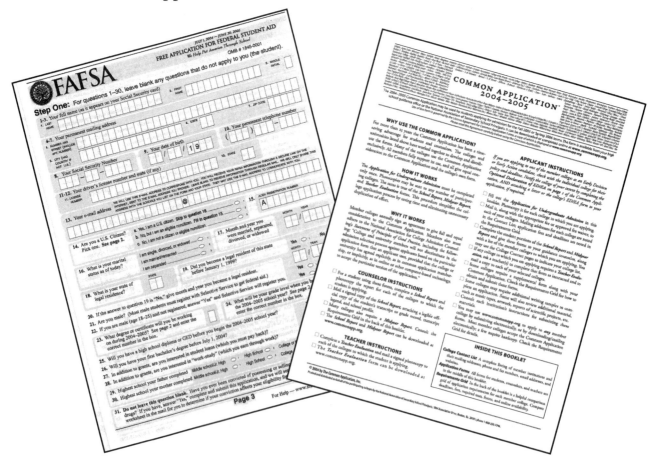

College Literacy Quiz

1. What are AP and IB courses?

2. When are AP exams given and what scores typically qualify for college credit?

3. Who administers the AP and IB Programs?

4. What does the 'weight,' of such courses mean?

5. Is the Ivy League an athletic or academic grouping of colleges?

6. How many colleges make up the Ivy League?

7. What does HBCU stand for?

8. How many HBCUs are there?

9. What is the difference between the SAT, SAT Subject Test, and the ACT and what is the top score for each exam?

10. How many times can you take the SAT and ACT?

11. Which type of high school classes will best prepare you for success on the Critical Reading and Writing Sections of the SAT?

12. What advantage, if any, is there to taking the SAT or ACT more than once?

13. What does PSAT stand for and in which grade (i.e., 9th, 10th, 11th, or 12th) do the scores qualify students as National Merit or National Achievement Scholars?

14. What does GPA mean?

15. What is a weighted GPA?

Notes:

16. With what organization does a college-bound athlete have to register?

17. What is the significance of taking classes for high school credit while in middle school?

18. What is joint enrollment?

19. What is the significance of taking advanced math classes in middle school?

20. What is the most important academic skill that colleges want incoming students to demonstrate?

21. Does a student from a top private school have a significantly better chance of being admitted to college over a student from an average public high school?

22. What are complementary sports and how can they increase your college admissions opportunities?

23. Will being a top academic achiever and having high SAT/ACT scores guarantee that you will be accepted into the college of your choice?

24. Will average grades and average SAT/ACT scores guarantee that you will not be accepted into the college of your choice?

25. Who is a legacy student?

26. What is FAFSA, why is it important, and when should you complete it?

27. What is EFC?

28. What is Need-based—Need-blind admissions?

29. What is an articulation agreement?

30. How many colleges can a student apply to under the Early Decision program?

What You Have to Do

All of the information contained within this book, resources and web sites to which you will be referred, and ideas and strategies are directed toward the singular mission of attending and graduating from college. As you progress through the book, refer to the *workbook* and complete the forms and track your grades and test scores. As a high school student you do not have to have a perfect plan. You do not have to know what you want to study, what career you want to pursue, or even what you aspire to do after graduating from college. You do, however, need a general sense of the type of college experience you want and the amount of work you are willing to do.

Begin with the End in Mind

What are your dreams and aspirations—the places you want to go, things you want to experience, changes you want to make in your home, community, or in the world itself? Where do you find your joy? What type of people do you prefer being around? What type of job would you do even if you did not get paid to do it? Or, better yet, what is your purpose? Are you passionate about music, art, science, math, sports, or social issues? Do you prefer working with people or  in isolation? Do you have a passion to coach on the field or run front-office operations? Do you have a passion to teach elementary school children or inspire college students? Would you prefer to write a book, give a lecture, or both?

Notes:

Answering such questions as you enter high school will help you to identify the classes that will expand your knowledge, nurture your passions, and best prepare you for the college experience you are interested in pursuing.

Answering such questions will also greatly enhance your college search as you begin looking for and focusing on colleges that will provide you with the opportunity to pursue your dreams and aspirations. While many students think in terms of attending their "dream college," you will be on your way to attending the "college that will help you to pursue your dreams."

In the book, *Follow Your Dreams: Lessons That I Learned in School,* I share my experiences growing up in poverty and  the academic, social, and emotional struggles experienced from elementary through high school. I thought you went to college so you could get a good job. Subsequently, I entered college in the pursuit of a career (electrical engineering). However, a college education enabled me to do more than just get a job, it enabled me to discover and pursue my second-grade passion—writing and talking! If I had known that my elementary school passions could have become my career, I would have chosen different high school classes, a different college major, and explored a much broader range of colleges and universities.

Your dreams, and the colleges that may best help you to pursue those dreams should guide your efforts in planning your high school schedule of classes, extracurricular activities, and involvement in student and community organizations.

Your Life List

The book, *Chicken Soup for the Soul*, shares the story of a young boy, who, at fifteen years old sat down at his kitchen table in Los Angeles, California, and wrote three words at the top of a yellow pad: 'My Life List.' On his Life List, John Goddard, an adventurer and explorer, wrote 127 goals. On the following pages is this fifteen-year-old's list of his 127 life goals. Few people would create such a list; fewer yet would even know the type of things that are on the list. However, all of us, perhaps not as extensively, can develop our own life list.

After reviewing this comprehensive and extensive list, take a moment to reflect on what your life list would be. Use the following questions to guide you:

1. What would you like to explore?

2. What would you like to study?

3. Where would you like to visit?

4. What would you like to accomplish?

After answering such questions and developing your own life list, try to answer the following:

What type of college experience would help you to pursue the things on your list?

Life List of a Fifteen-year-old

Explore:

*1.   Nile River
*2.   Amazon River
*3.   Congo River
*4.   Colorado River
5.   Yangtze River, China
6.   Niger River
7.   Orinoco River, Venezuela
*8.   Rio Coco, Nicaragua

Study Cultures In:

*9.   The Congo
*10.   New Guinea
*11.   Brazil
*12.   Borneo
*13.   The Sudan (nearly buried alive in a sandstorm)
*14.   Australia
*15.   Kenya
*16.   The Philippines
*17.   Tanganyika (now Tanzania)
*18.   Ethiopia
*19.   Nigeria
*20.   Alaska

Climb:

21.   Mount Everest
22.   Mount Aconcagua, Argentina
23.   Mount McKinley
*24.   Mount Huascaran, Peru
*25.   Mount Kilimanjaro
*26.   Mount Ararat, Turkey

* Indicates items that have been completed or achieved.

*27. Mount Kenya
28. Mount Cook, New Zealand
*29. Mount Popocatepetl, Mexico
*30. The Matterhorn
*31. Mount Rainier
*32. Mount Fuji
*33. Mount Vesuvius
*34. Mount Bromo, Java
*35. Grand Tetons
*36. Mount Baldy, California

Do:

*37. Carry out careers in medicine and exploration (studied pre-med and treats illnesses among primitive tribes)
38. Visit every country in the world (30 to go)
*39. Study Navaho and Hopi Indians
*40. Learn to fly a plane
*41. Ride horse in Rose Parade

Photograph:

*42. Iguaçu Falls, Brazil
*43. Victoria Falls, Rhodesia (chased by a warthog in the process)
*44. Sutherland Falls, New Zealand
*45. Yosemite Falls
*46. Niagara Falls
*47. Retrace travels of Marco Polo and Alexander the Great

Explore Underwater:

*48. Coral reefs of Florida
*49. Great Barrier Reef, Australia (photographed a 300-pound clam)

* Indicates items that have been completed or achieved.

Notes:

*50. Red Sea

*51. Fiji Islands

*52. The Bahamas

*53. Explore Okefenokee Swamp and the Everglades

Visit:

54. North and South Poles

*55. Great Wall of China

*56. Panama and Suez Canals

*57. Easter Island

*58. The Galapagos Islands

*59. Vatican City (saw the pope)

*60. The Taj Mahal

*61. The Eiffel Tower

*62. Blue Grotto

*63. The Tower of London

*64. The Leaning Tower of Pisa

*65. The Sacred Well of Chicken-Itza, Mexico

*66. Climb Ayers Rock in Australia

67. Follow river Jordan from Sea of Galilee to Dead Sea

Swim In:

*68. Lake Victoria

*69. Lake Superior

*70. Lake Tanganyika

*71. Lake Titicaca, South America

*72. Lake Nicaragua

Accomplish:

*73. Become an Eagle Scout

*74. Dive in a submarine

*75. Land on and take off from an aircraft carrier

*76. Fly in a blimp, hot air balloon and glider

* Indicates items that have been completed or achieved.

*77.   Ride an elephant, camel, ostrich and bronco

*78.   Skin dive to 40 feet and hold breath two and a half
         minutes underwater

*79.   Catch a ten-pound lobster and a ten-inch abalone

*80.   Play flute and violin

*81.   Type 50 words a minute

*82.   Take a parachute jump

*83.   Learn water and snow skiing

*84.   Go on a church mission

*85.   Follow the John Muir Trail

*86.   Study native medicines and bring back useful ones

*87.   Bag camera trophies of elephant, lion, rhino, cheetah,
         Cape buffalo and whale

*88.   Learn to fence

*89.   Learn jujitsu

*90.   Teach a college course

*91.   Watch a cremation ceremony in Bali

*92.   Explore depths of the sea

93.   Appear in a Tarzan movie (he now considers this an
         irrelevant boyhood dream)

94.   Own a horse, chimpanzee, cheetah, ocelot and coyote
         (yet to own a chimp or cheetah)

95.   Become a ham radio operator

*96.   Build own telescope

*97.   Write a book (on Nile trip)

*98.   Publish an article in National Geographic Magazine

*99.   High jump five feet

*100. Broad jump 15 feet

*101. Run a mile in five minutes

*102. Weigh 175 pounds stripped (still does)

*103. Perform 200 sit-ups and 20 pull-ups

*104. Learn French, Spanish and Arabic

105.   Study dragon lizards on Komodo Island (boat broke
         down within 20 miles of island)

*106. Visit birthplace of Grandfather Sorenson in Denmark

* Indicates items that have been completed or achieved.

Notes:

Notes:

*107. Visit birthplace of Grandfather Goddard in England

*108. Ship aboard a freighter as a seaman

109. Read the entire Encyclopedia Britannica (has read extensive parts in each volume)

*110. Read the Bible from cover to cover

*111. Read the works of Shakespeare, Plato, Aristotle, Dickens, Thoreau, Poe, Rousseau, Bacon, Hemingway, Twain, Burroughs, Conrad, Talmage, Tolstoi, Longfellow, Keats, Whittier and Emerson (not every work of each)

*112. Become familiar with the compositions of Bach, Beethoven, Debussy, Ibert, Mendelssohn, Lalo, Rimski-Korsakov, Respighi, Liszt, Rachmaninoff, Stravinsky, Toch, Tschaikovsky, Verdi

*113. Become proficient in the use of a plane, motorcycle, tractor, surfboard, rifle, pistol, canoe, microscope, football, basketball, bow and arrow, lariat and boomerang

*114. Compose music

*115. Play Claire de lune on the piano

*116. Watch fire-walking ceremony (in Bali and Surinam)

*117. Milk a poisonous snake (bitten by a diamond back during a photo session)

*118. Light a match with a .22 rifle

*119. Visit a movie studio

*120. Climb Cheops' pyramid

*121. Become a member of the Explorers' Club and the Adventurers' Club

*122. Learn to play polo

*123. Travel through the Grand Canyon on foot and by boat

*124. Circumnavigate the globe (four times)

125. Visit the moon ("Someday if God wills")

*126. Marry and have children (has five children)

*127. Live to see the 21st Century (he will be 75)

* Indicates items that have been completed or achieved.

What Do You Want Out of College?

Notes:

While there are many resources to assist you in evaluating, assessing, and choosing a college, here are some suggestions to consider as you begin gathering information:

1. Make a list of things you most enjoy doing, e.g., traveling, shopping, sports, surfing, roller skating, music, dressing up, dressing down, cooking, eating, telling jokes, talking on the phone, socializing, dancing, solving puzzles, writing poetry, drawing cartoons, playing computer games, lifting weights, studying martial arts, running marathons, sailing, flying an airplane, camping, fishing, golfing, competing, creating, etc.

2. Make a list of the type of people and places you enjoy, e.g., large crowds, small groups, debating/discussing political and social issues, attending concerts or sporting events, bodybuilding, theatrical performances, building businesses, working on an assembly-line, pursuing a spiritual journey, attending social functions, exploring and discovering, creating and developing, living in a penthouse, living on a farm, etc.

3. Make a list of the types of careers that will allow you to do those things on your first list and work with the type of people or live in the places on your second list.

Another approach to this activity would be to get a poster board, together with magazines and pictures that depict your interests, and create a collage of words and images that reflect your hopes and dreams.

Use these three lists or your collage to guide your college search!

Notes:

Rather than choosing Harvard, Yale, or Princeton because they are part of the Ivy League—MIT, Stanford, Caltech, or Duke because they are on everyone's top-ten list—Spelman, Fisk, Howard, or FAMU because they are some of the most renowned HBCUs—choose a college that will allow you to pursue your passions, surround you with the type of people you enjoy, and nurture your intellectual development, creative capacity, and social consciousness. In essence, carefully choose a place to live, grow, and enjoy life for the four years following high school.

Why Would a College Want to Admit You?

The question for you to ask yourself as you begin the process of developing your high school plan is, "Four years from now, why would a college want to admit me into its freshman class? What will be special about me and what will I be able to contribute to its school community?"

Asking that question as you enter high school will help you to better understand how to take advantage of the many programs and opportunities available at your high school and accessible to aspiring college students over the course of your four-year high school experience. Whether you are passionate about athletics, politics, dance, music, science, mathematics, journalism, poetry, art, philosophy, social issues, technology, or speech and debate, your high school years will have a significant impact on the scope and depth of the college application packages that you prepare as a high school junior and senior. Entering high school with the passionate desire to pursue something, become something, discover something, change something, or fulfill some purpose will guide your intellectual, spiritual, moral, physical, and creative development in ways, that, four years from now, will enable you to sit in a college interview and say, "I have had a passion to do ... since I entered high school; this is what I have done and why I want to continue my studies at your college."

This focus will provide the framework for all the work that follows. Your academic record, extracurricular activities, community service, employment history, teacher recommendations, awards, and achievements will all provide testimony to the pursuit of your passions and the discovery of your dreams.

Michele A. Hernandez, former Assistant Director of Admissions at Dartmouth College, notes in her book, *A is for Admission*:

> *With perhaps some rare exceptions, neither position, nor wealth, nor an elite prep school, nor connections can single-handedly guarantee admission to an Ivy League school. In fact, some of these factors could work against the applicant in the Ivy admissions process. There is never anyone who is guaranteed admission. There are cases of valedictorians with double 800 SATs who are not admitted into their top-choice colleges, just as there are lower-ranked students with mid-500 scores who are admitted.*

The uniqueness of your school performance, extracurricular activities, standardized test scores, hobbies, interests, leadership abilities, personal achievements, race, gender, culture, family background, and life experiences not only define who you are, but make a statement as to why you are different. Many prep school students, whose families have provided access into the most prestigious private schools, private tutors, thousands of dollars in SAT/ACT prep classes, travel abroad, and access to the most powerful and influential people in America, are exasperated at the thought of a low-income, unprivileged student, from a low-performing school, with average SAT/ACT scores being admitted into "their" first-choice school while they, themselves, are denied admissions!

If you are a prep school student, do not allow yourself to become one of the prep school carbon copies, one of the masses of students who dress alike (even when they are not

Notes:

wearing their uniforms), talk alike, read the same books, participate in the same clubs, propagate the same ideas, enroll in the same classes, play the same sports, and earn nearly the same grades and SAT scores. Do not become an undeniably great student, but fail to distinguish yourself in any meaningful way from the millions of other great students. Whether you are an affluent private school student or an impoverished public school student, you must develop a plan that distinguishes you from your peers, defines who you are, and, most importantly, who you have the potential to become.

Resist the temptation to follow the crowd or to blend in while attending high school. Four years from now, you will be attempting to separate yourself from the masses of college applicants. The best colleges are looking for a diverse student population—one that represents a broad spectrum of gender, ethnicity, culture, talents, interests, abilities, ideas, opinions, and passions.

Important Relationships

Developing and executing an effective high school plan will require that you build relationships with several groups of people. Colleges will evaluate your application in part based

on recommendations from your teachers and counselor; your meaningful involvement in clubs, organizations, school and community service projects; and your involvement in sports, band, cheerleading, or other special-interest activities. The relationships you develop with tutors and study groups will also greatly contribute to your academic success throughout high school.

Typically, students begin pulling away from parents during middle school and oftentimes push parents away during ninth and tenth grades. Resist the temptation to follow this

path as your relationship with your parent(s) may represent the most important bond of all. The open and honest communication with your parent(s) is critical to your successfully dealing with the many

decisions that you must make during your four years of high school. Drugs, alcohol, cigarettes, sex, and even driving or riding in an automobile represent but a few of the many daily decisions that could delay, deny, or destroy your college-bound dreams. Each school day students are becoming pregnant, becoming infected with AIDS or STDs, dying of drug overdoses, committing suicide, engaging in violent conflicts with other students, and being killed or injured in

Notes:

automobile accidents due to their decisions or those of their peers—decisions that may have been different if students had open communication with a parent or concerned adult.

As a writer and consultant I have to travel often. However, when I am not traveling, I make a point of driving my older son to school and taking time to talk to him each day after school. We talk about his classes, friends, football practice, hopes, and dreams. We do not always agree, yet we always find time to talk. He does not share everything that is going on in his life, but he knows that I am always willing to listen.

Prepare for the Work Ahead

Preparing for the work ahead requires that you establish a place to store all of your high school information as well as all of the college and financial-aid information you gather over the next four years.

- Set up a binder and label it "College Planning Notebook."

You are going to use this binder to store such information as grades, test scores, awards, and recommendations received throughout high school and to which you will refer when applying for scholarships and putting together your college admissions packages.

- Set up four file folders for:
    - Academics
    - Programs & Camps
    - Scholarships
    - Awards, Competitions, & Internships

- Set up two boxes for:
    - College Information
    - Financial-Aid Information

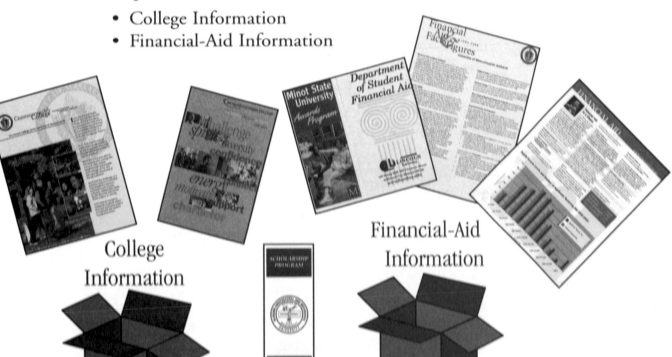

Notes:

Identify Your Team

If you are planning on going to college, then you need to affirm that you are going to college. This means that you have to begin talking about college to your family, friends, teachers, counselors, coaches, mentors, and tutors. The more you talk about college, the more information people with share with you. The more they will confirm or challenge what you think about college, what you are thinking about doing with your life, and whether or not what you are doing now is consistent with where you say you are planning to go. In the book, *Follow Your Dreams: Lessons That I Learned in School*, I described four groups of students at my high school and the choices they were making:

In the eleventh grade I began to see four groups of people beginning to develop in school. One group was made up of students who were working hard, getting good grades, and planning to go to a four-year college or university. Another group was talking about a trade school, junior college or joining the armed forces (Army, Navy, Marines, Air Force). The third group wasn't talking about anything and didn't have a clue about what they were going to do when they graduated. Maybe they would get married, get a job or just stay at home until they either figured out what to do or their parents forced them to get out. The fourth group was just chill'in and hanging out. They were the gang bangers, street hustlers or thugs. Most of them had been to jail or were going to jail. Many people in this group didn't believe that they were going to live past 21, so they weren't planning on a long future and they weren't making good decisions. The only thing that each of these four groups had in common was that all of the people within each of these groups got to choose whether or not to join that particular group. Some people have more choices than others, but they all had a choice.

Your high school counselor (or in some cases a mentor or private counselor) is going to be one of the most important people with whom to share your college dreams. Along with this book, he or she should become an invaluable source of information. It is your counselor's job to provide you with, or direct you to, the information you need to fulfill your college aspirations. Your counselor may be able to make your work a lot easier by identifying where to get the information you need, assisting in completing the necessary financial-aid forms, and ensuring you fulfill your high school graduation requirements. Eventually, you will have to turn your college application packages in to your counselor, who will have to order and enclose your high school transcript prior to mailing your materials to the colleges to which you apply. In addition to identifying your counselor's information, each U.S. high school has a school code that will be required on college applications; on your SAT, SAT Subject Test, and ACT registrations; the NCAA Clearinghouse forms; and financial-aid forms.

Notes:

Working with friends, booster clubs, mentoring programs, organizations, places of worship, and other families will allow you to accomplish much more than by working alone. Develop teams or committees to focus on specific areas:

- College Admissions

- College Fairs

- Scholarships

- Summer Camps

- Internships

- Recruited-athletes

- College Programs for Juniors and Seniors

- Special Interest Programs (e.g., athletics, arts, music, math, science, literary, leadership, etc.)

- Local, National, and International Competitions

- Tutors

- SAT, SAT Subject Test, PSAT, and ACT Prep Programs

- Organizing the Application Packages

Put Yourself in a Position to Be Blessed

As you prepare to develop your high school plan, keep in mind that no matter what you do, you may simply be blessed with a highly unusual opportunity. Thousands of students are contacted by or admitted into a particular college, but not because they are among the highest ranked, have the highest GPA, or have followed the strategies outlined in this book. They are blessed to attract the attention of the college—they play a particular position on an athletic team, they play a musical instrument and the college orchestra is in need of a violinist, they helped a little old lady across the street and her son happened to be a college admissions officer, they received national notoriety as the result of a heroic act, their parent attended the college, their uncle belongs to the same country club as the college's president, their family donated a new athletic facility, or their parents are celebrities. Whatever the reason, you may be one of those students who get *invited* to a particular college or university.

If such a situation presents itself, you want to be in a position to take advantage of the opportunity.

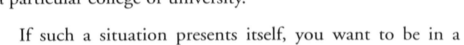

There were twins who, as football players, were offered full academic scholarships to Duke University (at a current value of $37,555 per year each). Unfortunately, while both young men had worked hard during their four years of high school in preparing to be successful at football, neither had focused on preparing for college. Neither had taken the SAT and neither had registered with the NCAA Clearinghouse.

Unfortunately, they were unable to enroll at Duke University, the dream school of thousands of aspiring college students, and take advantage of the opportunity of receiving over $300,000.00 in scholarships ($150,220.00 each).

As you begin high school, imagine beginning an NBA or WNBA career. Every pass, steal, free throw, three-pointer, blocked shot, and playoff game—every statistic is going to become part of your permanent NBA/WNBA stat sheet. Your college application package will represent your high school stat sheet—SAT/ACT scores, class rank, GPA, course work, extracurricular activities, recommendation letters, job history, summer camps, special programs, and awards.

As NFL, NHL, NBA, WNBA, and Major League Baseball players track their statistics, so too, must you track of your statistics as you go through high school. When you go into a college interview, you should be able to point out your strengths and explain your weaknesses. You should know your GPA, test scores, and class rank as a baseball player knows his batting average, walks, strikeouts, stolen bases, and errors.

A friend of mine graduated from USC (University of Southern California). He attended a prestigious, highly competitive, Catholic high school in Los Angeles, California. Students from his high school are routinely accepted into their first-choice colleges. When his children were in the third and fourth grades he donated $50,000.00 to his former high school to establish a scholarship fund, virtually guaranteeing that his children would be accepted when they applied in the 9th grade. He also knew that 'legacy' children (children whose parent(s) graduated from the college where students are applying) nearly always receive preferred status during the admissions process. Whether or not his children are among the highest academic achievers, they are virtually guaranteed admission into one of the country's best high schools and will have a clear advantage of being accepted into one of the country's best universities.

Develop your plan and prepare yourself to be blessed.

Section I
Academics

30

Chapter 1

Performance in a rigorous curriculum is the single most important aspect of the college application. Colleges want to see a challenging course load through the senior year and an incoming GPA commensurate with their average incoming GPA (3.7, un-weighted at Emory). Emory bases many of its decisions on the history of the high school and on the student's performance in relation to that context.

— *[Rock Hard Apps]*

Academics

There is a reason that the first area of focus in your high school plan is academics and not because it falls first in alphabetical order. Your high school transcript is the most important part of your application package. Whether you are a star athlete, president of the student council, brilliant musician, or most popular student in your high school, college success, ultimately, comes down to your ability to successfully complete the course work.

Athletics, leadership positions, creative or artistic talent, awards and community involvement may all influence the final decision of a college admissions committee; however, once you are accepted, you will have to complete the course work to receive your college degree. In the final analysis, your academic ability is still the most important aspect of your college preparation. Far too many aspiring athletes discount or dismiss class work as they put all of their eggs into the proverbial professional sports basket. For every successful NBA player there are over one hundred thousand aspiring high school athletes who will never play at that level. Not to mention that for every professional athlete who develops star talent and is subsequently rewarded with countless millions of dollars in a professional sports contract, there are far too many who squander their money and their extraordinary opportunity because they lack the education and critical-thinking skills to manage, invest, and secure their financial future.

Do not become one of the thousands of high school students for whom academics is an afterthought. Do not spend your 9th-, 10th-, and 11th-grade years focusing exclusively on being popular, hanging out with the "in" crowd, playing sports, and enjoying the high school social experience so much that you forget about the most important prerequisite of college admissions—grades and course work!

Your academic performance include:

- Meeting high school graduation requirements (which may include passing high school exit exams)

- Meeting college admissions standards

- Course work, grades, class ranking, and high school profile

- SAT, SAT Subject Test, ACT, AP, or IB exam scores

- Awards, honors, noteworthy academic achievements and recognition

Begin with a College Focus

It is important to begin high school with a college focus. Whether you are considering going into the military, pursuing a trade, or simply getting a job after high school, you should begin high school with a college focus. Doing so will ensure that you do as much as possible to prepare yourself for college

Notes:

Develop a college-bound wall or room. Decorate the wall or room with:

- *Pennant flags*

- *College mascots*

- *Brochures*

- *Sample forms*

- *Newspaper articles*

- *College-related periodicals*

- *Map of schools attended by former students, staff, mentors, and mentees*

Notes:

Median Weekly Earnings in 2008

Level of Education

Doctoral: $1,555

Professional: $1,522

Master's: $1,228

Bachelor's: $978

Associate's: $736

Some College: $645

High School: $591

Source: U.S. Department of Labor

should you decide to attend college after graduating from high school. While the primary focus of this book is on college admissions, keep in mind that for high school students, there are many postsecondary educational opportunities that may lead to something other than a four-year university. A student's passion for cooking may lead to a culinary school, a passion for computer programming may lead to a computer programming or technical school, a passion for a trade may lead to an internship or trade school. Pursuing an education beyond high school will lead you into higher levels of knowledge, higher level careers, and greater opportunities than would be available to you with simply a high school diploma.

Focusing on where you are going will help define the necessary relationships, experiences, and knowledge needed to get you there. Coaches begin the season with a focus on making the playoffs and winning the championship. They prepare players, develop skills, prepare their game plan, and adjust their strategy as needed with a clear purpose or mission, translated into a clear focus or vision. Your *vision* must be to prepare for and be accepted into your first-choice college and your *mission* must be to graduate.

Your vision will guide your efforts toward gathering information that will enable you to narrow your college choices, develop relationships with your first-choice colleges, and keep the lines of communication open so that you increase your opportunities of getting in and getting the money needed to pay all your expenses.

Which Colleges?

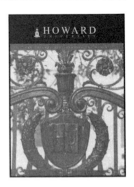

Research and carefully assess the programs, people, and communities of the colleges you are considering. Look for schools where you can envision yourself developing a life-long relationship and that are highly regarded in the field you are interested in studying or the career you are interested in pursuing. In essence, choose colleges where you would encourage your own children to attend. If they do, they will be considered legacy applicants, who oftentimes have an advantage over other applicants. Colleges view alumni and their children as having life-long relationships and subsequently give legacy students preferred admission status.

The primary sources of your college information will be:

- *Your high school guidance office*
- *College fairs*
- *College visits*
- *Information you request through a college's web site*

- *Unsolicited information, which will be plenty, that you will begin receiving based on your answers to the SAT, ACT, and PSAT questionnaires*
- *Offer letters and contact by recruiters if you are a recruited-athlete or have a highly regarded talent in art, music or dance, or have distinguished yourself by being recognized in such prestigious competitions as the Westinghouse Competition, as a Presidential Scholar, or as a National Merit/National Achievement Scholar*

Develop a filing system to organize information by first-, second-, and third-choice colleges (or A, B, and C schools). Do not throw away anything as your college and career choices may change several times over the course of your four years of high school. You may discover that colleges you place onto your 'C' list as a ninth-grader make their way onto your 'A' list by your junior or senior year.

The book, *A Middle School Plan for Students with College-Bound Dreams*, outlines how to identify your personality type, learning styles, best/worst learning situations, and other areas that define the divinely unique person you are. Understanding who you are and what your unique gifts, interests, dreams, and aspirations are can help narrow your

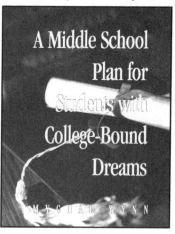

list of colleges to those that offer the type of school community, values, diversity, and learning environment that is best for you. Gather as many college brochures, college guides, course catalogs, viewbooks, and as much information as you can. Keep in mind that brochures are meant to portray a college in the best possible light. They are like food advertisements: the dish that is served may only vaguely resemble the dish that is in the picture. That is why you should never make your college choices based on pictures and brochures; use them only as a means of gathering information for you and your parents to review.

Following is a list of helpful sources:

- *Campus Dirt (www.campusdirt.com)*
- *Campus Tours (www.campustours.com)*
- *College Board (www.collegeboard.com)*
- *College Bound (www.collegeboundnews.com)*
- *College Prowler (www.collegeprowler.com)*
- *My College Guide (www.mycollegeguide.org)*
- *School Guides: (www.schoolguides.com)*
- *The Fiske guide to Colleges: (www.fiskeguide.com)*
- *U.S. News & World Reports Annual Listing of the Best Colleges: (www.usnews.com)*

The National Center for Educational Statistics web site provides comprehensive information on all U.S. colleges and universities (www.nces.ed.gov/ipeds).

When you submit your college application, you want to separate yourself from the thousands of other applicants by making a personal connection to the college based on your research. You want to be able to communicate through your essay or your interview why you believe that this particular college would be a good school for you and why you would be a good student for the college's student community.

Contact Schools and Programs

As soon as you begin to develop an idea of the types of colleges in which you are interested, or colleges that offer fields of study in your areas of interest, begin making contact. Colleges keep track of whom, and how often, prospective students contact them. It is never too early in the process to let potential schools know that you have an interest in their programs. Write, call, or e-mail admissions officers, professors, coaches, departments, or programs to request information. Once you are in their database, they will begin mailing or e-mailing you information on a regular basis. As you begin receiving information, give extra or unwanted information to your high school counselor so that he or she can use it in the guidance office or counseling center.

College Affiliations

You can make an important connection to a college through a teacher, counselor, principal, members from your place of worship, or friend of the family who is a member of the college's alumni association or who has a professional affiliation with the college.

Make note of:

- The college they attended

- Any contacts they may still have at the school

- Any information or insight they may have to assist you in the admissions process

- Any scholarships, grants, or special programs of which they are aware

Develop a college affiliations wall with the name, affiliation, degree, major, and graduation year of family members, mentors, friends, members from your place of worship members, teachers, and coaches.

The Ivy League

The "Ivy League" is an extension of the original Ivy League Agreement, which provided the framework for a group of schools competing against each other in football in 1945. In February 1954, the Ivy League was formally established with the basic intent to improve and foster intercollegiate athletics while keeping the emphasis on such competition in harmony with the educational purpose of the institutions.

Eight schools make up the Ivy League and are considered among the most prestigious universities in the world and are the most competitive in which to be admitted:

1. Brown (Providence, RI) (www.brown.edu)
2. Columbia (New York, NY) (www.columbia.edu)
3. Cornell (Ithaca, NY) (www.cornell.edu)
4. Dartmouth (Hanover, NH) (www.dartmouth.edu)
5. Harvard (Cambridge, MA) (www.harvard.edu)
6. Penn (Philadelphia, PA) (www.upenn.edu)
7. Princeton (Princeton, NJ) (www.princeton.edu)
8. Yale (New Haven, CT) (www.yale.edu)

The Big Ten

The Big Ten is comprised of actually 11 schools:

1. Illinois (www.uiuc.edu)
2. Indiana (www.indiana.edu)
3. Iowa (www.uiowa.edu)
4. Michigan (www.umich.edu)
5. Michigan State (www.msu.edu)
6. Minnesota (www1.umn.edu/twincities)
7. Northwestern (www.library.northwestern.edu)
8. Ohio State (www.osu.edu)
9. Penn State (www.psu.edu)
10. Purdue (www.purdue.edu)
11. Wisconsin (www.uwsa.edu)

Historically Black Colleges & Universities

Historically Black Colleges and Universities (also referred to as HBCUs) offer a wide range of undergraduate, graduate, and doctoral programs. These institutions were established prior to 1964 with a primary mission of providing a college education for black Americans. There are approximately 230,000 black students enrolled in the 105 HBCUs [*National Center for Education Statistics*] across the country.

For students considering HBCUs, develop a calendar of HBCU sports classics, band competitions, college fairs, and college tours.

Over 35 percent of black lawyers, 50 percent of black engineers, and 65 percent of black physicians graduated from HBCUs. About 18 percent of black college students are enrolled at HBCUs, which award 23 percent of the bachelor's degrees earned by African-Americans.

Notes:

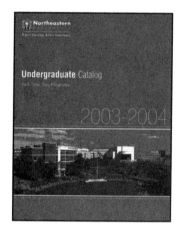

Learn more about Historically Black Colleges and Universities at the U.S. Department of the Interior web site: *http://www.doi.gov/hrm/black.html.*

Cooperative Education Programs

Northeastern University in Boston, Massachusetts (www.northeastern.edu) has the largest cooperative education program in the world with over 50,000 students at its combined campuses. Coop schools provide programs where you attend school half of the year and work full time in your field of study the other half of the year, thereby allowing you to earn money to pay tuition and other costs while gaining invaluable professional and on-the-job experience.

I attended Northeastern University. I began as an electrical engineering major and later switched my major to Business Administration with a concentration in accounting and computer science. For my coop experience I worked on the commercial audit staff of Arthur Andersen & Company, which, at that time, was one of the foremost public accounting and business consulting companies in the world. Upon graduation, the work experience at Arthur Andersen & Company helped me to receive job offers from Boston to San Francisco. I eventually accepted a position with IBM at their Santa Teresa Laboratory facility in San Jose, California as a financial systems analyst. For a full listing of schools visit the National Commission for Cooperative Education *(www.co-op.edu).*

Tuition-free Schools

The following schools are tuition-free: West Point, Naval Academy, Coast Guard, Air Force Academy, Merchant Marine, Webb Institute in Long Island, New York (marine engineering and naval architecture), Cooper Union in New York (art, architecture, and engineering), Deep Springs College in Nevada ("service and idealism"), College of the Ozarks in Missouri, and Berea College in Kentucky.

Top Ten Rankings

The national college rankings vary from year to year. Below are the 2010, *U.S. News & World Reports* rankings of National Universities and Liberal Arts Colleges.

The Princeton Review (www.princetonreview.com) provides college rankings based on such criteria as *happiest students, most beautiful campuses, America's best value colleges,* and *best colleges by region.* You can also research information for a specific college in regard to such areas as school history, enrollment statistics, application deadlines, ranking, cost of attendance, and financial aid.

National Universities		
	School	**Acceptance Rate**
1.	Harvard University (www.harvard.edu)	7.9%
1.	Princeton University (www.princeton.edu)	9.9%
3.	Yale University (www.yale.edu)	8.6%
4.	Caltech (www.caltech.edu)	17.4%
4.	MIT (www.mit.edu)	11.9%
4.	Stanford University (www.stanford.edu)	9.5%
4.	University of Pennsylvania (www.upenn.edu)	16.9%
8.	Columbia (www.columbia.edu)	10.0%
8.	University of Chicago (www.uchicago.edu)	27.9%
10.	Duke University (www.duke.edu)	22.4%

Liberal Arts Colleges		
	School	**Acceptance Rate**
1.	Williams College (www.williams.edu)	17.0%
2.	Amherst College (www.amherst.edu)	14.8%
3.	Swarthmore College (www.swarthmore.edu)	15.7%
4.	Middlebury College (www.middlebury.edu)	16.8%
4.	Wellesley College (www.wellesley.edu)	36.0%
6.	Bowdoin College (www.bowdoin.edu)	18.6%
6.	Pomona College (www.pomona.edu)	15.6%
8.	Carleton College (www.carleton.edu)	27.5%
8.	Davidson College (www.davidson.edu)	25.7%
10.	Haverford College (www.haverford.edu)	27.0%

U.S. News & World Reports 2010 National University and Liberal Arts College Rankings

Visit

When I enrolled into Boston's Northeastern University, I was more committed to leaving Chicago than going to Boston. I wanted to leave Chicago so badly that I never visited Boston. While in high school, the only college trip I took was to the campus of the University of Illinois at Urbana-Champaign; however, I was committed to leaving the city of Chicago, the state of Illinois, and the entire Midwest. Attending college would represent my first real opportunity to travel and experience life in another part of the country.

Visit as many college campuses as you can during the time that school is in session and get a feel for the atmosphere, student body, and community surrounding the college where you will spend four or more years of your life. If you do not like cold weather, do not go to schools in the Northeast or Midwest. If you are afraid of earthquakes, then rule out California. If you have allergies, then you may have to rule out schools in the South and Southeast. If you do not like crowds, then you may want to focus on small intimate college settings rather than large informal ones. College campuses can range from a few hundred to over 30,000 students.

Shopping for a college is in many ways analogous to shopping for a car—do your research, compare other models, look into the history, read independent assessments, and go for a test drive. Visit the campus, go into the buildings, examine the library and the research facilities, and check out the athletic facilities, cafeteria, dormitories, and classrooms. Talk to students, meet professors, and talk to the people in the admissions and financial-aid office. Do not expect to pay sticker price (published tuition and fees) once you are accepted and be prepared to negotiate your financial-aid package.

Campus Visits

Nearly all colleges provide campus tours and some, such as Carnegie Mellon in Pittsburgh, Pennsylvania, provide overnight visits.

By attending a Sleeping Bag Weekend, you will have the opportunity to live like a Carnegie Mellon student. You will stay overnight in a residence hall with a current student (do not forget your sleeping bag!), eat on campus and attend classes. You will also have a chance to tour our campus, explore the surrounding neighborhoods, and interact with current students and faculty to get a feel for the academic atmosphere at Carnegie Mellon. [www.cmu.edu]

Wesleyan University in Middletown, Connecticut, provides overnight stays for high school seniors (www.wesleyan.edu).

College Tours

Students can, for a fee, sign up for college tours sponsored by private companies, places of worship, Boys & Girls Clubs, YMCAs, and community organizations; experience "virtual tours" through online web sites; or take video tours through companies like Collegiate Choice (www.collegiatechoice.com).

Some of the companies sponsoring college or online tours are:

- *Campus Tours (www.campustours.com)*
- *eCampus Tours (www.ecampustours.com)*
- *CollegeSurfing.com (www.collegesurfing.com)*
- *College Visits (www.college-visits.com)*
- *Collegiate Explorations (www.cetours.com)*
- *Soul of American Tours (www.soulofamerica.com)*

Take the *Workbook* with you on your college visits:

Facilities:

- ❑ *Dorms & laundry facilities*
- ❑ *Cafeteria*
- ❑ *Athletic facilities*
- ❑ *Classrooms*
- ❑ *Libraries*
- ❑ *Study halls*
- ❑ *Student Union*

Support Services:

- ❑ *Financial-Aid office*
- ❑ *Dean of Students*
- ❑ *Admissions*
- ❑ *Local entertainment*
- ❑ *Health Services*
- ❑ *Shopping*
- ❑ *Bank/ATM*

People:

- ❑ *Students*
- ❑ *Professors*
- ❑ *Sororities & fraternities*
- ❑ *Campus & local law enforcement*
- ❑ *Surrounding community*
- ❑ *Diversity*

College Fairs

In the article, *The College Fair for College Choice,* Elisa Kronish notes:

Make note of the dates of College Fairs in your area and attend at least one per year during each of your four years of high school.

> *When choosing a college, you need all the information you can get. But visiting each campus can be expensive. And who has time to call each school individually?*
>
> *That's where college fairs come in. "College fairs are a 'one-stop shopping' kind of experience," says Greg Ferguson, director of the National College Fairs program of the National Association for College Admission Counseling (NACAC). It is a mini-convention for students and college representatives, designed to give students a chance to explore all their options quickly and efficiently.*

Where you find out about college fairs

- Your guidance counselor can tell you about college fairs in your area. The National College Fairs Program (a division of NACAC) sponsors about 35 college fairs at convention centers around the country each year. Six to eight weeks before each fair, NACAC sends a mailing to high school counselors in the area. Ask your counselor or check NACAC's web site for schedules at *http://www.nacacnet.org.*

What you should expect to learn

- College fairs will help you to better evaluate potential colleges. Like a shopping mall, they provide an opportunity to visit many stores within one location. You are able to compare programs, admission requirements, and extracurricular activities side-by-side. The college representatives at the fair tend to have a broad range of knowledge, can provide on-the-spot answers to questions, may be able to provide you with an important contact if you decide to apply, or take your application right on the spot.

Materials college reps will give you

- You will be able to collect brochures, viewbooks, applications for admissions and financial-aid forms from most visiting colleges. You may also receive a calendar with important application and admissions dates and an application fee waiver.

How you should prepare

- Some college fairs—like the college fair held at Chicago's McCormick Place—are huge events. There are hundreds of colleges and universities represented and a wealth of information offered. Before attending the fair you should get a listing of the colleges that will be represented with a floor plan of the exhibit area. Develop a list of the colleges and universities that offer programs in which you are interested.

- Take a parent or a friend. While you will not have time to speak with all the reps, you should try to get as much information as you can so that you can review it at a later time. Divide the exhibit area by the number of parents or friends and assign each person an area to cover to ensure that you gather as much information as possible.

What you need to bring

- Take your college-planning notebook with you. Carry it in a sturdy backpack just as if you are going to school. You never know what type of opportunity you may have or whom you will meet. If you are an art student, take your portfolio. Your college-planning notebook will allow a college representative to immediately assess if you would be a highly qualified student for admissions into the college's program. You also want a note pad and pen so you can take notes and record important contact information.

Notes:

Questions you should ask

The best thing about college fairs is the one-on-one contact you get with college representatives. Use this time to your advantage. Come prepared with questions:

- What are the application deadlines for admissions and financial aid?
- What is the application fee?
- What is the cost of tuition? Room and Board? Books?
- Will I have a faculty advisor?
- Are SAT Subject Tests required? If so, how many?
- What is the average GPA and SAT/ACT scores for admitted students?
- What is your enrollment and your ratio of students to full-time faculty?
- What are your 4-year and 6-year graduation rates?

Pick Your Top 10 Schools

My Top-Ten List:

Amherst College

Art Center College of Design

Dartmouth

Fisk University

Milwaukee Institute of Art and Design

Morehouse College

Savannah College of Art and Design

UMass Amherst

University of Maryland Baltimore County

Yale

Refer to your 'Life List.' Use your hopes and dreams, your passions and aspirations to guide your efforts in sorting through all your college information to arrive at your top ten schools. As you gather information, talk to people, and visit campuses, your list is likely to change as you drop some schools and add new ones.

To the left was our older son's top-ten list as he entered his junior year of high school. He was initially interested in pursuing studies in Fine Arts, however, fascinated by his 12th grade AP Psychology class he expanded his college major to include psychology. He visited such Ivy League schools as Yale, Harvard, and Dartmouth (where he attended a 3-week program at the Tuck School of Business), such HBCUs as Fisk, Xavier, and Morehouse College, and took three trips to Amherst College (where he ultimately enrolled). The admissions requirements and reputations are different at each school, however, each school provides courses of study related to his interests.

The community at each of the colleges on his list represent a very different experience over the course of four years. The Yale philosophy is to provide a residential community that students experience during their entire four years—Amherst College is part of a five-school consortium (Amherst College, UMass Amherst, Smith, Mount Holyoke, and Hampshire College) located in rural Massachusetts; Fisk, Xavier, and Morehouse enjoy a rich tradition of graduating some of the country's most scholarly and successful African-Americans; the University of Maryland Baltimore County, under the leadership of Dr. Freeman Hrabowski, provides an academically nurturing environment through the Meyerhoff Scholars Program, which graduates more African-American Ph.D.'s than any other university in the U.S.

These are the types of decisions you must make. Your top-ten list of schools should reflect places and programs where you can envision yourself developing lasting relationships with professors as well as a desire to return to the campus to inspire hope in future students and share the sense of pride you should have in becoming one of your school's distinguished alumni.

Venita Polyne is an alumna of Xavier University (1983). One of her college professors attended her wedding and wrote her recommendation to Law School. Her ties to her alma mater are so strong that she recalls passing a Nun who recognized her in a local shopping mall nearly ten years after graduation!

John and Ruth Strong, graduates of Lane College [Jackson, TN] (1952/55) with Master Degrees from Tennessee State University (1960/61), and Doctorates in Education from the University of Tennessee Knoxville (1963) have such strong ties to their alma mater that neither has missed the annual Tennessee State–Jackson State football game since its inception.

Notes:

By focusing on whether or not a school will meet your needs rather than its national ranking, your list is likely to include schools in each of the following categories:

- *Reach Schools:* the most highly competitive schools where you may stand less than a 10 percent chance of being accepted.

- *Competitive Schools:* schools where you meet the admission requirements.

- *Safety Schools:* schools where you stand your strongest chance of being accepted.

Place your top-ten list in your college-planning notebook, on a wall, or onto your refrigerator—someplace where you will be continually reminded of your high school focus until you can begin checking off those schools where you have been accepted.

Chapter 2

States that require high-school graduation exams: Alabama, Florida, Georgia, Indiana, Louisiana, Maryland, Massachusetts, Minnesota, Mississippi, Nevada, New Jersey, New Mexico, New York, North Carolina, Ohio, South Carolina, Tennessee, Texas, and Virginia. States phasing in exit exams by 2008, but not yet withholding diplomas: Alaska, Arizona, California, Utah, and Washington.

— [Center on Education Policy]

High School Graduation Requirements

High school graduation requirements vary by state. Sometimes the requirements vary by district within the state and even by school within the district. It is important for you to identify and understand your state or school district's graduation requirements and track your progress throughout high school.

Course Requirements

Fully understanding your high school course requirements will require that you meet with your counselor, read your school district's curriculum guide, and understand your state department of education's high school graduation course requirements, which will specify the number of classes that you must pass within such areas as:

- *Math:* Math requirements vary from 3 to 4 years of math with minimum subject-area requirements such as Algebra I (keep in mind that your state math requirements may be much lower than the requirements of the colleges on your top-ten list).

Notes:

- *English:* Requirements vary from 3 to 4 years of classes such as literature, English, Writing and Composition.

- *Science:* Requirements vary from 3 to 4 years of classes such as biology, chemistry, physics, and physical science. As in math, your state science requirements may vary significantly from those required by the colleges to which you apply.

- *Social Studies:* The number of required classes in subjects like history, economics, and psychology.

- *Foreign Language:* Most states require two consecutive years of a foreign language.

- *Physical Education, electives, and other required classes.*

If you are pursuing a specialized diploma, e.g., college preparatory, International Baccalaureate, college prep–technical diploma, magnet seal, etc., you must also understand and track your progress toward fulfilling the graduation requirements in these specialized areas.

To illustrate the type of information that you must gather, on the following pages are sample schedules to meet course requirements of the Fulton County Schools in Georgia. After reviewing the sample course requirements, identify the unique requirements within your school or school district.

College Preparatory Diploma

Students must complete 23 units (21 standard units plus two additional units in the core areas: language arts, math, science, social studies, foreign language or Fine Arts). The College Preparatory Diploma meets the entrance requirements of every college in the University System of Georgia and qualifies students to earn the Georgia Board of Education's College Preparatory diploma:

Language Arts   (4)
    Language Arts Core (3)
        9th Grade Literature
        10th Grade Literature
        11th Grade American Literature
    Language Arts Selective (1)

        AP Literature and Composition
        AP Language and Composition
        College English

Mathematics   (4)
    Algebra I
    Algebra II
    Geometry or Applied Geometry
    Selective (Above Algebra II)

Science   (4)
    Biology
    Physical Science of Physics
    2 Selective (science)

Social Studies   (3)
    U.S. History
    World History
    American Government/Economics

Foreign Language   (2)
Electives   (5)
Health and Physical Education   (1)

    Total Graduation Credits   **(23)**

Graduation Tests

There are many well-publicized stories of students in states that require high school exit exams having their college-bound dreams deferred or destroyed as a result of their failure to pass the exams. At many high schools, students earn A's and B's in their classes and yet fail their state's high school graduation exams. In the state of Florida, many students are accepted into college only to fail the high school exit exam and, therefore, not receive their high school diploma.

BOSTON, Massachusetts (AP) -- Four attempts. Two points shy.

The numbers plague Karl Kearns, a senior at Burke High School in Boston. This was the first year in which seniors statewide were denied diplomas if they failed the state's high school test, the Massachusetts Comprehensive Assessment System exam, or MCAS.

Kearns was one of some 4,800 seniors who didn't make the cut.

Despite maintaining a "B" average, winning an award for "most improved" in his class, being captain of his football team and overcoming the challenges of a broken home and a reading disability, he didn't score high enough to get a diploma and graduate with his classmates.

[AP Sunday, June 15, 2003]

Diplomas Denied as Seniors Fail Exit Exams

This spring, thousands of high school seniors across the country weren't awarded a high school diploma because they failed to pass their state's exit exam. Lawmakers in states such as California, Florida, Massachusetts, Nevada, and North Carolina have instituted the high-stakes tests to ensure graduates are competent in basic skills, but now they face pressure from angry students and parents to delay or scrap the tests. Students say the tests do not reflect the curriculum covered in school.

"The stuff on the test doesn't equate to anything that I've learned in school," 18-year-old Robyn Collins of Sparks, Nevada protested to the Washington Post. A student with a solid academic record and a 3.0 grade point average, Collins had just failed on her fifth attempt to pass the math portion of the state's exit exam.

[School Reform News, September 1, 2003]

Do not take your high school graduation requirements for granted or assume that your classes or teachers have adequately prepared you. Meet with your counselor and get all the necessary information to ensure that you are fulfilling the graduation requirements in your school district and that you are enrolled in the necessary classes to prepare you for the end-of-grade exam or high school graduation tests in your state.

In the state of Georgia, a high school student must meet the state board of education's curriculum requirements AND pass graduation tests in the following areas before receiving his or her high school diploma:

- English/Language arts

- Writing

- Mathematics

- Social Studies

- Science

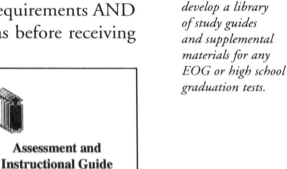

Assessment and
Instructional Guide
for the
Georgia High School
Writing Test

Students take the writing test in the fall and the other four tests in the spring of their junior year with five opportunities to retest before the end of 12th grade.

- Go to your state department of education web site and download any student-parent guidelines and practice tests.

- Research test assessment or preparation classes offered at your high school, through your local library, or through private companies.

- Try Googling your state's high school graduation exams (i.e., "GHSGT" for prep programs for the Georgia High School Graduation Test) to aid your efforts in identifying test preparation programs and materials.

Notes:

Identify tutors and develop a library of study guides and supplemental materials for any EOG or high school graduation tests.

- Assess your skill level or subject-area knowledge at least a year before you are scheduled to take required high school graduation tests.

- Take several practice tests in each of the exam areas to identify your strengths and weaknesses.

After gathering the available materials relating to the tests, such as scoring criteria, length of time allowed, and expected content knowledge, meet with your teacher, tutor, counselor, or someone who can assist you in ensuring that you are prepared to pass each required test.

Special Requirements for College-Bound Athletes

If you are planning on participating in college athletics at a Division I or II school during your freshman year in college, you must register with the NCAA Clearinghouse (www.ncaaclearinghouse.net). Many athletes register during the summer between their junior and senior year after receiving their junior-year high school transcript. The Clearinghouse outlines the full range of classes, grades, test scores, and recruiting guidelines as shown in the NCAA Guide for College-Bound Athletes.

For example, the NCAA eligibility rules for Division I is 16 core courses and 14 core courses for Division II in the following breakdown:

- 4 years of English for D-I and 3 years for D-II

- 3 years of mathematics for D-I and 2 years for D-II (Algebra I or higher)

- 2 years of natural/physical science (one must be a lab science)

- 1 year of additional English, math or science for D-I and 2 years for D-II

- 2 years of social studies

- 4 years of additional core courses for D-I and 3 years for D-II (from any area listed above, or from foreign language, non-doctrinal religion or philosophy)

Carefully review the *NCAA Guide for the College-Bound Student-Athlete* so you fully understand recruiting guidelines, eligibility requirements, and registration dates. It is possible to fulfill the graduation requirements for your high school and not meet the NCAA eligibility requirements, which would mean that you would not be able to receive a scholarship or be eligible to compete as a college student-athlete.

In order to participate in athletics and receive athletically-based financial aid at an NCAA Division I or II school, you must register with the NCAA Initial-Eligibility Clearinghouse and meet eligibility standards.

For further information, or to download the current copy of the *Guide for the College-Bound Student-Athlete* go to:

www.ncaaclearinghouse.org

Chapter 3

As competition grows tougher at all the top colleges, the game of getting into these schools has become more and more complex. No matter who you are or how good your grades and test scores are, there is no guarantee that you will be admitted to your desired schools. You must commit yourself to putting in a valiant effort if you want to compete in this game where students and college counselors are increasingly using sophisticated timing, marketing, and information-relaying strategies in order to get ahead.

In order to be confident that you will do your best in the process, you must research your college and program options, finding those that best fit your needs and desires; understand college admissions, recognizing application options such as Early Decision and identifying the goals or philosophies of the admissions officers at your target schools; and then, based on information gained during these first two tasks, launch a sophisticated application and marketing strategy.

— *[How to Get into the Top Colleges]*

Course Work

 You and your parents must take an active role in planning, scheduling, and sequencing your high school classes. Class requirements vary by high school and can range from unrestricted open enrollment to highly restricted–highly selective student enrollment that requires counselor and teacher approval.

Questions that must be considered when planning a high school course schedule are:

* What are the enrollment restrictions such as prerequisite classes, student enrollment, teacher recommendations, grades in previous classes, etc.?

- What is the school district policy for students who do not meet all of the class enrollment criteria, such as providing a signed parent waiver, taking a placement test, etc.?

- Are classes offered during certain semesters?

- Can required, elective, or enrichment classes be taken online, in night school, or during summer school?

- What are the enrollment restrictions for summer school classes (e.g., opened only to students who failed the class, seniors, etc.)?

- What classes must be taken in a particular sequence, such as Algebra I, Geometry, Algebra II, Pre-Calculus, Calculus?

- Do classes have to be taken in combination with other classes, such as Algebra II and Chemistry?

- Are classes embedded with other classes, such as AP U.S. History and 11th Grade Literature, that alternate days, with each class meeting every other day?

- Do any classes have mandatory parent meetings prior to student enrollment?

During eighth grade your middle school counselor will submit a suggested class schedule to the high school that you will be attending. Nearing the end of eighth grade or during the summer before enrolling in high school, you will receive your high school class schedule. Carefully review your ninth grade class schedule to ensure that you will begin on track toward taking the classes that you would like to take during your four years of high school.

Some students will develop high school plans that have them enrolled in AP classes during the 9th and 10th grades. Other students will take a less rigorous and more conservative

Notes:

approach by scheduling honors classes during 9th and 10th grades leading into AP classes during 11th and 12th grades. Other students will not pay attention to their course schedules and find themselves on either a vocational track or in classes that will not meet the admissions requirements for four-year universities and will require enrolling into a junior college as part of a student's overall college-bound plan.

Another important area of consideration in planning your high school schedule is to understand how classes build upon what is called, "preexisting knowledge." Important information is taught, study skills are developed, and higher-level thinking skills are strengthened in 9th and 10th grade classes, which enhance your opportunity to succeed in the more difficult 11th and 12th grade classes.

The level of classes that you take (i.e., regular, honors, AP, or IB), and your grades in such classes will have a tremendous impact on your college choices and scholarship opportunities.

When planning your course schedule, do not be afraid to enroll in academically rigorous classes such as honors or AP classes. The sooner that you enroll in the higher-level classes, the more higher-level classes you will have the opportunity to take throughout high school. If you developed a challenging middle school course schedule, you may find yourself, as a high school freshman and sophomore, in higher-level math and science classes with juniors and seniors. Consider yourself fortunate to be as many as two years ahead and well on the way to developing an impressive high school transcript.

Reading, Writing, and Communicating

Perhaps the most important skills that you can develop as a high school student in preparation for admission into and success in college is the ability to communicate your thoughts and ideas verbally and in writing.

In the book, *College Admissions Trade Secrets,* Andrew Allen notes:

> *The dean of admissions for Princeton once said that the best advice he could give to parents is to encourage their children to read. It is that easy and that complex. Most top colleges are more interested in good readers than anything else. A student with an 800-math and a 620-verbal is much more likely to be rejected from a top college than one with an 800-verbal, 620-math.*

Michele A. Hernandez, in the book, *A is for Admission,* notes:

> *Over the summer, read, read, and read in your spare time: novels, newspapers, scientific journals, etc. By reading many different literary styles and genres, you will be doing the best kind of preparation for the SAT verbal section. This is much cheaper than taking a Stanley Kaplan course, and it is equally effective in many cases. The more you read, the more your vocabulary and reading comprehension will increase and the more you will be able to raise your score on the SAT verbal section.*

When planning your high school course schedule, you should strongly consider such courses as literature, history, philosophy, and statistics. While many students may not find such classes as exciting or as much fun as P.E., Recreational Games, Weight Training, or Badminton, the more challenging courses provide the foundation for success in top-ranked colleges. Classes such as Forensics, Statistics, AP U.S. History,

AP Literature, and AP Psychology develop a student's reading, writing, critical thinking, and analytical skills. Students who enter high school with weaknesses in their reading and writing skills may take regular classes during their freshman year and more challenging honors classes during their sophomore year in preparation for the most challenging classes during their junior and senior years. Such a transcript (provided that you achieve good grades) not only will be impressive for college admissions committees, but also would greatly enhance your writing and language skills for your junior-year PSAT, SAT, and ACT exams.

What Admissions Committees Look For

When you submit your college application packages, you will be submitting your information along with thousands of other students from throughout the country, and depending on the colleges to which you apply, from throughout the world. Colleges will be looking for a diverse student body; hence, their admissions criteria will reflect a number of components: grades, test scores, types of classes, activities, interests, student backgrounds, community service, and any number of other criteria unique to the needs of the college or university to which you apply. Your high school transcript will reflect not only your academic success in high school, but also your willingness to be challenged and your areas of interest. The type of classes—math, science, language arts, social studies, and electives—and the level of those classes—honors, AP, IB—will be considered along with your grades.

Students who choose to load their schedules with easy classes and electives severely limit their college choices. Admissions committees at the nation's top colleges will be looking for a challenging academic schedule and examples—either in your course work or in your teacher recommendations—of your participation in classroom discussions, debates, and active involvement in furthering ideas and opinions. Colleges want students who can contribute to classroom discussions, share ideas and opinions, and effectively communicate with professors

and classmates. Admissions officers at the top colleges are assigned to regions of the country. They are familiar with the high schools within their region and communicate with high school counselors. The admissions officer assigned to your region may ask your counselor whether or not you are taking the most demanding, very demanding, demanding, average, or a below-average class schedule. Keep in mind that a *demanding* class schedule for a student who is not involved in any extracurricular activities may be considered by an admissions officer as a *very demanding* schedule for a student who plays one or more varsity sports or is involved in clubs and student organizations.

Notes:

College Prep Classes

As was outlined in the previous chapter, a strong college-prep schedule includes a mix of subjects:

- *English:* four years

- *Math:* three to four years

- *Foreign language:* two to three years

- *Science:* three to four years (two lab sciences)

- *Social Studies:* three to four years

Fitting an extra class into a full course load or taking math and science classes that exceed your high school graduation requirements will count in your favor. Honors or other types of advanced classes, assuming, of course, that you earn at least a 'B,' will also count in your favor.

During the first semester of our son's sophomore year, the class schedule that he received from his school was not as academically challenging as it needed to be to make him competitive for admissions into a top college:

10th-grade, first-semester schedule received from school:

- *Algebra II*
- *World History*
- *Physical Science*
- *Recreational Games (Bowling)*

After discussing the schedule with his counselor, his schedule was changed to:

- *Honors Algebra II*
- *Honors 10th Grade Literature*
- *Honors Spanish IV*
- *Drawing/Painting I/II*

The meeting with his counselor revealed that his enrollment in Honors Algebra II was prerequisite for enrollment into

Honors Pre-Calculus, both of which would provide stronger preparation for the SAT, SAT Subject Tests, and ACT exams.

As a result of his academically challenging first-semester class schedule, he had the following second-semester schedule:

- *Honors Pre-Calculus*
- *AP Computer Science*
- *Chemistry*
- *Drawing/Painting III/IV*

In addition to a more academically challenging class schedule than was initially received from the school, the honors and AP classes resulted in an additional 7 points, per class, being added to his numerical grade (i.e., his AP Computer Science grade of '90' resulted in a '97' being used to calculate his weighted-GPA). These additional points increased his class ranking.

Dear Sir:

I am currently a junior at North Springs High School in Atlanta, Georgia. I am currently enrolled in the Math and Science magnet program and will be graduating with a College Preparatory Diploma with Distinction with the Math and Science Magnet Seal.

My current GPA is 3.25 and as a sophomore, I took the ACT and scored a composite score of 25. I have plans to retake both exams during my junior year.

I am currently on course to take additional math and science classes beyond my graduation requirements and I will be attending the Math/Science camp at Duke University this summer.

I would appreciate any information that you can provide relative to your Biology and Psychology departments, math and science majors, and admissions criteria for biology majors.

I currently participate in three varsity sports—football (linebacker/running back), track and field (400, 200, 4 x 100, 4 x 400), and lacrosse.

Thanking you in advanced for any information or assistance that you can provide in helping me identify the best university setting to continue the pursuit of my dreams and aspirations.

Sincerely,

Based on your current class schedule and academic performance, what would you say in a query letter to a prospective college?

Specialized Majors

If you are planning to pursue a specialized major such as engineering, business, education, architectural design, or nursing school, you must inquire into any specific college admissions requirements, such as additional math and science or economics and psychology classes. Be sure to review the admissions requirements for your major and call or write each school on your top-ten list to ensure that you fully understand the requirements. Indicating a major on your application may be to your advantage if the college is looking to increase the number of students in a particular program, e.g., nursing, art, engineering, micro biology, etc.

Academic Quality of Your High School

Admissions committees pay attention to the classes that are offered at your high school and those that you chose to take. Many of the colleges that you apply to will request a "School Profile" from your counselor, which outlines the types of classes offered, total number of available honors and AP classes, state ranking, average SAT scores, etc. The college admissions committee will raise the question, "Did this

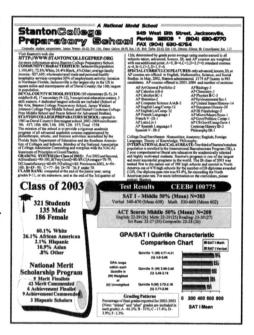

student take the most challenging classes offered at his or her high school?"

The academic quality of your high school will impact your college application in the following ways:

- *Class rank:* Great schools often have highly-motivated and high academically performing students making it more difficult to be among the school's top-ranked students.

- *Available classes:* Some schools offer a wide range of honors, AP, or IB classes. Along with the greater number of classes come expectations from colleges that you challenge yourself by enrolling in the most challenging courses.

- *SAT/ACT scores:* Your SAT/ACT scores will be evaluated within the context of the average SAT/ACT scores for your school. Students from high-performing schools are expected to have higher SAT/ACT scores.

If you are a student who attends what is considered a low-performing high school with low graduation rates and a limited selection of honors or AP classes, do not be discouraged. Factor this into your plan:

- Take the most challenging classes available at your high school and look into joint or dual enrollment opportunities at local colleges.

- Do not be influenced by peer pressure that does not encourage or support academic achievement. Make sure that you are among your school's top students.

- Talk to your teachers to let them know that you plan to go to college and ask them to make sure that you are learning what you need to know to score highly on the SAT, ACT, SAT Subject Tests, and any state-required end-of-grade or exit exams.

- Get involved in clubs, organizations, or activities to make your school better and assume a leadership role (i.e., officer, committee chairperson, board member, etc.).

- Identify at least 4 teachers who will write you a glowing recommendation.

- Strive to become a star student.

Notes:

My high school was one of the lowest-performing high schools in Chicago. My high school did not offer honors, AP, calculus, or physics classes. Yet, by being ranked within the top 5 percent of graduating seniors, I was still able to be accepted into the only college to which I applied.

Honors

Identify tutors, support, and supplemental materials for each honors subject.

Admissions committees will assess a higher value to honors classes. Depending on the subject or teacher, the class may move at a faster pace, involve more work, or require more effort on the part of the student. As a result of the increased difficulty, many school districts provide additional points that are credited to the student's overall GPA. For example, a school district may award

North Springs High School			
Grd 10 5/2004 Term: S2			
Atlanta, GA			
11.0160010			
	AP Computer Sci A	90	0.500
27.0670040			
	Pre Calculus H	80	0.500
40.4510000			
	Chemistry	86	0.500
50.4313062			
	Draw/Paint 2 M	86	0.500
Crd Att: 2.000 Cmp: 2.000	Numeric Avg: 89.0000		

an additional 7 points to the class numerical grade for honors classes. In such classes, a final numerical grade of 70 would result in 77 being posted to the student's grade point average; 90 results in a 97; and 100 results in a 107. This procedure permits students on a 4.0 scale to post GPAs higher than the scale, e.g., 5.25, 5.5, etc.

Do not be afraid to enroll in honors classes or take on the additional work. You may be surprised to discover that honors classes are more fun, more engaging, and provide an overall more positive learning experience, as a result of fewer students, fewer classroom disruptions, students who are more serious about learning, and teachers who have a passion for the subject and are genuinely interested in student success.

Find out what the honors credit policy is for your school district and if honors credit is received at all grade levels. In some school districts, 9th grade honors classes do not receive the additional honors credit; however, the classes can still be important in providing the necessary foundation for future success or may be a required prerequisite for other classes. Identify all of the honors classes that are offered and identify those classes or subjects in which you are interested or have performed well in the past.

AP (Advanced Placement): What it is

Advanced Placement, or what is more commonly referred to as 'AP' classes, is a program of college-level courses, offered as regular high school classes. Students who take such classes have the opportunity to receive advanced placement or college credit. The AP program is administered by the College Board (www.collegeboard.org). AP classes are considered the most difficult and demanding high school classes and are designed to prepare students for AP exit exams. AP exams are administered once a year in May and usually take two to three hours to complete. While many students take the exams at the end of their senior year, it is advisable to take the exam as soon as possible after completing the AP course work.

The AP class provides a course grade like any other high school class; however, many high schools provide additional points (usually 5 to 7 points) that are added to the student's final numerical course grade, and many colleges will award students college credit if they score 3 or higher on the AP exam. While students are encouraged to take the AP class prior to taking the AP exam, taking the class is not required to take the exam. Any student can register for, pay the $86 fee, and take any of the AP exams. However, many school districts pay the examination fee for students who take the AP class.

Identify tutors and create a library of each AP exam course description or portfolio requirement.

Contact the College Board (www. collegeboard.com) for the latest AP Prep materials.

Notes:

You will have to check with your counselor to ensure that your school district pays the fee for the AP exam.

There are over 37 college-level courses in 20 subjects available through the AP program (*http://apcentral.collegeboard.com/apc/public/courses/index.html*).

If your school or school district does not offer any or all of the AP classes, you can prepare for the AP exam by taking classes online, at other schools, through distance-learning programs, or through self-study. Colleges that award credit for AP classes will do so as long as the AP exam score (usually 3 or higher) meets their requirements.

Due to the increased popularity of AP classes and competition for student enrollment, you should become familiar with your school district's policy. Important questions are:

1. Is a teacher recommendation required for enrollment in AP classes?

2. Are there prerequisite classes, and, if I have not taken the prerequisite classes, can my parents sign a waiver that will allow me to enroll in the class?

3. Are there mandatory student or parent meetings prior to enrollment?

4. Is the class limited to certain grades, i.e., junior, seniors, etc.?

5. Will the school district pay the AP exam fee?

Meet with your counselor so that you fully understand your school and school district's policy for enrollment into honors, AP classes, or other types of advanced classes.

AP (Advanced Placement): Why you take them

Many students raise the question, "Should I take regular classes and get A's, honors classes and get B's, or AP classes and get C's?" One of the admissions officers at Yale responded to this question by saying, "At Yale we expect you to take AP classes and get A's!" The top colleges want to see you challenge yourself. They want to see you take the more difficult classes and succeed.

There is a card in Monopoly^{TM} that reads, "Go to Jail. Do Not Pass Go. Do Not Collect $200.00." This card could read, "If you do not take AP classes, do not apply to competitive colleges. Do not save thousands of dollars in tuition!" AP classes can be vitally important to your overall college plan.

Following, are some of the more compelling reasons to put yourself on track to take as many AP classes as you can handle.

- If your high school offers AP classes, competitive colleges and universities "expect" you to take some of the classes offered. If you do not, they will want to know why you did not take the classes.

- The AP class prepares you for the AP exam. Your score on the AP exam determines what, if any, college credit you will receive, potentially saving you thousands of dollars in tuition.

- The AP exam is scored on a scale from 1 to 5, with a 3 being considered a passing grade. Schools such as Harvard University, which does not give credit for AP classes, have a policy that allows you to enter as a sophomore if you score a "5" on a minimum of 5 AP exams. At the University of Massachusetts (Amherst), where in-state-tuition, room, and board is over $18,000.00 per year and out-of-state costs are

Notes:

nearly $30,000.00 per year, AP scores of 3 receive one course credit and AP scores of 5 receive two course credits.

5 AP classes and a score of '5' on each AP exam can save $50,550.00 in freshman tuition, fees, room, and board at Yale by enabling a student to achieve advanced standing and enter as a sophomore:

2009-2010 Yale COA = $50,550.00

- The course content and challenge of AP courses will provide excellent preparation for the SAT, SAT Subject Tests, and ACT exams.

- The additional "Weight" of AP classes, which may contribute 3 to 7 additional points to your GPA, depending on your school district, will increase your overall class ranking (provided that your final grade is at least as high as it would have been in a regular class).

- Receive academic recognition through the *AP Scholars* program based on the number of exams taken and scores received.

- The number of AP classes successfully completed adds a competitive edge to your total student profile.

- When planning the number and type of AP classes you take, keep in mind how the classes are viewed by the colleges on your top-ten list. For example, Harvard does not place the same value on AP classes in Psychology, Studio Art, and Geography as it does on Chemistry, BC Calculus, and European History. Since there are over 30 AP courses offered and it is unlikely that you will take all of them, consider focusing on those classes where you have an interest, where you believe that you can perform your best, and that are highly regarded by the colleges on your top-ten list.

AP Grade Reports

AP grade reports (transcripts) are sent out in July to those colleges that you specify and include your grades for all of the AP exams that you have ever taken. AP exams are scored on a scale of 1-5.

AP Grade	Qualification
5	Extremely Well Qualified
4	Well Qualified
3	Qualified
2	Possibly Qualified
1	No Recommendation

Students with a grade of 3 or higher are recommended to receive advanced placement in college or credit for a college course. However, as previously stated, your score on the AP exam does not guarantee that you will receive college credit. While many colleges will provide credit, requirements vary by school.

AP Scholar

AP exams have impressive recognition levels that may have a positive influence on your college application. In the fall, following the May AP exams, notification is sent out to recipients of the AP Scholar Awards.

AP Scholar: Grades of 3 or higher on 3 or more AP Exams on full-year courses.

AP Scholar with Honor: Average grade of 3.25 on all AP exams taken, and grades of 3 or higher on 4 or more of these exams on full-year courses.

Notes:

AP Scholar with Distinction: Average grade of at least 3.5 on all AP exams taken, and grades of 3 or higher on 5 or more of these exams on full-year courses.

AP State Scholar: One female and one male student in each U.S. state and the District of Columbia with the highest average grade (at least 3.5) on all AP exams taken, and grades of 3 or higher on the greatest number of exams. The minimum requirement is a grade of 3 or higher on 3 exams on full-year courses.

National AP Scholar: Students in the United States who receive an average grade of at least 4 on all AP exams taken, and grades of 4 or higher on 8 or more of these exams on full-year courses.

Department of Defense for Education Activity (DoDEA) Scholar: One female and one male student attending DoDEA schools with the highest average grade on the greatest number of AP exams. The minimum requirement is a grade of 3 or higher on 3 exams on full-year courses.

AP International Scholar: One male and one female student attending an American international school (that is not a DoDEA school) outside the U.S. and Canada with the highest average grade on the greatest number of AP exams. The minimum requirement is a grade of 3 or higher on 3 exams on full-year courses.

Refer to the College Board web site (www.collegeboard. org) for a complete description of the AP program and the most current listing of AP subjects.

AP exam fees are $86.00 per exam; however, keep in mind that some schools or school districts pay the fee. The College Board also provides a fee reduction for students who can demonstrate a financial need. Check with your counselor for complete details and options at your school.

Advanced Placement courses and exams are available in the following areas:

Art (No exam required for Studio Art; Portfolio only)

Art History
Studio: Drawing Portfolio
Studio: 2-D Design
Studio: 3-D Design

Computer Science (A/AB)

Foreign Language

Chinese, French, German, Italian, Japanese, Latin, Spanish

Language Arts

Literature and Composition
Language and Composition

Mathematics

Calculus (AB/BC)
Statistics

Music Theory

Science

Biology
Chemistry
Environmental Science
Physics (B/C)

Social Studies

Economics (Macro/Micro)
European History
U.S. Government and Politics
Comparative Government and Politics
Human Geography
Psychology
U.S. History
World History

Notes: **IB (International Baccalaureate) Program**

The IB program is a rigorous college-preparatory curriculum of study that is designed and regulated by the International Baccalaureate Organization (www.ibo.org) established in 1968. The IBO offers 3 IB programs: The Primary Years Program for students ages 3-12; the Middle Years Program for students ages 11-16; and the Diploma Program for students ages 16-18. There are 1,746 schools in 122 countries offering the IB program.

IB classes are designed to help students think critically, write well, speak articulately, and manage extremely demanding schedules. The IB Diploma is an internationally-recognized and accepted diploma for college admission throughout North America, western Europe, and Australia. Students enrolled in IB classes receive an IB certificate for the completion of individual courses and the IB Diploma for the successful completion of the entire course of study. For students seriously considering studying abroad, the IB Diploma is usually required by colleges outside the United States.

College Credit

Similar to AP classes, individual colleges handle IB certificates and the IB diploma differently. Some colleges prefer an IB diploma to a standard high school diploma and award course credit for IB certificates.

IB Exams

IB Diploma-program students generally take six exams in the following areas:

- Literature in the student's native language

- Foreign Language

- Social Studies

- Experimental Science

- Mathematics

- Art

The exam results are sent in July for the May session and in January for the November session. IB exams are scored on a scale of 1-7 with 7 being highest.

Pursuing an IB Diploma

If your school district offers an IB Diploma, you must meet with your counselor to identify the essential and prerequisite course or admission requirements. Since the IB program itself is a two-year program, many school districts will have prerequisite courses during 9th and 10th grades that lead into the 11th- and 12th-grade IB course of study.

Joint Enrollment/Postsecondary Programs

Joint Enrollment programs provide opportunities to enroll in college while completing high school. Joint enrollment programs will vary by state and by school district within the state.

Some of the benefits of joint enrollment classes:

- they qualify for college credit with some also qualifying for high school credit, thereby allowing students to take college classes in place of certain high school classes

- they are usually paid for by the state, college, or local school district

- they provide students with an opportunity to experience college-level classes while still in high school, thereby helping them to know what to expect when they enroll in college full-time

Notes:

• they enhance a student's college application by demonstrating that the student is capable of college-level work and may provide early admissions preference at the joint enrollment college

• they provide an opportunity for students to learn from college professors

You will need to discuss joint enrollment opportunities with your high school counselor as the policies and procedures will vary by state. For example, at North Springs High School [Georgia], there are three colleges that offer joint enrollment for juniors and seniors, each with very different qualifying criteria. Students applying to the joint enrollment program must apply by April 10 for enrollment in the Fall Semester and by November 1 for enrollment in the Spring Semester.

Georgia Perimeter College

- *Junior or senior; currently enrolled in high school*
- *Minimum GPA of 3.0 or higher in core classes*
- *SAT scores (minimum) Critical Reading 530, Math 530 or ACT scores (minimum) English 23, Math 22: Composite 20*
- *The only college courses that may be used to fulfill both high school and college degree requirements are Math (4th unit), English (4th unit), and Social Studies (3rd unit)*
- *Deadline for fall admission is April 10*
- *Deadline for spring admission is November 1*
- *Joint Enrollment classes last one semester and earn one semester of college credit*

Georgia Tech

- *Junior or senior; currently enrolled in high school*
- *Minimum GPA of 3.6 or higher in core classes*
- *SAT scores (Critical Reading and Math) 1360*
- *Deadline for fall admission is April 1*
- *Joint Enrollment classes last one semester and earn one semester of college credit*
- *Students may take a maximum of 8 semester hours in courses that are not available at their high school*

Georgia State

- *Junior or senior; currently enrolled in high school*
- *Minimum GPA of 3.0 or higher in college prep courses*
- *SAT scores (minimum) Critical Reading 530, Math 530 or ACT scores (minimum) English 23, Math 22*
- *The only college courses that may be used to fulfill both high school and college degree requirements are Math (4th unit), English (4th unit), and Social Studies (3rd unit)*

Notes:

Unlike AP classes, which qualify for college credit at a broad range of colleges and universities, you must evaluate whether the credits earned through joint enrollment programs are transferable to those colleges on your top-ten list. Some colleges do not accept college transfer credit for students entering as freshmen. Also, the grades in some joint enrollment courses do not count toward your high school GPA as AP course grades do.

Grades

If you have the academic ability to be an 'A' student, then be an 'A' student. If you are an athlete and your teammates do not take academic achievement seriously, do not allow them to keep you from performing at the level of your academic potential. Put yourself in the best possible position to qualify first, for admission, and secondly, for financial aid.

Balancing your high school class schedule with extracurricular activities can be particularly stressful. If you play a varsity sport or are involved in an activity such as band, cheerleading, drama, math/science club, or orchestra, you are likely to have a schedule that involves before- or after-school practice as well as local, national, or international travel. Organizing yourself from the opening bell is going to be critical to ensuring your academic success.

The book, *A Middle School Plan for Students with College-Bound Dreams,* outlines ten important steps to preparing for academic success:

1. ***Get organized:*** Set up binders for each subject and pay close attention to the course syllabus and grading policy for each class.

2. ***Develop your before- and after-school routine:*** Set up a routine, based on your class schedule and extracurricular activities, that will maximize your study, homework, and test preparation time.

3. ***Develop consistent classroom routines:*** Set up a routine that keeps you organized, ensures that you make note of homework assignments and test dates, and helps you keep your subject-area binders in order.

4. ***Learn how to take good notes:*** Effective note-taking is critical to high school academic success.

5. ***Daily review/summary:*** Establish a time within your daily routine for a review of your notes from each class.

6. ***Review your agenda:*** Establish a time within your daily routine to review your agenda to ensure that you are aware of announced test, quizzes, and project due dates.

7. ***Test preparation:*** If you are consistently following your routines, then you should be preparing yourself for announced tests and quizzes.

8. ***Put your homework where it goes:*** The grades of many high school students suffer, due to misplaced, forgotten, or lost homework assignments.

9. ***Develop your vocabulary, writing, and grammar skills:*** Writing and language skills are critical to high school success and success on the SAT/ACT exams. Take advantage of every opportunity to continue expanding your vocabulary and developing your writing skills.

10. ***Become a critical thinker:*** Continue developing and expanding your critical-thinking skills. Consciously go through the process of investigation, interpretation, and judgment when formulating ideas and making decisions.

Notes:

GPA (Grade Point Average)

When coaches prepare their game plan, they want to put their team in a position to win. Sometimes, they just want to keep the score close until the final quarter so their team has an opportunity to win. Good coaches teach their players the importance of conditioning and "Execution." Your academic record is your scoreboard. In the final analysis it is the stat sheet of your high school course work. Like batting averages, rushing/passing yards, quarterback efficiency ratings, earned run averages, goals scored/allowed, free throw/field goal percentages, stolen bases, and your 100-meter time, your record is there for the world to see. There is no additional analysis, "Were the bases stolen against the best pitchers? Were the yards gained against the conference's strongest teams? Were the passes competed against the best defense?" No one knows and no one cares with the following exceptions:

1. How does your high school rank? Impressive grades at a highly-ranked high school are really impressive. Unimpressive grades at a low-ranked high school are really unimpressive.

2. What types of classes did you take? Good grades in honors, AP, and IB classes are oftentimes weighed more highly than great grades in regular or lower-level classes.

Do not be among the thousands of students who do not pay attention to their GPA until their junior year. By then you have two years of grades that can either prop your GPA up or weigh it down.

Weighted-GPA

A weighted-GPA reflects a student's actual GPA plus any additional points awarded from honors, AP, or IB classes. Some colleges do not count your weighted grade point average. They use your actual grade point average for their comparisons against other students. An exception to this policy is those colleges that have their own formula to allow additional credit or weight for grades achieved in honors or AP classes. Check with each of the schools on your top-ten list for their policy. Even if the college does not consider your weighted grade point average, the additional weight will positively impact your class ranking and the additional challenge of the weighted classes will have a positive impact on your application package.

Notes:

Upward Trend in Grades

One salvation for the student who struggles or does not take school seriously in the 9th and 10th grades is that junior-year grades are very important and improvement will be noticed. A student who does not perform well in his or her freshman year of high school may be given the benefit of the doubt if his or her grades show improvement during the sophomore, junior, and senior years.

A Solid Senior Year

Do not approach your senior year as an opportunity to coast once your college applications are in the mail. College admissions committees do not think much of students who take tough classes during their early years of high school and then try to take easy classes through their later years. Admissions committees will notice if you drop AP classes or take an easy schedule during your senior year.

Rather than a time to take easy classes, your senior year is your final opportunity to challenge and prepare yourself for the rigor of college. Stay focused on the mission, "Graduating from College." A rigorous course schedule from the 9th through the 11th grade may provide you with joint enrollment, internship opportunities, or independent study projects during your senior year. Students attending high schools that operate on block schedules are frequently able to meet their graduation course requirements by the end of their junior year. Students on traditional schedules who take advantage of summer school, night school, or online opportunities may also meet their high school graduation requirements by the end of their junior year. Such students may qualify for early college admission in the fall or spring semester of their senior year. Students who have identified their dreams and are pursuing passionate interests in music, art, economics, sports training, education, etc., should take advantage of the opportunity to attend college classes or enroll in special programs. Students who are planning on becoming student-athletes should explore the opportunity to participate in specialized training or work with personal trainers following the end of their varsity sport season.

Class Rank

Class rank is one of those very important, little discussed, statistics. Some colleges establish their primary admissions criteria based on class rank (e.g., top 5 percent, top 10 percent, etc.). States such as California, Florida, and Texas guarantee resident-students admission into the state's public universities based on the student's class ranking. One of the most highly-publicized states, Texas, has a law that guarantee's  resident-students who rank in the top ten percent of their high school's graduating class admission into the student's choice of the state's public universities.

House Bill 588, Sec. 51.803 (1997). AUTOMATIC ADMISSION: ALL INSTITUTIONS.

Each general academic teaching institution shall admit an applicant for admission to the institution as an undergraduate student if the applicant graduated in one of the two school years preceding the academic year for which the applicant is applying for admission from a public or private high school in this state [Texas] accredited by a generally recognized accrediting organization with a grade point average in the top 10 percent of the student's high school graduating class.

The decision confronting students and parents is whether to enroll in a low-performing high school where good students are assured a high class ranking or to enroll in a high-performing, competitive high school where even the best students may rank outside of the top 10 percent of their class. This is a tough choice and there is no clear answer. Our decision as parents was to enroll our sons into what we believed

to be the best high school for them, which happened to be a highly-ranked high school—ranked among the top high schools in the U.S. and in the top-ten SAT scores in the state. While our older son did not rank in the top 10 percent of his graduating class, he had the opportunity to pursue four years of his passion in art, play three varsity sports, and be surrounded by other students who were pursuing their passions in art, theater, math, science, and general studies.

Whatever decision you and your parents make, keep in mind that if your high school is considered a low-performing high school, then you have to separate yourself from any low-performing friends who are not encouraging you to do your schoolwork. In a low-performing school, you must work as hard as you can to be a top student so that you definitely rank in the top 5 percent, if not top 1 percent of your graduating class. It will be easier for a student attending a highly-competitive high school to explain a low class rank than it will be for a student attending a low-performing high school.

You must also keep in mind that if your school district awards additional points for honors, AP, IB or other types of advanced classes, then you must carefully consider course selections. Your goal should be to achieve the highest possible class ranking. For example, if an 'A' is worth 4 points in a regular class and '5' points for an honors or AP class, you must make a decision whether or not to take the regular, honors,

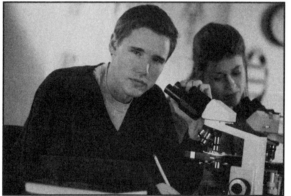

or AP version of a particular class—that is, chemistry, honors chemistry, or AP chemistry. Students who take honors and AP chemistry have an opportunity to earn 10 points if they are able to earn an 'A' in each class. Students who take chemistry and physical science (as opposed to honors chemistry and AP chemistry), even with 'A' grades, can earn a maximum of 8 points, thereby being ranked behind the student who took the honors and AP chemistry classes.

Over the course of four years of high school, the points earned as a result of your grades and course selections will impact your weighted-GPA, class ranking, and strength of schedule (i.e., most demanding, demanding, not very demanding, weak, etc.).

Meet with your counselor to explore the full range of class selections and program opportunities.

Chapter 4

Your academic profile consists of two parts: your high school record and your performance on standardized tests. These data together function like a key that can open the gateway of possibility for admission to a top college—but if the key does not fit, the door will most likely remain closed to you. There is no way of getting around the fact that for almost all candidates, intellectual ability is the most important criterion upon which you will be evaluated for college admission.

— *[How to Get into the Top Colleges]*

Academic Support

As you enter high school, you must openly and honestly assess your strengths and weaknesses. Do you have difficulty with math? Is science one of your weakest areas? Do you struggle with doing research and writing papers? Are you having difficulty grasping a foreign language? Do not allow yourself to get off to a slow start and do not shrug off your weaknesses, "I am just not good at math." You must identify what and whom you need to ensure your academic success throughout high school. Do not make the mistake of believing that a music major will not have to succeed in college math or that an athlete will not have to write a college paper. Even a star athlete, concert pianist, or brilliant artist will need a solid academic foundation to succeed in and graduate from college.

On September 1, 2003, the NCAA issued a report pertaining to the graduation rates of student-athletes. The report found that in 1995 and 1996, only half of Division I-A male basketball and football players graduated from college.

Notes:

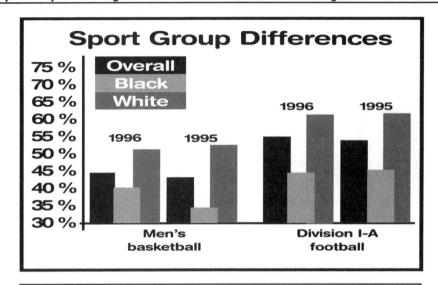

| NCAA Division I-A Student-Athlete Graduation Rates |

While female basketball players graduated at a slightly higher rate (66 percent), over a third did not graduate!

Division I-A football student-athletes in the 1996 cohort graduated at a 54 percent rate, one percentage point higher than the 1995 class but seven percentage points below the 1996 student body. Men's basketball players overall were at 44 percent for the 1996 class compared to 43 percent for 1995. Neither group has graduated at a higher rate than the student body in any year since graduation rates began being tracked with the 1984 class, but both have experienced increases in each of the last two classes. It is also important to note that these groups of student-athletes do tend to graduate at higher rates than their gender and ethnic group counterparts in the student body.

Rates continue to be high in women's basketball, as the 1996 class posted a rate of 66 percent, one percentage point higher than the 1995 group.

The NCAA report is further evidence that students who do not consciously work to overcome academic weaknesses in high school may significantly reduce the odds of their succeeding in college.

Study Groups

As you enter high school, you are going to be developing relationships with all types of students. They are going to be involved in all types of activities. They are going to have a wide range of contacts, from older siblings who are currently attending college to parents who are gathering information for their college plan. Yes, your friends are going to be headed in all types of directions—some toward college and others toward alternative school or dropping out of school. Some will be developing leadership skills while others will be constantly getting into trouble. Some will be developing their bodies and expanding their minds while others will begin abusing their bodies with drugs, tobacco, or alcohol.

If you are college-bound, then you should try to develop relationships with other college-bound students—students with similar hopes, dreams, and aspirations. If your high school plan includes taking honors and AP classes, then you are going to be in classes with other students who have high aspirations and who are willing to put forth the time and effort to be successful academically. Such individuals may or may not be among your current friends. While some students perform well by reviewing their class notes and studying independently, many students benefit from study

groups where they discuss class notes, share ideas, review their work and prepare for tests and exams as a group.

As you enter college, you will find many study groups. When I was in my first year of college as an electrical engineering major, my girlfriend was also an engineering major. We were taking the same classes and we belonged to a study group comprised of engineering students. Later in college I became a tutor and I led study groups in Accounting, Business Policy, and Statistics.

Since you are likely to join a study group in college, it would be a good idea to form study groups during high school. You may find them particularly beneficial in your more challenging classes—those classes or subjects where you are experiencing difficulty or have an acknowledged weakness.

Tutors

Do not get left behind. You are not always going to make a connection with all of your teachers. Sometimes you will experience a teaching-style–learning-style match and at other times you will experience a teaching-style–learning-style mismatch. In classes like math and science, which are challenging subjects in themselves, you may find yourself experiencing difficulty fully understanding concepts or equations that are being covered. This does not necessarily have anything to do with your intelligence or the teacher's effectiveness. However, it is your grades that admissions officers are going to be reviewing so it is your responsibility to let the teacher know when you are having difficulty. If you continue to find yourself struggling, it is your responsibility to find a tutor. Oftentimes, a tutor will have more time to explain problems and concepts in greater detail than what the teacher covers in class.

Finding a tutor can be a difficult task. Not every tutor will be the right one for you. However, unlike your classroom teacher, you can continue changing tutors until you find the one who best meets your needs or makes the best connection with your learning-style. Once you find the right tutor for each subject, you may find yourself working with a particular tutor through multiple classes. For example, a knowledgeable math tutor may be able to help you through Algebra I, Algebra II, Geometry, and Calculus. Next to your counselor, your tutor may become one of the most important members of your team.

Our son's Pre-Calculus tutor is a former math teacher and provides help in all of the math classes including AP Statistics. She also provides SAT and SAT Subject Test preparation. She was referred by the chairperson of the math department at our son's high school and provided invaluable support to our son. In addition to the once-per-week tutorial session, she worked with him prior to exams and was available for e-mail support to answer homework questions. The support that she provided enabled our son to bring his course grade from an 'F' to a 'B.' By working with her he was able to score an 'A' on his Pre-Calculus final exam. Our younger son utilized the same tutor during each year of middle school. This helped him to enroll in the highest level math classes, qualify for the honor roll each semester of middle school, pass the end-of-grade test in mathematics each year, and maintain the 80+ average required to be accepted into the high school Math/Science Magnet Program, and to begin high school in a honors level math class.

Notes:

Having or needing a tutor is nothing to be embarrassed about. Some of the highest academically-achieving students have tutors in every subject. In fact, the highest achieving students are themselves the most readily available and easily accessible tutors. Even when they do not serve as tutors, they oftentimes can provide recommendations to knowledgeable tutors for a variety of subjects. You may also be able to find a tutor through your teacher or through the department chairperson. The Math, Science, English, and Foreign Language department chairpersons frequently have a list of tutors whom they recommend. Many students choose to limit their after-school or extracurricular activities to concentrate more time on studying; however, keep in mind that admissions officers at top colleges are looking for students who have good grades AND are involved in extracurricular activities. An effective tutor may provide you with the opportunity to do both.

Academic Clubs

Consider joining clubs related to your academic areas—science, math, computer programming, foreign language, etc. Students involved in these clubs have probably taken classes that you are going to take and will have comments and information about teachers, tutors, course content, and how to succeed.

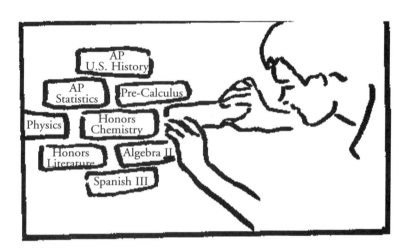

Chapter 5

Some of the most competitive schools now look for special intellectual passion in applicants as another way of distinguishing between superb candidates and more-than-superb candidates. It has, in fact, become nearly imperative to show special intellectual prowess beyond classroom participation to be admitted to some of the top schools. MIT, for example, rates all applicants on a scale of 1 to 5, with 5 being the best rating, in four separate areas: Academics, Co-curricular Activities, Extracurricular Activities, and Interpersonal Skills. Co-curricular Activities are described as "learning-oriented activities that take place outside the classroom." Applicants must be able to show that they participate in academic pursuits beyond what is required of them at school in order to stay in the running for admission at MIT.

— *[College Admissions Trade Secrets]*

Academic Honors

Begin high school with a focus on the types of honors, awards, and recognition that you would like to receive. Each state, local district, and high school recognizes student achievement differently. Identifying the available awards as you enter high school will help you to establish goals that include awards in a broad range of areas. Many colleges are interested in developing a diverse and well-rounded college community. Keep in mind that no award or recognition is too small to be overlooked.

There are many opportunities for high school students to be recognized by their school, or local community, local government, religious, civic, and professional organizations. To ensure that you do not miss anything when it is time to complete your college application, establish a routine of making note of your awards in your college-planning notebook

Notes:

and filing your award in your awards box immediately upon receiving or being notified of the award.

Following is a listing of the awards and honors common in many high schools. Research available awards and honors at your high school and within your community.

- **AP Scholars:** Seniors completing five or more AP courses in at least four areas of study.

- **Faculty Cup:** Selected by entire staff and presented to graduating senior.

- **Honor Roll:** Overall average of 85 or higher.

- **Journal Cup:** Selected by entire staff and presented to best all-around senior.

- **Legion of Honor:** Students qualifying for principal's list each of previous four quarters.

- **Legion of Scholars:** Students maintaining honor roll during the previous 4 quarters.

- **PTSA Cup:** Senior Journal Cup runner-up.

- **Principal's List:** No grade below C.

- **Salutatorian:** #2 ranked student.

- **Sigma Alpha Tau:** Seniors earning a composite SAT score of 1200 or higher.

- **Star Student:** Senior with highest SAT score.

- **Super Honor Roll:** Overall average of 90 or higher.

- **Valedictorian:** #1 ranked student.

- **VIP Night:** Students who have made a positive contribution to school climate and are recommended by teachers, coaches, and sponsors.

State, Federal, and National Awards

There are many local, state, and national awards available to students in recognition of academic and artistic achievement. Just being recommended for such awards can enhance your profile and college application. Ask your counselor about any local, state, and national awards for which you may qualify.

Robert C. Byrd Honors Scholarship

The Robert C. Byrd Honors Scholarship Program is a federally-funded, state-administered program to recognize exceptionally able high school seniors who show promise of continued excellence in postsecondary education. This scholarship is designed to support high school graduates for their study at the postsecondary level through an award amount of $1,500 per academic year. For more information, go to *www.ed.gov/programs/iduesbyrd/index.html* or ask your counselor for an application.

National Merit Scholar

The National Merit Scholarship Corporation (NMSC) is an independent, not-for-profit organization that conducts the National Merit Scholarship Program and the National Achievement Scholarship Program—annual competitions for recognizing outstanding students and awarding college undergraduate scholarships. The National Merit Scholarship Program is an academic competition that began in 1955. High school students enter the National Merit Program by taking the PSAT/NMSQT— a test that serves as an initial screening of approximately 1.3 million entrants each year— and by meeting published program entry/participation requirements.

The NMSC has recognized 2.4 million students and provided close to 300,000 scholarships worth more than one billion dollars.

Student Entry Requirements

To participate in the National Merit Scholarship Program, a student must:

- take the PSAT/NMSQT in the specified year of the high school program and no later than the third year in grades 9 through 12, regardless of grade classification or educational pattern;

- be enrolled full time as a high school student, progressing normally toward graduation or completion of high school, and planning to enter college no later than the fall following completion of high school; and

- be a citizen of the United States; or be a permanent U.S. resident (or have applied for permanent residency) and intend to become a U.S. citizen at the earliest opportunity allowed by law.

The student's responses to items on the PSAT/NMSQT answer sheet that are specific to NMSC program entry determine whether the individual meets requirements to participate in the National Merit Scholarship Program. Score reports provided for test takers and their schools indicate whether the student meets program entry requirements.

Program Recognition

Of the 1.3 million entrants, some 50,000 with the highest PSAT/NMSQT Selection Index scores (verbal + math + writing skills scores) will qualify for recognition in the National Merit Scholarship Program. In April following the fall test, high-scoring participants from every state will be invited to name two colleges or universities, which they would like to be referred by NMSC. In September, these high scorers will be notified through their schools that they have qualified as either a Commended Student or Semifinalist.

Commended Students

In late September, more than two-thirds or about 34,000 of the approximately 50,000 high scorers on the PSAT/

NMSQT will receive Letters of Commendation in recognition of their outstanding academic promise, but they will not continue in the competition for Merit Scholarship® awards. Some of these students, however, will be candidates for Special Scholarships sponsored by corporations and businesses.

Semifinalists

In early September, about 16,000 students, or approximately one-third of the 50,000 high scorers, will be notified that they have qualified as Semifinalists. To ensure that academically able young people from all parts of the United States are included in this talent pool, Semifinalists are designated on a state representational basis. NMSC will provide scholarship application materials to Semifinalists through their high schools. To be considered for a Merit Scholarship award, Semifinalists must advance to Finalist standing in the competition by meeting high academic standards and all other requirements explained in the materials provided to each Semifinalist.

Finalists

In February, some 15,000 Semifinalists will be notified by mail at their home addresses that they have advanced to Finalist standing. High school principals will be notified and provided with a certificate to present to each Finalist.

Winner Selection

A variety of information is available for NMSC selectors to evaluate—the Finalist's academic record, information about the school's curricula and grading system, two sets of test scores, school recommendation, information about the student's activities and leadership, and the Finalist's own essay. All winners of Merit Scholarship® awards (Merit Scholar® designees) will be chosen from the Finalist group, based on their abilities, skills, and accomplishments.

Merit Scholar Designees

Beginning in March, NMSC will notify approximately 8,000 Finalists that they have been selected to receive a Merit Scholarship award. Merit Scholarship awards are of three types:

- *National Merit Scholarships:* Every Finalist competes for single-payment $2500 scholarships, which are awarded on a state representational basis.

- *Corporate-sponsored Merit Scholarship Awards:* Corporate sponsors designate their awards for children of their employees or members, for residents of a community where a company has operations, or for Finalists with career plans the sponsor wishes to encourage. These scholarships may be either renewable for four years of undergraduate study or one-time awards.

- *College-sponsored Merit Scholarship Awards:* Officials of each sponsor college select winners of their awards from Finalists who have been accepted for admission and have informed NMSC by the published deadlines that the sponsor college or university is their first choice. These awards are renewable for up to four years of undergraduate study.

Merit Scholarship Awards are supported by some 550 independent sponsors and by NMSC's own funds. Sponsor organizations include corporations and businesses, company foundations, professional associations, and colleges and universities.

Special Scholarship Candidates

Every year, some 1,600 National Merit Program participants who are outstanding, but not Finalists, are awarded Special Scholarships provided by corporations and business organizations for students who meet the sponsor's criteria. To be considered for a Special Scholarship, students must meet the sponsor's criteria and entry requirements of the National Merit Scholarship Program. They also must file an entry form directly with the sponsor organization, which forwards the forms to NMSC. NMSC subsequently contacts a pool of high-scoring candidates through their high schools. These students and their school officials submit detailed scholarship applications. A committee from the NMSC evaluates information about candidates' abilities, skills, and accomplishments and chooses winners of the sponsor's Special Scholarships. These scholarships may be either renewable for four years of undergraduate study or one-time awards.

A list of corporate organizations that sponsor both Merit Scholarship and Special Scholarship awards is given in the PSAT/NMSQT Student Bulletin. For more information, go to *www.collegeboard.com/student/testing/psat/about.html.*

National Achievement Scholars

The National Achievement[SM] Scholarship Program is an academic competition established in 1964 to provide recognition for outstanding Black American high school students. Black students may enter both the National Achievement Program and the National Merit Program by taking the PSAT/ NMSQT and meeting other published requirements for participation. The two  annual programs are conducted simultaneously, but operated and funded separately. A student's standing is determined independently in each program. Black American students can qualify for recognition and be honored as Scholars in both the National Merit Program and the National Achievement Program, but can receive only one monetary award from NMSC. For more information, go to *www.nationalmerit. org/nasp.html.*

Student Entry Requirements

To participate in the National Achievement[SM] Scholarship Program, a student must:

- take the PSAT/NMSQT in the specified year of the high school program and no later than the third year in grades 9 through 12, regardless of grade classification or educational pattern;

- request entry to the National Achievement Program by marking the specific space provided on the PSAT/ NMSQT answer sheet;

- be enrolled full time as a high school student, progressing normally toward graduation or

Notes:

completion of high school, and planning to enter college no later than the fall following completion of high school; and

- be a citizen of the United States; or be a permanent U.S. resident (or have applied for permanent residency) and intend to become a U.S. citizen at the earliest opportunity allowed by law.

Information supplied by the student on the PSAT/ NMSQT answer sheet determines whether the individual meets requirements for participation in the National Achievement Program. The PSAT/NMSQT Student Bulletin, which high schools receive for distribution to their students before the test administration date, shows all sections of the answer sheet that apply to NMSC program entry requirements, including the section Black American students must mark to request consideration in the National Achievement Program. A school official or the student should report immediately to NMSC any error or change that may affect participation.

Program Recognition

Of the more than 120,000 students who currently enter the National Achievement[SM] Program each year, approximately 4,600 will be honored. A group of about 3,000 will be referred to colleges for their academic promise. A smaller group of about 1,600 will be named Semifinalists, the only students who have an  opportunity to advance in the competition for Achievement Scholarship® awards.

Participants Referred to Colleges

Each year, up to 3,000 National Achievement[SM] Program participants are brought to the attention of about 1,500 four-year U.S. colleges and universities. In late September, a roster of these students' names, high schools, and tentative college majors and career choices will be sent to higher education officials to enhance the admission and financial-aid opportunities of these academically promising students.

Semifinalists

At least 1,600 top-performing participants in each year's National Achievement[SM] Scholarship Program are designated Semifinalists. To ensure that able Black American students throughout the nation will be included in the pool, Semifinalists are named on a regional representational basis. Semifinalists are the highest-scoring program participants in the states that constitute each region. Application materials will be sent to Semifinalists through their high schools. Before being considered for an Achievement Scholarship Award, a Semifinalist must advance to Finalist standing in the competition by meeting high academic standards and other requirements explained in materials provided to each Semifinalist.

Finalists

In late January, approximately 1,300 Semifinalists will be notified by mail at their home addresses that they have qualified as Finalists. High school principals will be notified and provided with a certificate to present to each Finalist. All Achievement Scholarship Award winners (Achievement Scholar designees) will be selected from the group of able Finalists based on their abilities, skills and accomplishments.

Achievement Scholar Designees

Beginning in mid-February, the National Achievement[SM] Program will notify more than 775 Finalists that they have been selected to receive Achievement Scholarship® Awards.

Achievement Scholarship Awards are of two types:

- *National Achievement $2500 Scholarships:* Every Finalist competes for these single-payment scholarships, which are awarded on a regional representational basis.

- *Corporate-sponsored Achievement Scholarship Awards:* Over 100 corporate-sponsored awards that may be either renewable for four years of undergraduate study or one-time awards.

Presidential Scholar

The United States Presidential Scholars Program was established in 1964, by Executive Order of the President, to recognize and honor our nation's most distinguished high school students. In 1979, the program was extended to recognize students who demonstrate exceptional talent in the visual, creative, and performing arts.

Each year, 141 high school seniors are named *Presidential Scholars*. These students are chosen on the basis of academic and artistic success, leadership, and involvement in school and community affairs.

There are two ways to become a Presidential Scholar:

- 121 students are chosen on the basis of "broad academic achievement."

- 20 students are selected as arts scholars, on the basis of excellence in visual, performing, or creative arts, in addition to scholastic achievement.

Notes:

For more information on the Presidential Scholars program go to *www.presidentialscholars.org*.

Governor's Honors

Many states have differing versions of the Governor's Honors program, which provides extended-learning opportunities and financial awards for students and is based on academic, artistic, or community service criteria established by the state. Go to your state department of education's web site for information pertaining to such programs as:

- *Georgia Governor's Honors Program (www.doe.k12. ga.us/support/sss/scholarships.asp)*

  A six-week summer instructional program for juniors and seniors, based on teacher recommendations, and designed to provide intellectually gifted and artistically talented high school students with challenging and enriching educational opportunities.

- *California Governor's Honors Program (www. scholarshare.com/gsp/index.html)*

  Provides $1,000 scholarships to students who demonstrate high academic achievement on certain exams in the Standardized Testing and Reporting (STAR) program in the 9th, 10th, or 11th grades as reported by the testing services that administer the exams each spring.

- *West Virginia Governor Honor's Academy (www. wvgovschools.org/gha/)*

  Offered to students who are currently juniors in high school. Recipients live and learn with 164 other outstanding West Virginia scholars in a three-week residential experience.

N o t e s :

- *Utah Governor's Honors Academy (www.suu.edu/ss/ admission/gha/)*

  The Academy is organized to provide Utah high school students with an opportunity to learn from and interact with some of the foremost leaders in business, technology, humanities, science, education, communication and social science.

State Scholar Programs

Go to your state department of education's web site to identify what, if any, types of state scholarship programs are available and what the requirements are. Many states offer programs such as:

- *Georgia Scholars Awards (www.doe.k12.ga.us/support/ sss/scholarships.asp)*

- *Indiana's Hoosier Scholar Awards (www.in.gov/ssaci/ programs/hsa.html)*

  A $500 non-renewable award available to students who rank within the top 20 percent of their class and who are selected by their high school guidance counselor.

- *Florida's Bright Future Scholars Awards (www.firn.edu/ doe/bin00072/home0072.htm)*

- *Maryland's Distinguished Scholar Award (www.mhec. state.md.us/financialAid/ProgramDescriptions/prog_ ds.asp)*

  Available to current high school juniors who may apply or may be nominated by their high schools.

Finalists in the National Merit Scholarship and National Achievement Scholarship programs will automatically receive the award if they attend a Maryland institution.

United States Senate Youth Program

The United States Senate Youth Program was created for outstanding high school students to help broaden their knowledge and understanding of Congress and the legislative process in our nation's Capitol; to demonstrate the importance of a freely elected legislature in the perpetuation of an effective democratic system of government; and, to dramatize in particular the crucial role the Senate performs in the maintenance of our government (check with your state department of education).

Siemens Westinghouse Competition

The leading science and mathematics research-based competition for high school students in the United States, The Siemens Foundation, in partnership with the College Board, established the Siemens Westinghouse Competition to promote excellence by encouraging students to undertake individual or team research projects in science, mathematics, engineering and technology or in combinations of these disciplines. For more information, go to *www.siemens-foundation.org/scholarship*.

Research Available Programs

Identify the honors and awards that you would like to earn in high school and research some of the many available programs and opportunities. As you are recommended for, or are awarded honors, list them on worksheets in the *workbook*. If you keep track of these as you progress through high school, you will have all the information that you need to complete your résumé and college applications. Remember that a recommendation or consideration for an award can be just as impressive as receiving the award itself.

Many people do many great things and make important contributions to their community, but are embarrassed by public recognition. They serve from their hearts, not for awards or recognition. However, you have to accept that awards, honors, and formal recognition are important. There are many people who do good deeds ONLY so that they can be recognized and build impressive-looking application packages. These will be some of the people with whom you will be competing for college admission. Do not get left behind. Get recognized!

Notes:

There are many local, state, national, and international academic and scholarship competitions that reflect a broad range of academic areas and student interests.

As there are local, state, national, and international competitions in dance and sports, there are programs and competitions that relate to a student's passion in math, science, literature, geography, speech and debate, and other academic areas.

Chapter 6

The increasing number of students who met GPA and minimum course requirements caused university admissions officers to pay closer attention to the composition of the high school transcript and the number and type of academic courses that applicants took. Next, they scrutinized more closely the challenge level of the academic courses. Were they honors courses? In what other ways did the students demonstrate intellectual rigor? Gradually, more weight was placed on Advanced Placement (AP) courses, and more recently, on the International Baccalaureate (IB) program. The effect of increased emphasis on AP has been particularly striking. An outstanding student in the mid-1980s might have taken one or two AP courses. Now, the transcripts of comparable students commonly contain five or six such courses.

— *[College Knowledge: What It Really Takes for Students to Succeed and What We Can Do to Get Them Ready]*

Plan Your Schedule

After familiarizing yourself with your school district's graduation requirements, types of diplomas offered, and the amount of academic preparation that your top-ten colleges want to see in students admitted into their freshman class, you must develop your four-year high school schedule accordingly. If you began your college planning in middle school, your high school schedule will represent the final four years of the seven-year schedule that you outlined in middle school. If you are only beginning the process of developing your high school schedule, then you should plan to discuss or revise your schedule as needed with your counselor or career advisor.

You may find developing a high school schedule a more difficult task than developing a college schedule. In college, a student is likely to take no more than four or five courses per quarter or semester (at Dartmouth College students take only three classes per quarter), whereas on a traditional high school schedule, a student is likely to take six to eight classes. Also, at many colleges a student has the opportunity to sit in on classes for a week or more to determine if he or she likes the instructor or is really interested in the course, whereas high school students rarely have choices of teachers or the flexibility of sitting in on a class before making a commitment to taking the class.

What You Want to Achieve

Your high school class schedule should:

1. Meet the mandatory graduation requirements within your school district.

2. Reflect as many advanced classes, which you can handle, to maximize your GPA and achieve a higher class ranking.

3. Meet the mandatory admissions requirements at the college(s) you are applying to (and the NCAA Clearinghouse requirements, if you are planning on becoming a student-athlete).

4. Demonstrate to a college admissions committee your willingness to challenge yourself by taking the most demanding classes offered in your high school.

5. Reflect electives that provide an underlying academic or special-interest focus area that will support your college application or essay.

North Springs
High School

Home of the "Spartans"

Course Offerings
2003-2004

Notes:

Review your school's or school district's course catalog and meet with your counselor to ensure that you understand the prerequisites, enrollment criteria, and correct sequencing of classes to develop your academic and elective schedule.

Important Resources

All of the information that you need to evaluate classes and plan your high school course schedule is contained within one or more publications available from your high school, school district's offices, or from your state department of education. Course descriptions, GPA calculations, AP course offerings, and exit exam criteria can usually be found through the following resources:

- *Student Planner/Agenda*

- *School District Curriculum Handbook*

- *High School Course Offerings*

- *School District web site*

- *State Department of Education web site*

- *College Board web site for description of AP classes (www.collegeboard.com)*

- *International Baccalaureate Organization web site for description of IB classes (www.ibo.org)*

- *Local college, community college, and junior college course catalogs and joint enrollment program descriptions*

Summer School, Night School, Online Classes

Your four-year high school course schedule should be viewed as your ticket to the dance. The classes that you take and the grades that you receive will either enhance or hinder

Admit One to First-Choice College or University

your opportunity to get through the admissions process and into the college of your choice.

The mention of summer school conjures up images of rows of struggling students. However, more students are using summer school as an opportunity to take classes that are required for graduation—Social Studies, P.E., Health, Electives, etc.—to free their schedule during the school year for additional math, science, language arts, honors, or AP classes. Other students take classes in summer school as a means of meeting their graduation requirements by the end of their junior year or the first semester of their senior year. This approach allows for early graduation, college enrollment, or internship opportunities. Discuss the full range of options with your counselor.

Night school, junior college, or online programs may provide other opportunities to take required, elective, or special-focus classes. Some school districts offer online classes or have agreements with neighboring school districts offering such classes. Many students find the online learning experience an enjoyable and engaging one. Those students who spend a great deal of time on their computers playing video games or in chat rooms oftentimes find themselves more engaged in online classes than in their regular classes. As in the case of summer school, night school, or junior college, online programs provide an opportunity to take a greater number of math, science, honors, or AP classes during the normal school year.

Our son took Health & Fitness and honors Economics through our school district's online summer school program. The online program allowed him to fulfill his P.E. requirement and one of his social science requirements.

Extended Learning Opportunities

Extended learning opportunities are just that—opportunities to participate in programs that may not be offered or are not readily available to students at your high school. Oftentimes, only a few people know about such opportunities: parents with children who participated in the past, students with a sibling or friend who told them about the program, or parents/students who have a relationship with a teacher or counselor who gives them the inside track to these oftentimes little-publicized programs, camps, or enrichment opportunities.

Some of the extended learning opportunities may include:

- Internships
- Independent study
- Taking the school's yearbook class, developing the school's web site, or working on the staff of the school newspaper
- Exchange programs with other schools
- Community-service projects
- Working on a political campaign
- Enrolling in an academic or pre-college camp
- Attending Space Camp
- After-school jobs that can be designed to become internships like working at a nail salon for entrepreneurial studies, working at a senior citizen home for nursing studies, designing brochures for graphic arts studies, writing/publishing a book, etc.

9th Grade

Beginning in 9th grade, take the most challenging classes. Whether you are one of those students who experience difficulty making the 9th-grade transition into high school or one of those students who immediately become involved in sports, student organizations, and extracurricular activities, you must develop the class schedule that is most appropriate for you. Consider all options when planning your course schedule so you do not overburden yourself. Take the most challenging schedule, which you believe you can achieve the highest grades.

Most school districts require only two years of a foreign language, but if you are interested in a foreign language, you should plan to take the same one during each of your four years of high school. Classes taken in each of the following areas will meet most high school graduation, college enrollment, and NCAA Clearinghouse requirements:

- 4 years of a foreign language
- 4 years of science (with two lab sciences)
- 4 years of math
- 4 years of English/literature

The additional requirements of social studies, health and fitness, art, music, or other electives can be scheduled around these core classes.

Take classes that improve your reading and writing skills. Classes in history, philosophy, and literature will strengthen your reading, writing, and language foundation. Enhance your thoughts, ideas, and communication skills by actively participating in class and group discussions. When you submit your college applications, you will be required to provide teacher recommendations. You want teachers to be able to recall your active participation in classroom discussions and allude to your insightful ideas and opinions.

Students who have a primary language other than English should explore the opportunities for taking four years of high school foreign language in their native language.

The high school course offerings can be particularly beneficial for students who are not as proficient at reading and writing in their native language as they are speaking the language. They can also benefit from four years of study leading to one or more of the available AP exams in Spanish, French, and German.

During Spring Break, plan to get two SAT Subject Test books and study for two SAT Subject Tests to be given in May. Pick your two best subjects. Identify a special-interest summer camp, pre-college program, or summer-school program to strengthen or enhance one of more academic areas. Continue reading, writing, and further developing your communication skills. You will also benefit by beginning to study a SAT vocabulary building book. Read newspapers, magazines, novels, and any other material that expands your vocabulary and comprehension skills.

10th Grade

Carefully select among honors and AP classes available to sophomores at your school. However, do not take such a rigorous course schedule that you cannot play a sport or become involved in other student or extracurricular activities. Colleges will look for students who were academically challenged as well as students who contributed to their school community through sports,  student government, extracurricular activities, and community service participation. Try to put yourself on track toward AP U.S. History in the 11th grade and AP Literature or College English by the 12th grade. You also want to continue in higher-level math and science classes.

Plan to take the SAT, ACT, and PSAT. All your scores will help to identify your strengths and weaknesses. Remember that your 11th-grade PSAT scores are used to qualify for National Merit or National Achievement Scholar Recognition.

By Spring Break begin preparing for at least two more SAT Subject Tests. Again, choose your best subjects. Use the summer months to continue strengthening your areas of interests and preparing yourself academically for the challenging classes that you plan to take during your junior year. Continue summer camp, pre-college, or summer-school opportunities to push yourself academically.

11th Grade

Hopefully you will be on track to take a full schedule of the most demanding classes available at your high school during your junior and senior year. You can arrive at this point only if you pushed yourself during your 9th- and 10th-grade years with challenging classes. Your advanced course schedule should have prepared you to do well on the SAT, ACT, and PSAT. Begin working on your application and financial-aid essays. If you have enrolled in honors or AP Literature, your teacher may be willing to critique your essays.

Identify any remaining SAT Subject Tests that are required by the colleges on your top-ten list. If you have met their requirements, then plan to take two more SAT Subject Tests in your favorite subjects. Many colleges may require one specific SAT Subject Test and allow you to submit two or three of your choice. You want to submit your highest scores. Plan to take any final SAT Subject Tests in May or June.

12th Grade

Avoid believing that taking a challenging course load in 9th through 11th grade allows you to take easy classes during your senior year. A bodybuilder would not maintain a healthy diet, five-day-a-week workouts, extensive cardiovascular training, only to take a year off. One year off may take three years to regain his or her physique, form, and muscular definition. Your rigorous high school schedule has been designed not simply to get you admitted into college, but to enable you to succeed while there.

Notes:

Schedule and College Choice

As you plan your high school schedule, you must keep in mind your top-ten list of colleges. Different colleges are interested in different academic backgrounds. No matter what college interests you, you should avoid taking too many easy classes and electives during your 9th- through 10th-grade years. You do not want to miss taking any necessary prerequisites for advanced classes during your 11th- and 12th-grade years. As previously mentioned, take classes that will enhance your reading, writing, and critical-thinking skills, all of which will benefit you when taking the writing portion of the SAT and ACT, the writing portion of any required graduation exams, and when writing your college application and scholarship essays.

In the first chapter, you were encouraged to think about your interests and reflect on your dreams. As you develop your course schedule, consider balancing classes that relate directly to your passionate areas of interest with classes that strengthen your weaknesses and provide the best opportunity to expand your studies and career pursuits. While you may be totally focused on pursuing a career as an artist today, you are likely to explore many more options and opportunities as you meet people, take various classes, and are exposed to new ideas, places, and information. Use your high school schedule to explore other areas of interest and to further develop your many creative, artistic, and intellectual intelligences.

Today's fine artist may be inspired to become tomorrow's computer animator, automotive designer, architect, or plastic surgeon. Your artistic passion may be enhanced through

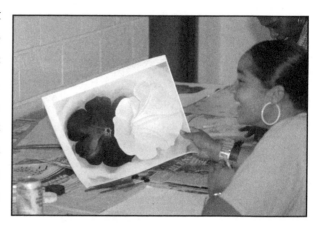

the study of anatomy, physics, calculus, literature, or history and may expand your artistic genius in ways previously unimaginable. Today's athlete may be inspired to become tomorrow's sports agent, personal trainer, nutritionist, sports

therapist, coach, physical education teacher, or health club owner. Your athletic passion may be enhanced through the study of anatomy, chemistry, physics, literature, economics, calculus, forensics, and statistics.

As you outline your course schedule, challenge yourself to develop the many regions and intellectual domains of your brain. Throughout this book, I have alluded to, and encouraged, your giving serious consideration to honors and AP classes. Now is the time for you to really think about what you want out of high school and the types of colleges where you are interested in applying. If you have a passion for sports or other extracurricular activities, you must take that desire into account when planning your course schedule. Also, if you are not interested in applying to top colleges, which are very competitive, you do not have to force yourself into such a rigorous academic schedule as to cause undue stress during your high school years when you should be enjoying your life and exploring your interests. Take time to sit and talk to your parents, coaches, teachers, counselor, or mentor to explore the type of life and future that is best for you. Consider the most challenging classes that you can handle as you develop your course schedule.

Meet with your counselor to ensure that you fully understand the prerequisite classes and enrollment criteria. Following are some questions to assist in guiding your

Notes:

discussions with your high school career or guidance counselor:

1. What are the required and recommended courses—for graduation and for college prep?

2. Are there any automatic admissions criteria for state colleges, for example, class rank?

3. Which elective courses do you recommend?

4. I have indicated the honors or AP courses that I am interested in taking and I would like to know if there is anything that I must do to meet all the prerequisites or enrollment requirements?

5. Can any of my elective or required classes be taken in summer school, night school, or online?

6. Are there tutors or is there a school-sponsored tutorial program that you would recommend?

7. What are your thoughts on the four-year schedule that I have developed?

8. When is the PSAT/NMSQT given?

9. Are there any after-school, evening, or special classes available for college planning or SAT/ACT preparation?

10. Do you have college handbooks or other guides that I may browse or borrow? Do you have a copy of the free "Taking the SAT" booklet that has a practice test in it?

11. Do you have a college-planning guide or calendar that outlines the types of things that I should be doing each year?

12. Is there a list of colleges that have a relationship with this school or actively recruit from this school?

13. Are there any college fairs at this school or nearby? And, if so, how can I find out when they are scheduled?

14. What are the requirements or standards for the honor society?

15. What clubs, organizations, community service, or student activities do you suggest that I consider joining or becoming involved in?

16. I have developed my top-ten list of schools. Do you have any information or are there any alumni from our school who can provide me with information about any of the schools on my list?

17. Are there any special scholarships or awards that I should be aware of so I can begin preparing myself?

18. How does our school compare to others, in terms of test scores, reputation, and ranking?

19. What is the deadline for submitting class requests for the next school year?

The critical areas to remember are:

• Take as many honors, AP, or advanced classes as you can

• Explore summer school, night school, joint or dual enrollment, and online opportunities

• Joint or dual enrollment classes may be good if you are planning to attend one of the colleges in your state, however, AP classes may be better if you are planning to apply to colleges outside of your state

• Fully understand prerequisite, enrollment criteria, sequencing and scheduling of classes

Refer to your school district's graduation requirements, diploma guidelines, and the sample schedules in the *workbook* to develop a preliminary draft of your four-year high school schedule.

Financial-Aid
Information

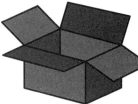

College
Information

As you sit down to develop your high school
schedule, begin with the end in mind.

Sample College Prep
Graduation Requirements

Language Arts   (4)

   Language Arts Core (3)
      9th Grade Literature
      10th Grade Literature
      11th Grade American Literature

   Language Arts Selective (1)

      AP Literature and Composition
      AP Language and Composition
      College English

Mathematics   (4)

   Algebra I
   Algebra II
   Geometry or Applied Geometry
   Selective (Above Algebra II)

Science   (3)

   Biology
   Physical Science
   Selective (science)
   or
   Biology
   Chemistry
   Physics

Social Studies   (3)
Health and Physical Education   (1)
Foreign Language   (2)
Electives   (5)

Total Graduation Credits   (22)

Chapter 7

One does not need to score 2400 to gain admission to the most selective schools in America, and that 25 percent of the students admitted to these schools have scores below the ranges some might consider Ivy League–type numbers. Twenty-five percent of Cornell's class of 2003—which in fact is about 800 students—had a best SAT score below 1270 (on the old SAT). It's safe to say that many more than 800 of the roughly 6500 plus students admitted to Cornell for the class of 2003 also had SAT scores below 1270 (on the old SAT). Students admitted to highly selective colleges who have scored below mid-range most likely have a major hook—exceptional personal qualities or some other facet that makes them compelling candidates for admission.

— *[What It Really Takes to Get into the Ivy League]*

Standardized Testing/Exit Exams

Most students and parents dread testing; however, it is a part of the educational landscape so you had better get used to it and you had better prepare for it. The major tests that students will take while attending high school are:

- **PSAT:** 9th, 10th, 11th grades (October)
- **SAT (also called the SAT Reasoning Test):** Offered several times a year
- **SAT Subject Test:** Subject tests that you should take close to completing the respective subject
- **ACT:** Offered five times a year
- **AP Exam:** Given in May
- **EOCT:** End-of-Course-Tests if required by state
- Graduation Tests if required by state

Avoid creating an unnecessary hurdle by not effectively preparing for college admissions tests or taking the tests too late. Begin preparing for the SAT and ACT as soon as you enter high school and take them no later than the end of 10th grade. Subsequently, you will have time to work on strengthening any weak areas and increasing your scores.

At our high school, the school year ends in May. While many of the underclassmen were preparing for their summer vacations, three football players were taking SAT and ACT prep classes. They each took the SAT and ACT in June of their sophomore year. They each scored high enough to meet the NCAA student-athlete eligibility requirements with one player scoring an 1120 on the old SAT and a 25 on the ACT. Both scores qualified for college admissions to all but the most selective colleges. Taking both exams

as sophomores provided each player with a valuable assessment of the areas of improvement needed and time to prepare for retaking the exams to increase their scores. All three players planned to retake the exams during the fall of their junior year, with one player scheduling an SAT prep class as part of his regular class schedule.

College admissions committees are trying to eliminate as many applications as possible to get to the right class size. Many colleges will eliminate thousands of applications to arrive at a class size of a few hundred students. Standardized test scores provide admissions committees with an easy way to eliminate applications.

Whether your first-choice college places a significant emphasis on test scores or not, it is in your best interest to do as well as you possibly can. This means preparation.

- If your school offers a test preparation class, take it.

- If your school does not offer a class, find a free class at a local library, place of worship, YMCA, or Boys and Girls Club.

- If you cannot find a free class, find one that you can afford, offered by one of the private companies:

  - *The Princeton Review (www.princetonreview.com)*
  - *Kaplan (www.kaplan.com)*
  - *Sylvan Learning Centers (www.educate.com)*
  - *The College Board (www.collegeboard.com)*

- If you cannot find a free class and you cannot afford to pay for one, pick up a test preparation book at the bookstore or local library and go onto the Internet and Google "SAT and ACT practice tests" and prepare yourself.

Take the SAT as early as your sophomore year—certainly by your junior year—to get your first assessment as to whether or not your scores qualify for admission into your top-

ten schools. If you are not satisfied with your scores, consider taking the test again, concentrating on one section (i.e., critical reading and writing, or the math). Hopefully, by concentrating your test preparation efforts on one section of the test, you will be prepared to take the test a third and final time, concentrating on the other section. Most colleges will accept the highest scores for each section, even if the tests were taken on different dates. Applying yourself and putting forth the effort to do your best work in your middle school and high school language arts and math classes will greatly enhance your preparation for the SAT and ACT.

Approach test preparation like an athlete preparing to run the 400 meters in a track meet. The 400-meter athlete who has not trained, has not had the proper nutrition, and who has not prepared himself or herself mentally is not going to perform well the day of the meet, no matter what happens the night before. However, the athlete who has trained (worked hard at his or her class work) maintained the proper nutrition (honors and AP classes) can benefit from 400-meter preparation. Such preparation may entail a walk around the track (reviewing what is going to be on the test), reviewing competitors' times (reviewing how much time is allowed for each section of the test), preparing himself or herself for each leg of the race (working out how much time to devote to each question within each section of the test), and showing up at the race mentally prepared to execute his or her game plan (being mentally ready to take the test).

Review Preparation

For students who are on an advanced math track, reviewing Algebra I, Algebra II and Geometry before taking the SAT and ACT is excellent preparation. Reviewing an SAT vocabulary book is also a good idea.

Notes:

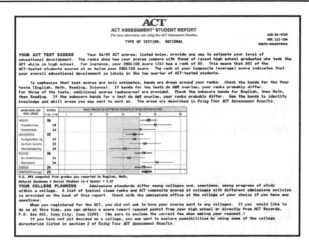

ACT

The ACT (American College Testing Exam) is a national college admission examination that consists of tests in English, Mathematics, Reading, Science, and an optional writing section.

ACT results are accepted by virtually all U.S. colleges and universities. The ACT includes 215 multiple-choice questions and takes approximately three hours and 30 minutes to complete with breaks.

Your score is based on the number of correct answers only, so if you are not sure, taking a guess does not hurt.

Actual testing time is two hours and 55 minutes. In the U.S., the ACT is administered on five national test dates—in October, December, February, April, and June. In selected states, the ACT is also offered in late September.

The ACT Assessment tests are curriculum-based. The ACT Assessment is not an aptitude or an I.Q. test. Instead, the questions on the ACT are directly related to what you should have learned in your high school courses in English, Reading, Mathematics, and Science. The scores on each section are averaged to create a composite score.

Many colleges accept the ACT in place of the combination of SAT and SAT Subject Tests. In 2003 the ACT reported that 79 of the 3,376 colleges surveyed for the ACT accepted it exclusively, 10 accepted the SAT exclusively, and all others accepted either.

An interactive CD-Rom is offered to assist students in test preparation.

ACT/SAT Conversion Table	
ACT	**SAT**
Score	
15	1060
16	1140
17	1210
18	1290
19	1350
20	1410
21	1500
22	1530
23	1590
24	1650
25	1700
26	1760
27	1820
28	1860
29	1920
30	1980
31	2040
32	2130
33	2190
34	2260
35	2340
36	2400

A perfect score is 36

ACT Registration
P.O. Box 168
2201 N. Dodge Street
Iowa City, IA 52243
(319) 337-1270
www.act.org

PSAT

The PSAT (Preliminary Scholastic Achievement Test) consists of two 25-minute Critical Reading sections, two 25-minute Math sections, and one 30-minute Writing skills section.

The PSAT provides practice for the SAT, an evaluation of your abilities in comparison with other college-bound students, an opportunity to enter scholarship competitions, a chance to learn about colleges interested in students with a profile similar to yours, and qualifies students for National Merit and National Achievement Scholarship consideration.

As a result of your answers to the PSAT questionnaire, you will begin receiving college information in the mail so be sure to answer the questions carefully and provide an accurate mailing address. The PSAT score range is between 20 and 80.

Junior-year scores are used to determine qualification for the National Merit and National Achievement Scholar programs.

A perfect score is 80

PSAT/NMSQT
P.O. Box 6720
Princeton, NJ 08541-6720
(609) 771-7070
www.collegeboard.com

SAT (SAT Reasoning Test)

The first SAT (Scholastic Aptitude Test) was administered in 1926 to 8,040 students. Today more than two million students annually take the SAT. The most recent change to the SAT occurred in 2005. The Verbal Section was replaced with the Writing and Critical Reading Sections. The Writing Section consists of a 35-minute multiple-choice section and a 25-minute essay. The Critical Reading Section consists of two 25-minute and one 20-minute sections. The Math Section consists of two 25-minute and one 20-minute sections. The SATs offered during October, November, December, January, March, May, and June.

The SAT carries a wrong answer penalty (either 1/4 or 1/3 point) with no deduction for blank answers.

While most colleges will allow students to combine their highest scores from different SATs—that is, their best writing, critical reading, and math scores—admissions officers receive all of your scores. Consider taking the SAT no more than three times. As a sophomore, you can obtain your baseline scores. This will help focus your test preparation efforts and strategies during your junior year. Some students will plan to take the test again, focusing all their energies and test preparation on one area, i.e., math or writing. If you are planning to take AP U.S. History or AP Literature, these classes will greatly enhance your writing, language, and communication skills and should help increase your SAT critical reading and writing scores. Following this, students may choose to take the SAT for a third and final time, concentrating all of their energies on the math section.

When you submit your ACT scores to colleges, they only see the scores from the testing date that you submit.

When you submit your SAT scores to colleges they see ALL of your scores from each SAT testing date. Although most colleges allow students to combine their highest scores from different testing dates, admissions officers will still see your lowest scores as well.

Each of the 3 sections (Math, Writing, and Critical Reading) has a top score of 800 points for a total top score of 2400.

SAT Program
(609) 771-7600
E-mail: sat@collegeboard.org
www.collegeboard.com

SAT Subject Test

The SAT Subject Test consists of tests offered in five Subject areas that are one-hour, mostly multiple-choice tests, designed to measure how much students know about a particular academic subject and how well they can apply that knowledge. Colleges use the test scores primarily for class placement; however, up to three tests may be required for some college admissions. The SAT Subject Test is offered during October, November, December, January, May, and June.

If you believe that you can perform well on SAT Subject Tests, then take them shortly after completing the subject in school while the information is still fresh in your mind. Include these scores with all of your scholarship and college applications. If you plan to apply to elite colleges, most will require 3 to 5 SAT Subject Tests. You should plan to begin taking them following the end of classes, beginning in the ninth grade so that by the time you start submitting your college applications, you will have taken the required number of SAT Subject Tests. Refer to your top-ten list of colleges and identify what and how many SAT Subject Tests each school requires. Focus on meeting the admission requirements and take the subject tests in your strongest areas.

Closely examine the admission requirements at the schools where you are applying. Some schools do not require SAT Subject Tests if the student is submitting an ACT score as opposed to an SAT score with his or her application.

Notes:

A perfect score is 800

SAT Subject Test Program
(609) 771-7600
E-mail: sat@collegeboard.org
www.collegeboard.com

Use the worksheets (located in the *workbook*) to track your high school progress and record your scores.

CLEP (College-Level Examination Program)

CLEP is the College-Level Examination Program that provides students with the opportunity to demonstrate college-level achievement through a program of exams in undergraduate college courses. There are 2,900 colleges that grant credit or advanced standing for CLEP exams. Each college publishes its qualifying criteria and number of credits awarded. The qualifying criteria and credits awarded will vary by college.

Talk to your counselor and log on to the college board web site for more information at *www.collegeboard.org*.

Average SAT/ACT College Admissions Scores

ACT Composite Score	College Selectivity	SAT I Total Score	Sample Colleges
17 – 20	Open Admissions	1210 – 1410	Bowie State University (MD) City College of New York City College of San Francisco Morgan State University (VA) Norfolk State University (VA)
18 – 21	Liberal Admissions	1290 – 1500	Villa Julie College (MD) Fairmont State College (WV) Bridgewater College (VA) Chowan College (NC)
20 – 23	Traditional	1410 – 1590	Frostburg University (MD) East Carolina University (NC) Hampton University (VA) George Mason University (VA) West Virginia University (WV)
22 – 27	Selective	1530 – 1820	Towson University (MD) Salisbury University (MD) University of Massachusetts Washington College (MD) Clemson University (SC) Spelman College (GA) Florida State University (FL)
27 – 36	Highly Selective	1820 – 2400	Yale University (CT) Amherst College (MA) Juilliard (NY) Cooper Union (NY) Duke University (NC) UNC Chapel Hill (NC) University of Virginia (VA) Georgetown University (DC) Harvard University (MA)

U.S. News and World Report provides a comprehensive college search and comparison web site:

http://colleges.usnews.rankingsandreviews.com/usnews/edu/college/rankings/rankindex_brief.php

Section II

Extracurricular

Activities

Chapter 8

Along with athletics, music is an extracurricular activity where admissions officers can evaluate an individual's talents and place a value on it in relation to the institutional needs and priorities. Highly selective institutions hold music in high regard, considering it both an academic pursuit and an extracurricular activity. NYU, Yale, and Columbia offer renowned conservatory programs in addition to their strong academic departments. Music departments at other schools offer individualized instruction and opportunities to perform on campus and within the music scene in the area.

— *[What it Really Takes to Get into The Ivy League & Other Highly Selective Colleges]*

Extracurricular Activities

Many of the country's top students, with the top grades and top SAT/ACT scores, do not get admitted into their first-choice colleges. Unfortunately, many of the top students are working so hard academically that they cannot find time to become involved in their school or community. It seems unfair that colleges want both scholarly students and students who are well-rounded as a result of their athletic, extracurricular activities, or community service involvement. However, that is exactly what they want.

There is no perfect GPA, SAT/ACT scores and extracurricular activity balance. Therefore, live your life! Play the sports that you enjoy, become involved in those student organizations that reflect your passions and interests, and perform community service because it is the right thing to do! College admissions officers are likely to value your passion, compassion, and contributions to your school or community.

Extracurricular Activities, College Admissions, & Financial Aid

As you apply to colleges, you will hear the term need-based financial aid. This will mean that a college will assist admitted students in meeting their full financial need based on their EFC (Expected Family Contribution). However, the financial-aid package may contain a combination of scholarships, grants, and loans. Your extracurricular activities may help to ensure that you maximize your scholarships and grants and minimize your need for loans. Unlike loans, scholarships and grants do not have to be repaid.

As you explore the wide range of extracurricular activities available both at your high school and within your community, civic, or clerical organizations, pay special attention to opportunities that can eventually lead to scholarship consideration. The obvious possibilities relate to athletics; however, there are many not-so-obvious opportunities that increase your chances of receiving a wide range of scholarship awards.

- Student Government

- Community Service

- Creative Arts (i.e., art, music, drama, etc.)

- Speech and Debate

- Science/Research Projects

- Faith-based and Membership Programs

Some scholarships actually require students to be involved in a particular activity such as student government. This is why you must begin your scholarship search as you enter high school. The information you gather may influence the activities, student organizations, and sports you choose. Recruited-athletes are perhaps the most visible and highly-publicized scholarship winners; however, your contribution to an extracurricular activity through leadership, creativity, innovation, or demonstration of character values may relate to or be reflective of highly valued attributes by a particular college. Identifying extracurricular activities that you will enjoy and 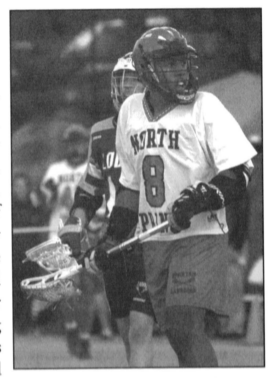 that also have scholarship potential can provide both a pleasurable experience and financial support for your college-bound dreams.

Your activity involvement must not be fly-by-night. Get involved, stay involved, and make a meaningful contribution.

Mychal Wynn • A High School Plan for Students with College-Bound Dreams

Notes:

Leadership

Academic preparation and standardized test scores have been covered in great detail because they undoubtedly are at the top of your stat sheet. They are the first things that the admissions officer will see and oftentimes will determine whether or not your application is rejected outright before he or she has had an opportunity to get to know who you are and the contribution you can make to his or her college community. If you make the first cut, your application will then be in a pile among hundreds, if not thousands, of other applications from students who are also academically qualified. It is at this point that who you are, what your interests are, and what contribution you can make to the college during your four years there and in society afterwards, will influence whether or not you are admitted.

- Sports
- Clubs
- Student Organizations
- Community Service
- Volunteer Hours
- Work Experience

True leadership is not reflected in how many offices you hold or the number of organizations you can claim membership, but by who you are and how your school, family, friends, and community have benefited from your skills, talents, gifts, abilities, and compassion. School districts spend huge amounts of money teaching character values to elementary and middle school students; now, as a high school student, you have the choice of standing for something or falling for anything. If your friends encourage rebellion against your parents or mean-spirited behavior toward other students,

Notes:

you have the opportunity to define yourself and discover your purpose—not as a sheep in the herd, but as a shepherd of the herd; not as a goose on a mindless migration, but as an eagle soaring high above the clouds.

Admissions officers are interested in not only that you played a sport, but that you were willing to accept the responsibility of being the captain or co-captain of the team, you organized a study hall, you tutored players, or encouraged teammates to focus on their academic preparation with the same passion as they prepared for athletic competition. An admissions officer is interested in not only that you belonged to organizations, but that your involvement resulted in meaningful contributions through innovation, creativity, and collaboration. When you submit your college essays and you are asked for words that describe your character, will such words as integrity, perseverance, compassion, collaboration, self-motivation, responsibility, and respect reflect who you are and what you stand for?

Look for leadership opportunities. Make a positive contribution to your high school and to your community so that when you leave, you will have made your mark and established your legacy. A legacy, measured not by the number of varsity letters on your jacket or by the number of offices that you held, but through the memories of those who knew the real you and your genuine deeds. A legacy that inspires others to provide testimony to your character. Nothing on your application shouts so loudly as, "What you have done!"

Extracurricular Activities/Clubs

Clubs & Organizations

21st Century Leaders
4-H
Academic Bowl
American Legion
 Auxiliary Boys
American Legion
 Auxiliary Girls
Aquarium
Art Club
Art Honor Society
Big Brothers/Big Sisters
Biology
Boys & Girls Club
Business Professionals
 of America
Chess
Choir
Civil Air Patrol
Color Guard
Computer Club
D.A.R.E.
Debate Team
DECA
DJ
Drama
Drill Team
Fellowship of
 Christian Athletes
Friends of the Library
Foreign Language
Future Business
 Leaders of America
Future Homemakers
 of America
Habitat for Humanity
Hugh O'Brian Youth
 Leadership
Junior Achievement
Junior Classical League
Junior Statesmen
 of America
Key
Letterman

Identify the full range of extracurricular activities (i.e., sports, clubs, organizations, community service, etc.) available at your high school and pick at least two you are willing to commit to for four years. Colleges are interested in your commitment and contribution to your activities. The greater the number of years that you demonstrate involvement in a particular activity, the more supportive it will be of your overall college application.

If some of the schools on your top-ten list are exclusive or highly-competitive colleges, then do some research and identify the clubs, student activities, or student organizations that are important to each school. Join one of the clubs or student organizations that would be highly thought of at your first-choice school and prepare to mention your involvement on your essay and during your interview. Otherwise, join a club or participate in an activity that you will enjoy and

make a contribution that can be mentioned prominently on your college application and in your personal bio.

Community Service

Community service is important to many colleges and it is a good thing to do. It builds personal character and strengthens your community. Again, your involvement should be with a project or activity where you commit the necessary time to make a meaningful contribution. You do not want to put on your college application, "I fed homeless people one year."

I coached youth basketball for my then, 10-year-old son and my 16-year-old son was an assistant coach during each of his first two years of high school. He learned to work well with young children and made a significant contribution to the overall youth sports program. He was also an instructor at a martial arts school where he learned to work with both adults and young children. His first job was in the capacity of, "Birthday Ninja." During birthday parties at the martial arts school, his job was to perform a martial arts demonstration. The room was totally black and he performed his demonstration with

weapons that glowed in the dark. He developed a reputation and birthday parties at the martial arts school became some of the most popular in the community. The owner of the martial arts school provided a glowing recommendation of his character, willingness to work with others, and effectiveness in working with children.

Identify a community service project that would be of value to your community and that you would enjoy. Consider your personal areas of interest and ask the question, "How can I do what I enjoy and use it to benefit my country, place of worship, school, or community?" Also consider becoming involved with a local sorority or fraternity, Big Brothers Big Sisters, civic, community, or mentoring organization.

Clubs & Organizations

Math Club
Math Honor Society
Model U.N.
Mu Alpha Theta
Music Honor Society
National Beta
National FFA
National Forensic League
National Honor Society
National Young Leaders
  Conference
Outdoors
Pep Squad
People to People Student
  Ambassador Program
Photography
Quill and Scroll Society
Quiz Bowl
R.O.T.C.
Scholastic Bowl
Science Club
Science Honor Society
Scouts: Boy/Girl
Service
Speech Team
Staff Member
  Newspaper
  Yearbook
  Literary Magazine
  Radio Show
  Television Show
Students Against Drunk
  Driving
Student Government
  Advisory Council
  Class Officer
  Student Council
  Class Representative
Technology
Temple Youth Group
Varsity
Vocational Industrial
  Club of America
Young Democrats
Young Republicans

Make a list of your:

- hobbies

- interests, e.g., photography, dance, producing music, cooking, sports, writing, modeling, playing computer games, building models, cycling, gardening, working with animals, drawing, painting, designing clothes, braiding hair, etc.

- special gifts, e.g., martial arts, playing an instrument, painting, illustration, carpentry, repairing automobile engines, automobile detailing, farming, etc.

Review your list and think of an opportunity in school, at a place of worship, in a senior citizen home, or within your community where you can teach or share your talents and interests. See your counselor or speak to someone at your place of worship or community organization about volunteer and community service opportunities.

Athletics

Athletics is one of the important parts of the college experience. Division I-A athletic teams generate millions of dollars annually in revenue that can represent a significant portion of a college's overall source of income. Although all colleges do not compete in Division I-A sports (which receive national television coverage), the vast majority of colleges offer intercollegiate or intramural athletic programs. Colleges are limited by NCAA rules as to the number of athletic scholarships they can offer, however, interest by a college coach for an intercollegiate sport or by an admissions committee for your potential contribution to the school's intramural sports programs may have a significant impact on your admissions status.

As was outlined in the foreword, if you have athletic abilities, you should consider developing them as a means of helping you to gain college admissions or possibly receiving a full or partial scholarship to offset the costs of college tuition, fees, room, and board.

Consider the following:

1. What areas of athletic competition do you most enjoy?

2. What athletic areas do you perform best, based on your talents and physical abilities?

3. What athletic opportunities or scholarships are available at the colleges that you are interested in attending?

Identify the complete range of athletic programs offered at your high school and the full range of athletic opportunities at the college level. Match your interests or talents with the available programs and arrange to meet the coaches of the sport that you are interested in playing. Every high school has athletic

traditions, some good and some not-so-good. Consequently, some of the varsity sports are very competitive and others have very little student interest and participation. Select the sport(s) that best fit(s) your talents, interests, and abilities and hopefully a coach who can provide you with the best personal and physical development. Do not limit yourself to those sports offered at your high school. Consider sports like lacrosse, swimming, cricket, ruby, and water polo that may be offered through private clubs or community organizations. Also consider AAU and USATF teams or sports offered at local YMCAs, Boys and Girls Clubs, parks and recreation centers, etc.

Estimated Probability of Competing in Athletics Beyond High School

Source: http://www.ncaa.org/research/prob_of_competing/

Student-Athletes	Men's Basketball	Women's Basketball	Football	Baseball	Men's Ice Hockey	Men's Soccer
High School Student-Athletes	549,500	456,900	983,600	455,300	29,900	321,400
High School Senior Student-Athletes	157,000	130,500	281,000	130,100	8,500	91,800
NCAA Student-Athletes	15,700	14,400	56,500	25,700	3,700	18,200
NCAA Freshman Roster Positions	4,500	4,100	16,200	7,300	1,100	5,200
NCAA Senior Student-Athletes	3,500	3,200	12,600	5,700	800	4,100
NCAA Student-Athletes Drafted	44	32	250	600	33	76
Percent High School to NCAA	2.9	3.1	5.8	5.6	12.9	5.7
Percent NCAA to Professional	1.3	1.0	2.0	10.5	4.1	1.9
Percent High School to Professional	0.03[1]	0.02	0.09[2]	0.5	0.4	0.08

1. Players must be at least 19 years old and out of high school one year to be eligible for the NBA draft.

2. Players must be at out of high school three years to be eligible for the NFL draft.

Related facts:

- Only 3 out of every 100 high school basketball players will play college basketball.

- Only 8 out of every 100,000 will be drafted into the NBA/WNBA.

- Only 6 out of every 100 high school football players will play college football.

- Only 25 out of every 100,000 will be drafted into the NFL.

NCAA Student and Student-Athlete Graduation Rates

Source: http://www.ncaa.org/grad_rates/2003/d1/index.html

School	1996-97		Four-year Average	
	All Students	Athletes	All Students	Athletes
Auburn	68	62	67	57
Bethune-Cookman	31	52	35	43
BYU	71	54	72	50
Brown	95	*	94	*
Dartmouth	95	*	94	*
Delaware State	30	54	29	39
Duke	93	88	93	89
Florida A&M	43	46	43	39
Georgetown	94	77	92	87
Georgia Tech	68	63	68	53
Howard	58	62	50	59
Loyola Marymount	70	73	70	68
UCLA	85	64	81	65
UMass Amherst	61	64	60	66
University of Connecticut	69	60	69	62
University of Georgia	70	60	67	64
University of Kentucky	58	48	56	45
Louisiana State	57	55	54	52
University of Miami (FL)	65	51	63	53
University of Michigan	84	82	83	73
UNC (Chapel Hill)	80	64	80	70
USC	76	56	73	61
Northwestern	93	87	92	89
North Carolina A&T	40	23	43	36
Notre Dame	95	92	94	87
Ohio State	59	60	56	59
Penn State	80	80	80	79
Rice	92	81	90	82
Rutgers	72	72	73	68
Syracuse	77	81	75	79
Stanford	93	84	92	87
Texas Tech	52	56	49	55
The Citadel	66	67	68	64
U.S. Air Force Academy	79	*	77	*
Vanderbilt	84	75	83	78
Wake Forest	87	79	87	76
Xavier	71	66	71	74
Yale	95	*	95	*

* Schools do not offer athletic scholarships

Notes:

NCAA Clearinghouse

Any prospective student-athlete who is interested in participating in collegiate athletics as a college freshman must meet all NCAA eligibility criteria, which include:

- Fulfilling academic eligibility requirements

- Following the NCAA guidelines during the recruitment process

- Maintaining an amateur athlete status

- Registering with the NCAA Clearinghouse

Any prospective student-athlete must become familiar with, and abide by, the NCAA student-athletes eligibility rules, which vary among Division I, Division II, and Division III schools. In order to participate in athletics and receive athletic-based financial aid, you must register with the NCAA Initial-Eligibility Clearinghouse and meet eligibility standards. For complete information, order a copy or download the *NCAA Guide for the College-Bound Student-Athlete.*

NCAA Clearinghouse
301 ACT Drive
Box 4043
Iowa City, IA 52243-4043
www.ncaaclearinghouse.net

Toll Free phone numbers (domestic callers only):
    Customer Service Line (877) 262-1492
    24-hour voice response (877) 861-3003

Phone numbers (international callers):
    Customer Service Line (319) 337-1492
    24-hour voice response (319) 339-3003

Fax Number (319) 337-1556

Consider Less Popular Sports

High schools are full of basketball, football, soccer, and baseball players. Do not limit yourself to the sports that are popular within your community or with your friends. Continue your strategy of looking for opportunities to separate yourself from the mass of college applicants. If everyone in your community is playing football, then perhaps you should consider playing lacrosse. If everyone in the local track club is running the 100 meters, then perhaps you should consider running the 400 meters.

Set yourself apart from other athletes. Consider less popular sports like water polo, Nordic skiing, rowing, and fencing. Colleges oftentimes recruit scholarship athletes from outside of the United States, due to low interest in these types of sports by American high school students. Review the complete listing of Division I, II, and III sports at the NCAA web site (www.ncaa.org/conferences) and seriously consider expanding your sports participation.

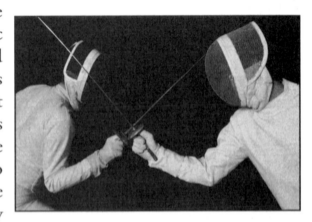

Colleges begin identifying high school athletes by their published statistics, newspaper articles, coaches' inquiries, and coaching referrals. Try to capture photographs or videos of your sporting events and practice sessions that highlight your special skills and abilities. Continue following the advice previously offered in regard to taking every opportunity to share your college aspirations with others. Take advantage of opportunities at sporting events, college fairs, and athletic camps to share your college athletic aspirations. Here are some of the books that may help you to develop an aggressive marketing strategy to get your name, statistics, and athletic profile in front of coaches:

- *Athletic Recruiting & Scholarship Guide* by Wayne Mazzoni *(www.mazzmarketing.com/about.html)*

- *Athletic Scholarships* by Mike Barber

- *Athletic Recruiting & College Scholarship Guide* by Robert L. Scott, Ed.D.

- *Peterson's Sports Scholarships & College Athletic Programs*

- *The Student Athlete's Handbook* by Bromwell and Gensler

- *College Scholarships:* www.collegescholarships.org/athletic.htm

Complementary Sports

Concentrate on becoming competitively successful at a particular sport, position, or event. Expose yourself to multiple sports and talk to coaches and trainers to develop a list of sports that provide a good match for your physical abilities. For example, football requires speed, strength, and agility. As a fall sport, football is a natural match with track and field or lacrosse, both of which are spring sports. For female athletes, softball is a fall sport requiring highly developed hand-eye coordination, speed, and agility. Soccer and lacrosse, as spring sports, provide a good match.

If you are one of the fortunate high school athletes to be offered a college scholarship, keep in mind that you should attempt to identify a college where you will enjoy both the athletic and academic programs. For the vast majority of scholarship athletes, a college athletic scholarship provides the opportunity to get a college education rather than entry into a career as a professional athlete.

If you aspire to become a college athlete, keep the following considerations in mind:

1. Identify good schools (i.e., academic reputation, majors in your area of interests, reputable campus life) that you would enjoy attending.

2. Review your top-ten listing of schools and identify those schools that offer athletic programs in the areas where you are interested in competing.

3. Follow the NCAA recruiting guidelines.

4. Market yourself to those schools by writing letters, sending e-mails, and talking to coaches.

5. Ensure that you are academically eligible.

6. Meet all the eligibility deadlines.

7. Prepare yourself for success athletically and academically.

8. Keep in mind that while your sports participation may not result in an athletic scholarship, it may help with your admission. Harvard University has 41 varsity-level sports, the broadest offering of any Division I school. And, while Harvard does not award athletic scholarships, your athletic talents may help you to be admitted into one of the country's most prestigious universities.

Notes:

Identify the following support persons or programs:

- *Sports training facilities*

- *Current and former competitive athletes*

- *Coaches*

- *Nutritionist*

- *Personal trainers*

- *Sports physicians*

- *Resource materials*

- *AAU, USATF, club teams*

9.   Speak to your high school coaches to ensure that you clearly understand the rules of participation and criteria for qualifying for a varsity letter in your sport.

Clubs & Band

As is the case in athletics, high schools have a broad range of opportunities in bands, clubs, student organizations, and activities. Some clubs or organizations have strong traditions and are very competitive. Other clubs and programs have weak traditions and little student interest. Choosing a club, organization, or student activity should reflect your interest and enhance your college plan. Just because a club or organization does not have much student interest at your high school does not mean that your involvement will not generate interest from colleges. For example, if the student government at your high school does not generate much student interest, your becoming involved and assuming a leadership position is impressive on your college application, even if it is not highly thought of in your high school. Any time there is a weak club or organization that does not generate a lot of student interest, you should see it as an opportunity. If you can revitalize a student activity or organization, you will have a powerful story to tell on your college or scholarship essay and to share during a college interview.

Identify all the clubs and student organizations available at your high school, even those that you may not be interested in at this time. As you move forward with developing your college plan, you may find that becoming involved in some of the clubs or organizations that you may not be interested in at this time may be important to helping you to be accepted into the college of your choice.

Playing a musical instrument and being a member of a successful marching band will oftentimes provide as much exposure as being a varsity athlete. Consider that many colleges have stronger band traditions than they do athletic traditions. Some fans attend football games with a stronger interest in the halftime show than in the game itself. While sports like basketball may have 12 players on a team, the college band may have over 200 members. Similar opportunities apply to cheerleading.

Special Programs/Activities

In addition to athletics, clubs, and student organizations, many high schools have special interest groups, intervention programs, and other activities available to students. Consider your participation in some of these activities as another opportunity to enhance your college application as well as contribute to your personal growth and development. The organizers, mentors, and faculty advisors in these organizations may also become people who can write recommendations, and provide introductions, to college admissions committees.

Identify mentors or advisors:

- *Actors/Actresses*
- *Musicians*
- *Artists*
- *Dancers*
- *Choreographers*
- *Directors*
- *Song writers*
- *Playwrights*
- *Coaches*
- *Politicians*
- *Entrepreneurs*
- *Law Enforcement*
- *Medical Professionals*
- *Educators*
- *Engineers*
- *Consultants*
- *Managers/ Supervisors*
- *Automotive Mechanics*
- *Computer Technicians*
- *Barbers/Hair Stylists*
- *Farmers*
- *Trades persons*

Notes:

Mentoring programs, community involvement programs, character development, student-student tutoring, designing sets for the drama department, taking photographs for the yearbook, recording statistics for the football team, running the concession stands, selling spirit wear, raising money for charities, building homes for Habitat for Humanity, all provide opportunities to enhance your college application and make a positive contribution to your high school and surrounding community. These kinds of involvement also provide opportunities to be formally recognized (another way of enhancing your college application).

Make a list of the programs and activities, which you are currently involved or have an interest in becoming involved. Keep in mind that there is always an opportunity for you to begin a new program at your high school or in your community.

Go to the worksheet section in the *workbook* and note your program and activity involvement as you go through high school. Keep track of every involvement—place of worship, community, school, YMCA, Boys & Girls Clubs, Boy/Girl Scouts, etc. Noting your involvement as you go through high school will be easier than trying to remember all your volunteer and community activities when you are under pressure to complete your college applications.

Competitions

Competitions provide additional opportunities to earn scholarship money, local and national recognition, and further enhance a college application. Competitions are available in athletic programs, cheerleading, band, academic areas, the arts, and a number of student-interest areas. Begin identifying the competitions that you may be interested in entering. Immediately note on your student worksheets your participation or any awards that you receive.

Jobs

Use the forms in the *workbook* to track your after-school and summer jobs. It is important to track the number of hours that you work and that you devote to extracurricular activities. Instead of bagging groceries, explore employment opportunities within areas of interest or areas that provide practical applications for some of your school course work. Following are examples of employment opportunities that relate to classes:

- *Typing:* Secretarial, office assistant, general office
- *Art:* Flyers, store window themes, brochures, signs
- *Weight Training:* Assisting personal trainers, stacking weights at a health club
- *Speech & Debate:* Sales, telemarketing, customer service
- *Math:* Accounting, tax preparation assistance, bookkeeping
- *Science:* Veterinarian's office, dental office, drug-store sales

9th Grade

Choose a sport where you have the talent, skill, or determination to play during each of your four years. Hopefully, this sport will enable you to earn a varsity letter in at least 3 of your 4 years. You should also look into programs such as the YMCA, Boys & Girls Clubs, and private clubs to continue your development during the high school off-season and summer months. You may also enhance your skills, abilities, and opportunities for award recognition through AAU or USATF teams.

Find an extracurricular activity that you can excel at such as art, music, model building, cheerleading, band, dance, or martial arts. Consider school, community, and parks and recreation activities.

10th Grade

Continue your sports, extracurricular, and community involvement. Explore opportunities to enroll in a summer camp or enter competitions in one of your areas of interest (i.e., athletic, artistic, academic, etc.).

11th Grade

Continue your sports, extracurricular, and community involvement. Further explore opportunities to enroll in

summer camps or other types of competitions. This is the final opportunity to develop the muscle mass, skills, and techniques that will enable you to excel during your senior year in varsity-level sports. Assume a leadership role as captain of a sports team, officer in a club or organization, or leadership position in an outside program or organization. Try to enroll in a leadership camp or internship during the summer.

12th Grade

Continue your sports, extracurricular, and community involvement, hopefully as a Captain or officer on a team or in a program. By this time you should have amassed between 300-400 community service hours and engaged in an internship opportunity. Review your sports, extracurricular activity, and community service involvement and identify the types of awards and recognition that you have received.

Section III

Honesty

Integrity

Justice

Resilience

Personal
Qualities

Chapter 9

Academic achievement is really only one factor in admissions; the college is also looking for integrity, maturity, initiative and, above all, creativity. No college wants to be boring! Your application is a sales package, and your 'hook' is your uniqueness. What makes you a superstar? Something does, I guarantee it. A good college counselor can find it. Your parents may know what it is. But something unique is within you, waiting to be brought out, developed, and packaged for colleges to consider. Do not try to tell a college that you are good at everything; tell them you are great at something.

— *[College Admissions Trade Secrets]*

Personal Qualities

No matter how you compare to others in terms of grades and test scores, who you are, what you have done, and what you stand for can become the defining factor that convinces an admissions officer that you are a student who would make a noteworthy contribution to his or her college community. Each day throughout your high school years you have the opportunity to separate yourself from the masses and define yourself. More than trying to make yourself into something, allow the divinely unique person whom you were created to be to come to the surface. Do not try to blend in and be like everyone else. Allow the divinely unique you to blossom. Not only will you distinguish yourself from the thousands of other applicants, but you will more likely identify the college community that would provide the best environment to nurture your artistic, personal, intellectual, and spiritual growth.

Leadership

Colleges are looking for leaders—students who can contribute to intellectual discussions, challenge professors, create music, explore science, provide creative and intellectual insight into the issues of today and contribute to their communities.

Questions that will help you to assess if you have been developing your leadership skills:

• Have you contributed to the creation of a new student club or organization?

• Have you been elected into office or served in a leadership capacity in an organization?

• Have you made a meaningful contribution to your school or community?

• Have you created a new approach or implemented a new way of doing things that has enhanced your school, place of worship, or community?

• Have you taught, tutored, coached, inspired, or encouraged others?

• Have you taken something that you have learned through a classroom experience and applied it through the creation of a new product or new way of doing things?

• Have you led a social cause or publicly lobbied for a legislative change?

Review the list of sports, clubs, organizations, and activities in which you are involved or have a desire to become involved. Identify the offices or leadership positions in which you are interested. Share your goals with coaches or faculty advisors to ensure that the leadership positions in which you are interested can be achieved and the likely year of school that you will be able to achieve your desired position.

Character

Your character defines who you are, what you stand for, and the beliefs and principles that guide your life. Do not allow yourself to be influenced by mean-spirited, self-centered, obnoxious people who go out of their way to ridicule, take advantage of, and hinder others. Do not follow the crowd or allow such people to define your character. What are your values, beliefs, and guiding principles? Take a moment and write down five values that define who you are. Ultimately, you will be known by your works. If these values truly define who you are in the ninth grade, then they will be evident in your works by the time you write your college essays in the eleventh grade.

Look over the words and phrases on the following list and circle five that define your character or your beliefs:

Integrity	Perseverance	Diligent
Compassionate	Fair	Excellence
Honest	Responsible	Intense
Passionate	Fortitude	Self-starter
Resilient	Spiritual	Dependable
Principled	Introspective	Determined
Focused	Leader	Collaborative
Sense of justice	Respectful	Team Player
Quality	Thoughtful	Creative
Self-motivated	Cooperative	Pensive

Many colleges will require teacher recommendations. Teachers will be asked to share their comments and insight into your personality and academic ability. Some schools will provide teachers with a checklist to rate such qualities as:

- personality

- curiosity

- academic promise

- self-confidence

- warmth of personality

- concern for others

Over the course of your four years of high school, take the time to get to know at least three teachers— people who would value the opportunity to write a letter telling the world what a wonderful person you are and attesting to your character and academic ability. Keep in mind that over the course of four years of high school, your participation in classroom discussions, contribution to group projects, and involvement in clubs and student organizations will provide many opportunities to develop relationships and contribute in a meaningful and relevant way to your school community. Admissions officers will view your involvement in your high school as indicative of your potential involvement in the vibrant life of their college community, which will offer an even broader range of clubs and organizations. Assess the character and leadership traits that you have demonstrated in the clubs, organizations, and activities through elementary and middle school.

Repeat this exercise for each club, organization, sport, or activity in which you participated through elementary and middle school. This information will provide a point of reflection of your past character and leadership qualities. As you enter high school, you should either continue demonstrating the qualities that distinguish you as a leader or begin identifying those qualities that you would like to define you as a leader through your four years of high school.

Take time to reflect on your personality. Understanding the uniqueness of your personality will help define your

role in clubs and activities. An introverted personality does not have to become an extraverted personality to assume a leadership role in an organization, on an athletic team, or in a student club. An extraverted personality may socialize easily and effortlessly meet, greet, and get to know people. The introverted personality may choose a behind-the-scenes leadership role. An extravert may enjoy lively group discussions and social gatherings, whereas the introvert may demonstrate leadership by conceptualizing new ways of gathering and analyzing information, creating web pages, or enhancing communications between student organizations. You do not have to become someone else to become a leader; just be the best you that you can be and unlock your own creative capacity.

In the book, *A Middle School Plan for Students with College-Bound Dreams,* the discussion on Multiple Intelligences provides ideas of how you can identify and use your unique talents and abilities to enhance your school and community. Whether you are an artist who paints murals, a musician who writes a new school song, a photographer who creates new photo collages for the yearbook, an investigative reporter who writes insightful and thought-provoking articles about school and social issues, or a student who builds bridges between student groups and the surrounding community, there will be many opportunities to utilize your unique talents, skills, and abilities.

Discipline Issues

To take full advantage of the range of high school opportunities, you have to take your school's policies and procedures seriously. Discipline infractions not only disrupt the high school experience for classmates, interfere with classroom instruction, and contribute negatively to your school's overall school climate and culture, but may cause you to forfeit your opportunity to participate in extracurricular activities, student organizations, or keep you from being recommended for programs and awards that would otherwise enhance your college application package.

Many high school students experience a difficult transition from middle school into the ninth grade. While suspensions at the middle school level are not likely to be reflected on your high school record, depending on your school district's

Notes:

policy, your high school record may contain a complete listing of your discipline infractions for each year of high school. You do not want to allow a split-second decision in the ninth grade to hinder your college application in the eleventh grade. An additional concern in the area of discipline infractions, is that a mandatory 3-, 5-, or 10-day suspension from classes can have a substantially negative impact on your grades. If you have been following the strategies outlined in the section on academics then you are likely to have a challenging course schedule from the opening bell in the ninth grade. An incident of fighting, which in many school districts carries a mandatory 10-day out-of-school suspension, can put you so far behind in your course work that you may not recover before the end of the grading period.

Fully understand your high school's policies regarding drugs, alcohol, firearms, fighting, sexual misconduct, inappropriate language, classroom disruptions, or other student behaviors that can result in suspensions, expulsions, or worst, criminal prosecution. You are likely to experience the full range of emotions during your high school years—joy, sadness, excitement, depression, enthusiasm and anger. Develop a strong network of parents, relatives, friends, mentors, teachers, and counselors who you can turn to for help or to simply share your joys and pains. The decisions that you make as a young adult in high school can have significant long-term ramifications.

Think before you act.

Think before you speak.

Think before you do anything.

Section IV

Intangibles

Chapter 10

Summer is your child's chance to win the edge, to beat the competition. The most important time for out-of-school enrichment is summer—when many opportunities exist to explore and develop interests. By fall, your son or daughter should possess an entirely new repertoire of abilities. Anything else is a waste.

Colleges ask on the applications what the applicant did every summer starting with the summer before ninth grade. This section should be filled with many exciting adventures, challenges, experiences, and extra learning that the high schools don't offer.

— *[What Colleges Don't Tell You and Other Parents Don't Want You to Know]*

Intangibles

Intangibles represent all of those areas not previously covered, which contribute to your uniqueness:

- Where you live

- Ethnicity, gender, and family structure

- Legacy status

- Experiences and circumstances

Where You Live

Your geographical area and community setting will have an impact on your application. Colleges typically seek to develop a diverse freshman class of students from different geographical regions—throughout the United States and other countries, and types of communities—urban, suburban, rural, liberal, conservative, etc. While in-state tuition is usually substantially less at public universities than out-of-state tuition, some students may be more easily accepted to out-of-state colleges looking for students from their geographical region.

It may appear extreme for an African-American student to move from Boston, Massachusetts to Bismarck, North Dakota. However, it is pretty safe to say that while Harvard has many applicants to choose from in the Boston–Cambridge area, an applicant may be the only African-American student to apply from Bismarck!

Ethnicity, Gender, and Family Structure

As colleges look for geographical diversity, they also look to develop well-balanced classes representing ethnic, gender, cultural, and socioeconomic diversity. A student from an affluent background may have more competition being accepted into some of the top schools where large numbers of students from similar socioeconomic backgrounds apply, whereas a student from a working-class or poor family may be among only a few applicants from similar socioeconomic backgrounds.

Another example would be an African-American male student applying to Morehouse College, an all-male historically black college. He will find himself competing for admissions with thousands of students from very similar backgrounds.

A student from a migrant family who is forced to move frequently and enroll into a number of schools and school districts has a very different educational experience than a student from a middle-class family of professional parents in a stable home environment. If both students develop similar academic credentials and test scores, the migrant student clearly has done so while having to overcome a more difficult set of circumstances than the middle class student.

The question that you must ask is, "If there is a large number of applications from students who have a similar ethnic, socioeconomic, and family background as myself, what can I do to distinguish myself?"

Legacy Status

As previously mentioned, some colleges provide preferential admissions status to students whose parents were graduates from the undergraduate program at the college. Such students are referred to as, "Legacy Students."

In the book, *Rock Hard Apps*, Katherine Cohen notes:

Students often do not realize a school's institutional priorities. For instance, Penn's legacy policy states that if an applicant's parent or grandparent is a Penn degree holder, and the student applies Early Decision, the Office of Admissions promises to give that candidate maximum consideration.

If you are applying to a college where one or both of your parents are graduates, then you should inquire into the college's legacy policy. Some schools prefer that legacy students apply via their Early Decision program.

If you are not a legacy student, then you should express in your essay or mention in your interview your desire to begin a lifelong relationship with the college so that your own children *will* one day become legacy students.

Experiences

Your experiences, such as where you have traveled, the type of communities where you have lived, the organizations with which you have been involved with, and programs or camps in which you have participated contribute to your intangibles. Your family experiences have uniquely contributed to who you are, whether your parents are millionaires or migrant workers, serving in law enforcement or political office, delivering mail or delivering babies, researching environmental issues or performing landscaping, teaching students in regular classrooms or prison inmates, serving children in school cafeterias or serving parishioners in a congregation. These experiences are the roots from which you have sprung and provide the substance of your hopes, dreams, perspectives, and perceptions of the world around you. Whether from privilege or from the projects, there is no shame in where you hail from; all geographical areas, ethnicity, and socioeconomic backgrounds reflect the diversity of the global landscape.

Career Interests and Aspirations

Your passionate areas of interest contribute to your uniqueness and may enhance the diversity of a college community. Do you teach martial arts? Do you coach little league baseball? Do you run a soccer clinic for inner-city kids during the summer? Do you volunteer for political campaigns? Are you a tutor in a literacy program at the Boys & Girls Club?

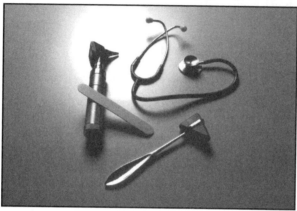

Such programs, involvement, and areas of interest help to shape your uniqueness. Many students will apply to colleges because of the college's rank or status. Such students are more concerned with getting admitted into a prestigious college than they are at pursuing some particular area of interest, dream, or aspiration. Your passionate interests and continued pursuit of your dreams and aspirations will separate your application from that of the masses.

Align your areas of interest with a college major. Use your research to assess the college's commitment to your field of study and its student diversity needs. For example, female students interested in pursuing such majors as engineering, mathematics, or science, which typically have fewer female applicants, may find themselves more aggressively recruited than female students interested in pursuing nursing, which has a large number of female applicants.

Students who have demonstrated a passion for art or music dating back to elementary school may have an advantage [in the college admissions process] over students who say that they are interested in pursing art, but took their first art class as a high school senior.

Summer Planning

The summer months between 8th grade and your senior year of high school should not be squandered. Take advantage of the many opportunities to explore your talents, interests, and abilities. Some of the many opportunities that you may explore, experience, or become involved in are:

- Traveling

- Working in a meaningful job related to an area of interest or through an internship

- Participating in a summer learning opportunity in an academic, artistic, or community service

- Participating in pre-college summer camps/programs

- Participating in an AAU, USATF, or club sport

- Participating in summer practice for a high school sport such as football, cross country, lacrosse, soccer, swimming, etc.

- Volunteering as a counselor, life guard, coach, or art instructor at a parks and recreation, Boys & Girls Club, or community program

- Taking some of your non-academic classes or electives in summer school to open your schedule for more honors or advanced classes during the regular school year

- Starting a business or working on a special project

Identifying a schedule of summer activities (8th through 12th grades) aligned with your areas of interest.

N o t e s:

Unlike the summer months during elementary and middle school, this is not the time to relax at grandma's house sitting back and watching television or playing video games. The summer months provide opportunities to attend camps or summer school, compete in AAU or USATF sports competitions, pursue internships, or otherwise engage in programs or opportunities that will enhance your college application package.

Camps, Internships, & Enrichment Programs

There are many summer enrichment, internship, and college program opportunities. The first two stops are your high school counselor's office and the web. Research programs related to your areas of interest and utilize the opportunity to increase your academic or athletic skills.

Try to concentrate first and foremost on those areas that relate directly to your college interests, whether in your major field of study or in sports that you intend to pursue on the college level.

Ask your guidance or career counselor for information regarding camps, enrichment programs, internships, work-study, and before- and after-school programs. These types of programs are usually offered through local colleges, community organizations, and clubs.

Students rehearse their roles in one of the school's theater productions.

Identify the camps, internships, enrichment programs, and extracurricular activities available at your high school related to your areas of interest. Identify the qualifying criteria for student participation, which may include participation in certain clubs, enrollment in certain classes, minimum grade point average, or recommendation by teachers or counselors.

Begin identifying summer programs in your area by Googling summer camps in your city, e.g., "Atlanta Summer Camps." Google programs hosted by or on the colleges on your list, and continue searching for programs at nearby colleges and cities, moving on to programs throughout your state, and as far away as you have the ability to travel.

Notes:

There are hundreds of summer programs for high school students offered nationwide. In the article, *"Summer Programs for High School and College Students,"* Mick Pugh notes twenty of the most popular programs:

Abbey Road Overseas Programs
www.goabbeyroad.com

Summer immersion programs for high school students designed to facilitate cross-cultural understanding. Students spend several weeks in either Spain, France or Italy, where they undergo intensive language immersion and travel to historic sites. The French and Spanish home-stay programs focus on linguistic and cultural immersion, while the pre-college programs in Cannes, France, and Florence, Italy, have a greater emphasis on academics (culture, history, art, literature, etc) and take place on college campuses.

Academic Connections at the University of California, San Diego
www.academicconnections.ucsd.edu

A three-week program where students immerse themselves in the study of a particular academic subject. Options include: engineering, biomedical sciences, humanities/arts, marine sciences, media/communication, mathematics/economics and social studies/law. Participants must be in high school and have a minimum GPA of 3.3.

American Collegiate Adventures
www.zfc-consulting.com/webprojects/americanadventures/index2.htm

Two-, three- and six-week summer programs held at the University of Wisconsin in Madison. Students enroll in two college-level courses and take them for either college credit or personal enrichment. American Collegiate Adventures also offers a four-week program in Spain.

Bentley College – Camp Bentley
www.bentley.edu/camp

A one-week residential summer program offered at Bentley College, located in Waltham, Massachusetts, for students entering the 10th, 11th and 12th grades—"Wall Street 101" and "Leadership Institute." Within a fun and interactive setting, the programs offer students an opportunity to learn about careers in business.

California State Summer School for Mathematics and Science
www.ucop.edu/cosmos

A four-week residential program that gives high school students a chance to take university-level math and science courses at one of three University of California campuses —Santa Cruz, UC Davis, and UC Irvine. Students live in campus housing with other program participants. Full and partial scholarships are available.

Columbia College of Chicago
www.colum.edu/admissions/hs_institute/index.html

A program for students who have a serious interest in the fine arts, performing arts, media arts or communication arts. Participants will choose from a selection of courses and earn 1-3 college credits. The program culminates in a showcase where  students share their finished work in a day of performances and exhibits. The program is open to current high school sophomores, juniors and seniors.

Concordia Language Villages
www.cord.edu/dept/clv

A world language and cultural education program whose mission is to prepare young people for responsible citizenship in the global community. With an annual enrollment reaching 9,500, Concordia Language Villages draws young people from every state and several countries. Villagers may choose from 12 world-language programs: Chinese, Danish, English, Finnish, French, French Voyageur, German, Japanese, Korean, Norwegian, Russian, Spanish, Italian or Swedish.

Cornell University - Summer Programs for High School Students
www.sce.cornell.edu/sc

High school students take Cornell courses for credit, live on campus, explore academic and career opportunities and learn what college is all about.

Duke University's Pre-College Program
www.tip.duke.edu

Duke's Pre-College Program (Part of Duke University's Talent Identification Program (TIP)), offers small classes

taught by Duke University faculty and a residential life program. Intensive, fast-paced courses are offered in the humanities, social studies, natural sciences, mathematics, and computer sciences.

Harvard Summer School Secondary School Program (SSP)

www.ssp.harvard.edu

Every summer approximately 1,000 high school students who have completed their junior or senior year spend eight weeks at Harvard University. (A limited number of sophomores are also accepted.) Living and learning with students from all areas of the United States and more than 90 countries around the world, SSP students take courses and earn college credit.

Indiana University - High School Journalism Institute

www.journalism.indiana.edu/workshops/HSJI

The High School Journalism Institute is designed for high school students interested in journalism. Participants examine the role of the media, analyze their own and other student publications and develop the skills needed to produce quality publications. Faculty members from Indiana University and guest lecturers from around the country guide student courses of study.

Notes:

LEAD (Leadership Education and Development)
www.leadnational.org

A national partnership of America's top corporations and business schools, the Leadership Education and Development Program in Business (LEAD) encourages outstanding high school students from diverse backgrounds to pursue careers in business. Each summer, 12 of the nation's top graduate business schools host an exciting, intensive program where junior high school students are introduced to career opportunities in a variety of disciplines.

Since 1980, LEAD's Summer Business Institutes (SBIs) have graduated more than 7,000 aspiring leaders, 65 percent of whom currently work in the business world.

Miami University of Ohio - Junior Scholars Program
www.units.muohio.edu/jrscholars

A six-week summer term for academically talented high school students. The Program provides a total collegiate experience, including courses for college credit, residence hall life, planned recreation programs and co-curricular seminars. Junior Scholars also receive scholarships in recognition of their scholastic achievements.

Mathcamp
www.mathcamp.org

An intensive five-week summer program where students receive dedicated instruction in various principles of mathematics. The program offers courses, problem-solving sessions and lectures by leading mathematicians. The program is open to high school and junior high students aged 13 to 18. A qualifying quiz is required of all applicants.

National Youth Science Camp

www.sciencecamp.org

An intense month-long camp for young scientists the summer after high school graduation. In a rustic setting, students from around the country are challenged in lectures, hands-on studies and an extensive outdoor program. Two students from each state are invited by their governor to participate in this all-expenses-paid program.

New York Film Academy's High School Workshop

www.nyfa.com

These immersion workshops range from four-week programs to full-year programs. They are designed to introduce students to the creative and technical demands of telling stories with moving images. Students have the opportunity to write, direct, shoot and edit short films. Award-winning instructors, abundant equipment and small classes provide students with the individual attention and support necessary to complete their own work.

Rhode Island School of Design Pre-College Program

www.risd.edu/precollege.cfm

The six-week RISD summer Pre-College Program introduces high school students to the focused curriculum of a college of art and design. Students live in residence halls, attend social activities and study a particular subject in the fine or visual arts. Participants must be high school students between thc ages of 16-18 years old.

Summer Study Programs

www.summerstudy.com/index.cfm

The Summer Study Programs at Penn State University, University of Colorado at Boulder, and The American University of Paris combine academically challenging courses with the experience of campus life. Students completing 9th, 10th or 11th grade can choose from several programs: three-and-one-half-week Summer Enrichment or six-week college credit Summer Study Program at Penn State University; a three-week enrichment program (no credit) or five-week college credit program at The American University of Paris; or a five-week college credit program at the University of Colorado at Boulder.

Summer Science Program (SSP) - Ojai, California
www.summerscience.org/home/index.php

The Summer Science Program in Ojai, California, exposes selected high school students to advanced topics in mathematics, astronomy and space science. SSP challenges its students to calculate the orbit of an asteroid using their own direct telescopic observations.

Telluride Association Summer Programs (TASP)
www.tellurideassociation.org

A six-week educational experience for high school juniors. Students participate in seminars led by college and university members and participate in educational and social activities outside the classroom. Telluride Association seeks students from all kinds of educational backgrounds who demonstrate intellectual curiosity and motivation. Telluride Association Summer Programs are free; every student awarded a place in a TASP attends the program on a full housing, dining and tuition scholarship.

Tufts Summer High School Program
www.ase.tufts.edu/summer/high_school_programs/hs2.htm

Since 1982, Tufts University has attracted top-caliber high school students who wish to spend their summers pursuing academic excellence and social maturity. Tufts programs are kept small so students receive individual attention from instructors. Two different programs are offered: Tufts Summit (Talloires, France) and Tufts Summer Study (Medford/ Boston).

University of Chicago Young Scholars Program

www.oca.uchicago.edu/workingtogether

The University of Chicago offers an enrichment program in mathematics for Chicago Public School students. Students attend daily seminars given by University professors and solve mathematics problems based on these seminars. Topics include number theory, geometry and probability. Students also learn computer skills. Tuition is free for those accepted.

University of Dallas Summer Study in Europe

www.udallas.edu/travel

The University of Dallas' programs use European travel to stimulate careful reading, writing and thinking about life's most serious questions. Courses are led by experienced University faculty and staff.

University of New Hampshire Upward Bound Summer Program

www.upwardbound.unh.edu

During their six-week summer program, students live on the campus of the University of New Hampshire and take five classes in the following areas: math, science, English, electives and "success studies" (SAT prep, study skills, etc). Small classes are designed to inspire excitement about academics and give students a head start on college.

University of Pennsylvania Programs for High School Students

www.upenn.edu/summer

Penn's summer programs combine rigorous classroom and lab work with a wide range of social activities, trips and

Notes:

tours. Opportunities are available for residential students, commuting students and distance learners. Each of Penn's summer programs for high school students offers a college-level experience that smoothes the transition from high school to college.

Upward Bound
www.ed.gov/programs/trioupbound/index.html

A federally-funded program that provides fundamental support to participants in their preparation for college entrance. The program provides opportunities for participants to succeed in pre-college performance, and

ultimately, in higher education pursuits. Upward Bound serves high school students from low-income families or from families where neither parent holds a bachelor's degree, and low-income, first-generation military veterans who are preparing to enter postsecondary education. The goal of Upward Bound is to increase the college enrollment and graduation rates of participants.

If you qualify, ask your counselor if your school has an Upward Bound program or if there are programs available in your area.

In addition to summer camps that provide academic or creative opportunities, there are sports camps that help those students passionate about sports competition to increase their odds of becoming a recruited-athlete.

For a comprehensive listing of summer program opportunities, go to *The Foundation for Ensuring Access and Equity* web site (www.accessandequity.org).

Chapter 11

The essay can be your ticket out of the faceless applicant hordes and into First-Choice University. And unlike everything else in your application—the grades, recommendations, and tests, which are by now out of your hands—you have real control over your writing, right up to the last frantic minute. Essays show the admissions committee who you are, and it's your chance to let fly, uninterrupted.

Even though we're all swamped every day with sloppy and deceitful language and bad writing, you can learn to say something simple and meaningful—and that's all a college essay asks.

— *[On Writing the College Scholarship Application Essay]*

Your Essay

Do not take your essay likely; it may represent the most important part of your entire application package. It will provide your opportunity to define who you are and state your case for admission into the college to which you are applying. It can take away from or enhance the overall picture of who you are, what you stand for, and why the admissions committee should give you an opportunity ahead of the thousands of other applicants. This is your opportunity to explain your grades; share your convictions, beliefs, philosophies, and guiding principles; tell what you know about the college's values, beliefs, and traditions; and merge your hopes, dreams, and aspirations.

Imagine your essay standing on a stage. The curtain pulls back and your essay walks from center stage to the podium. The spotlight shines, but there is talking and lack of interest throughout the room as thousands of other essays whisper, motion, and scream for attention, yet it is your essay standing alone at the podium as a Sunday morning preacher.

"I ain't where I wanna be

I ain't where I oughta be

I ain't where I need to be

But thank God,

I ain't where I was."

There is silence throughout the auditorium as all voices and distractions quiet. All discourse, debate, and discussions become still as a lake beneath the moonlight, as your essay captures, captivates, and presents a brilliant oratory on your behalf—sharing your hopes and your dreams, your achievements and your aspirations, your frailties and your uniqueness—your essay is the single ripple on the water carrying your message as the ripples widen and spread into the spirit, soul, and consciousness of the listener.

This moment is so pure, you dare not stain it with a lie. The listener is so eager to see your canvas painted with the broad strokes of your dreams and aspirations that you dare not squander the moment with a pathetic little story searching for sympathy or a handout. Gently take the listener's hand and lead him or her into your world. Whether your sounds are urban rhythms or rural country & western melodies, whether they represent the symphony of privilege or the penetrating beat of hip-hop, where you come from is who you are. Genuinely, unmistakably real. There are no knockoffs, copies, reruns or repeats. For this moment, your essay captures your spirit and presents the essence of who you are.

As fine wine deepens in color and becomes more robust in its fragrance as it matures and ages, so too must your essay. It cannot be thrown together as an after-thought, just to accompany a checked box in your application package. It stands alone at the podium with the script of your thoughts, ideas, hopes, and aspirations.

Many students find the college essay the most difficult part of the entire admissions process and will defer writing their essays until they actually need to be submitted with their college application. Writing a good essay requires practice, which should begin as early as middle school and continue throughout high school. By the time you write the essay that actually has to accompany a college application you should have had years of practice and proofing by teachers. Your essay should deliver a speech that has been practiced hundreds of times.

You should prepare yourself for this, perhaps the most important personal statement that you will make during your high school experience. From the opening bell in the ninth grade, your classes in literature, English, history, philosophy, and psychology will all prepare you for the moment when you sit down to share your thoughts, ideas, hopes, and dreams through your college essay. An extracurricular activity such as the Speech and Debate team will help you to develop the critical thinking and language skills needed to develop a compelling essay. Your teachers can become invaluable critics and editors.

An important part of the process of preparing and practicing requires that you read or listen to other essays.

Notes:

What you learn from reading good essays and bad essays can help you to create a great essay. Your goal from the beginning must be to create a great essay—not merely a good one, but a best seller—one that will leave a lasting impression. The essay is such an important component of your college admissions and scholarship application that you should not wait until the last minute to begin writing. Good essays are written months, if not years, in advance.

Following is an overview of the fine points of essay writing and preparation as part of your overall college plan. Take the time to review some of the many essay-writing books to help hone your essay-writing skills:

1. Practice.

2. Read other essays.

3. Read as many essay-preparation books as you need in order to understand the essay-writing process.

4. Write essays for extra credit throughout middle and high school and allow your teachers to assist with editing, grammar, punctuation, style, and content.

5. Keep in mind the basic admissions officer's question, "What does this applicant offer our college?"

6. Review the following listing of important themes and choose several themes to develop essays.

Important Themes

The sooner that you begin to assess your life based on some of the important essay themes, the faster you will begin to explore the important things about yourself and your character, the obstacles that you have had to overcome and what makes you uniquely the person that you are. A good essay written along the following themes can make a lasting impression on the readers of your essay:

- Hard work
- Overcoming obstacles
- Being of service
- Teamwork
- Perseverance
- Individual initiative
- Passion and enthusiasm
- Responsibility
- Civic duty
- Purpose
- Character or core value
- Autobiography
- Person you most admire
- Major challenge in your life
- Something significant that you want to accomplish
- Your strengths and weaknesses
- An issue of personal, local, national, or international concern
- Actions you would take if you were in a position of leadership, e.g., politician, principal, CEO, etc.

Heroes and Heroines

As your leadership skills, character, core values, and guiding principles provide the intangibles that define who you are, so too will your heroes and heroines. Are your heroes and heroines hip-hop, rap, or pop stars? Are you a groupie who admires and follows entertainers and athletes? Are those whom you most admire likely to reflect the core values and character traits that you value and which, ultimately, define who you are or who you aspire to become?

Some of the questions to be answered are:

- What stories have I read of leadership, personal sacrifice, or service that have inspired me?

- What people have demonstrated, through their lives or their ability to overcome obstacles, an example that I wish to follow?

- What people have left a legacy that has provided an example of the values that humanity should aspire toward?

- What people embody the values, beliefs, and ideals that define who I am or what I aspire to become?

- What people have, through their thoughts, words, or deeds, changed the course of human history in a meaningful and relevant way?

- With which historical figures would I value the opportunity to sit and discuss ideas, opinions, and views on the most pressing social or political issues of the day?

Make a list of the people whom you most admire in such areas as:

- Family or community

- Historical figures

- Political, civic, business, or religious leaders

- Educators (i.e., teachers, counselors, administrators, or coaches)

- Athletes, entertainers, and public figures

- Everyday people, e.g., custodians, cafeteria workers, farmers, brick masons, waiters or waitresses

Areas That Your Essay Should Explain or Highlight

Include in your essay thoughts about your course schedule, athletic achievements, musical or artistic competitions, community service projects, life-changing experiences, family, obstacles that you have had to overcome, and significant people whom have made a lasting impression on your life. As you prepare to write your essay, keep these questions in mind:

1. Who is my audience?

2. What type of essay am I going to write?

3. What do I want to communicate to the reader?

4. How will my essay reinforce my teacher recommendations, that I am, for example, humorous, purposeful, sensitive, passionate, driven, socially conscious, etc.?

5. What are my passions or aspirations?

6. What is it that only I can write about myself? What reflects my unique set of life experiences?

When to Begin

Begin as early as middle school. Keep a notebook or journal and start gathering your thoughts about those issues about which you feel passionate—life experiences and a wide range of issues about which you have an opinion. Increase your

Notes:

writing skills through letter writing. In this age of Internet jargon—LOL, KISS, BRB, CUL, SUL—losing your writing skills altogether is easy. The abbreviated conversations and acronyms of chat rooms will never replace a well-written

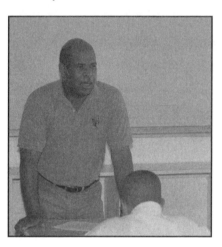

letter through which you can share your thoughts and ideas, your hopes and dreams, your passion and purpose.

Seek Your Teacher's Help

The reason that you want to begin experimenting with your essay writing in your early years of middle and high school is that it is an important skill to develop. You will benefit from not only your college applications and scholarship submissions, but also the reading and

writing components of the PSAT, SAT, ACT, and high school exit exams. This is your future. You must passionately share your story. It does not matter how well or badly written the first drafts of your essays are. You have your English, language

arts, and literature teachers to edit, critique, and provide invaluable feedback. You may even be able to earn extra credit for some of your writing. The way to become good at writing is to write often and to develop a willingness to accept constructive criticism. Consider writing a letter each week to a grandparent or friend living in another city.

Never throw away your work. Keep everything, good and bad. Keep it all and refer to it over and over again to continue perfecting your writing skills.

Formatting Your Essay

Pay close attention to the guidelines for formatting, number of words, content, or theme of your essay based on published admissions or scholarship guidelines.

While the widely accepted APA format is continually undergoing change, familiarize yourself with the current version and follow the standard guidelines:

- Double-space

- Use a common twelve-point font (etc., Times, Times New Roman, Helvetica)

- Set margins to 1-1 1/4" from the sides and 1" from the top and bottom

- Follow the APA (American Psychological Association) format for your title page, header, and footer

- Staple securely in the upper left-hand corner

- Develop a title that captures the reader's attention, e.g., "Lost Hope: A Teen's Challenge with Depression and Suicide" will catch your reader's attention more than "Teen's Have Issues."

- Place page numbers in the footer

- Make the appropriate footnotes, references, and citations

What is APA Format?

APA Format is a guide to writing student papers, writing articles for journal publishing, and citing references appropriately, as described in the American Psychological Association Publication Manual.

If you quote or refer to anyone else's ideas in your paper, whether from print sources, media or the Internet, it is essential to cite them according to established citation format. Failure to do so is plagiarism and a violation of copyright law.

Notes:

Personal Attributes

Try to incorporate words from the following list into your essay in reflecting who you are and in describing the issues, obstacles, and challenges that you have experienced in your life:

Passion	Purpose	Perseverance
Integrity	Diligence	Determination
Persistence	Dedication	Devotion
Commitment	Enthusiasm	Energy
Fortitude	Kindness	Humanity
Generosity	Selflessness	Tolerance
Awareness	Service	Leadership
Teamwork	Cooperation	Humor
Originality	Innovation	Imagination
Thoughtful	Judgment	Independence
Honor	Morality	Resilience
Experimentation	Idealism	Vision
Mission	Conceptualized	Created
Explored	Pursued	Discovered
Developed	Taught	Trained
Coached	Coordinated	Reformed
Respect	Responsibility	Established
Initiated	Compassion	Inspired
Founded	Tutored	Sense of duty
Collaborated	Led	Mission
Entrepreneurship	Was responsible for	Pursued

Use a Reference Guide

Do not just sit down and start writing. Take the time to prepare yourself mentally and identify the necessary resources to develop a well-thought-out and well-written essay. There are many essay-writing resources.

- Check with your English or language arts teachers for their recommended resources

- *On Writing the College Application Essay* by Harry Bauld

- *How to Write a Killer College Application: Rock Hard Apps* by Katherine Cohen

Create a Quality Product

When your essay steps to the podium, you do not want a hair out of place, food between his or her teeth, mud on his or her shoes, her slip showing, or his fly opened! You do not want anything to take away from the oratory. When you submit your essay, make it the best and highest quality. You will not be there to explain errors, mistakes, smudges, stains, or anything that will distract the listener from hearing your story and getting to know your hopes and your dreams. Before you submit your essay, find the person who never likes anything that you do—the one person who is always critical—and allow him or her to read your essay to see if he or she can find anything wrong. Invite the person to "let you have it," to be as critical as possible. If you can win him or her over, you are on your way to submitting an outstanding essay.

Notes:

Although previously stated, the point bears repeating that you should write your essay days, weeks, or even months in advance so that you can read it, have someone else read it, have a teacher proof it, and then read it again. Even after all the reading, you will find that you used "if" when you meant "of" or "and" when you meant "an" or "he" when you meant "the." Each time you read your essay, you are likely to find a misplaced or misused word. The one thing that you never want to find is a misspelled word!

Now is the time to begin your essay writing, based on the themes outlined in this chapter. Try to write one new essay per week until you have at least one good essay written for each major theme.

Video tape and critique your essay presentations.

Read Your Essay Aloud

What you have on paper has to inspire the reader. It has to allow him or her an opportunity to get to know you. Through your essay, you are having a conversation with the reader. You are telling him or her your hopes and your dreams or sharing your thoughts and ideas. You are telling him or her why you deserve to be admitted into his or her college or why you are deserving of his or her scholarship.

Stand in front of a mirror (your audience), looking at the reflection of your future, read your essay aloud and listen to yourself tell your story. If you can inspire yourself through your own words, your essay will be prepared to take center stage.

Section V

Application & Financial Aid

Chapter 12

By the time I headed off to college, I had applied for about three dozen merit scholarships, won more than two dozen of them, and amassed nearly $90,000 in scholarship winnings—funds that I could use at any school I desired. Thanks to these funds and some college credit I had earned in high school, virtually the entire cost of my Harvard education was covered.

— *[How to go to College Almost for Free]*

Financial Aid/Scholarships

Acquiring the needed financial aid to pay for the cost of college can be as simple as meeting state qualifying standards (such as obtaining a 3.0 GPA in a Georgia high school and qualifying for Georgia's Hope Scholarship to be used at Georgia colleges), as time-consuming as combing through the many scholarship books and web sites, or simply paying private scholarship consultants. Putting together your financial-aid treasure chest will require that you determine the best strategy for you based on your family's needs and your top-ten list of colleges.

As my wife and I sat down to gather our thoughts and prepare our financial-aid plan for our older son, we had books spread out all over the living room floor. We had purchased all of the books that we could find to help us develop our financial-aid plan and we had folders filled with information that we had printed from web sites. Of all the scholarship books that we reviewed, Ben Kaplan's book, *How to go to College Almost for Free* provided the most entertaining and insightful material. We also found the *Scholarship Book 2003* to provide the most comprehensive material of where to find and apply for scholarships.

While my wife and I began our financial planning when our son was born, we did not begin the scholarship research until our older son was a sophomore in high school. My advice is to begin this part of your plan much earlier. My wife and I plan to have the majority of our research for our younger son done by next year—his first year of middle school.

Updated versions of scholarship books are published each year. Most scholarship applications can be downloaded over the Internet.

Notes:

Gen and Kelly Tanabe in the book, *How to Find Great Scholarships*, note:

When we were searching for scholarships, we found them in nearly every place imaginable. Some we discovered in the dusty collection of books at our library. Others by serendipitous newspaper announcements of past winners. We even found an award advertised on a supermarket shopping bag.

Having personally spent hundreds of hours scouring the planet for scholarships and meeting dozens of other successful scholarship winners, we have learned where most scholarships are hidden.

Step 1: Set aside two boxes

Set aside two boxes for your scholarship information:

- One box for the scholarships that you apply to which will contain your essays and necessary application information

- The second box for your overflow of scholarship information that you may not be considering at this time

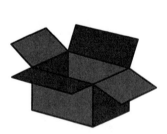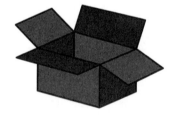

Show Me the Money

One of the hip-hop artists, Nelly, has a song with lyrics, "All money ain't good money, but no money ain't good!" As far as your scholarship search goes, "All money is good money." One of the big mistakes that students/ families make is their inability to take their sight off the big picture (i.e., $25,000 in tuition) and focus on one scholarship at a time (i.e., $500.00). As a student goes through school earning one 'A' at a time, taking one test at a time, turning in one homework

assignment at a time, and completing one class assignment at a time, the scholarship approach is no different—one application at a time.

The important thing is to start early so that one at a time becomes hundreds of entries by the time college enrollment comes around.

Step 2: Get a reliable mailing address

We live in a transient society. Jobs change, students transfer to different schools, apartment leases expire, families lose their homes or purchase homes. Once you begin applying for scholarships, your name and address will find its way onto many different mailing lists and into many different scholarship databases. You are going to begin receiving lots of mail. You need a stable address for the next FOUR years! We have a P.O. Box. No matter where we move, we will keep the same P.O. Box so that we do not miss an opportunity. Do not run the risk of changing your address before the big scholarship award comes in.

Step 3: Invest in a high-speed connection

There are more scholarships available on the web—more information and applications that can be downloaded than you will ever have the time to research. You have to invest in an Internet access account and a high-speed connection, i.e., DSL, Cable, Satellite, etc. I do all of my research on the Internet. Get as much computer power as you can afford—the fastest processor, largest hard disk, and fastest connection. You will also need a fast printer. There will be lots of files to download and forms to print.

Step 4: Get your paperwork together

Get your essays and paperwork together. Most scholarships only require that you complete an application, write an essay, include some paperwork, and submit the package by the deadline. Keep all of your original documents filed neatly in your box and keep copies in your binder under the appropriate tabs like grades, test scores, transcript, letters of recommendation, financial records, awards, essays, summaries of your extracurricular activities, etc.

If you completed the steps outlined in the previous sections and have maintained up-to-date worksheets, you should have all the necessary information.

Step 5: Fill out the necessary forms

There are some mandatory forms that you must complete so now is a good time to become familiar with completing the forms. The experience will also help you to understand what information—tax forms, social security numbers, employment income, assets, liabilities, etc.—is going to be required. If you or your parents treasure your privacy, then you are about to discover that your financial life is going to become an open book. The most important thing for you to keep in mind is do not guess. Also, do not lie! Get your facts straight and answer all of the questions truthfully.

1. Get a copy of the *Common Application* at *www. commonapp.org/* and complete it fully. The information that you provide on the Common Application will be referred to as you complete the many scholarship applications over the next four years.

2. Get a copy of the *FAFSA* (Free Application for Federal Student Aid) at *www.fafsa.ed.gov/* and complete it fully. This is the application that the federal government and your college will use to determine your eligibility for financial aid and the amount of aid that you are able to receive.

3. Submit your *FAFSA* as soon as possible after January 1 of your senior year. Expect to receive a SAR (Student Aid Report) in about four to six weeks after submitting your FAFSA. THIS WILL BECOME YOUR MOST IMPORTANT FINANCIAL-AID DOCUMENT—DO NOT LOSE IT!

4. Get a copy of *Funding Your Education*, a free publication from the U.S. Department of Education at *www.studentaid.ed.gov*. From the web site you can also set up a student financial-aid web account to assist in developing your financial-aid plan based on your current year in school.

    For more information, contact:

    Federal Student Aid Information Center
    P.O. Box 84
    Washington, DC 20044

5. Contact your state finance commission (e.g., Georgia Student Finance Commission) and request all available financial-aid information.

Step 6: Identify your niche

While you should apply for all types of general scholarships, identify the areas in which you uniquely qualify. Do you, for example, have special interest—art, web-page design, animation, film, drama, poetry, short stories, journalism, photography, etc.? Belong to a particular ethic group? Low income? Is anyone in your family a member of a particular religious group, professional organization, fraternity, sorority, or fraternal organization like the Masons or Shriners? Are you an athlete? Have you volunteered at the YMCA, Boys & Girls Club, recreation programs, community organizations, or at your place of worship?

Some of the readily identifiable niches are:

- Gender

- Ethnicity

- Disability

- Employment, hobbies, activities

- Competitions, i.e., talent shows, art, dance, etc.

- Religious Affiliation

- Organizational Affiliation

- Community Groups

- Local Businesses

- Local Dollars for Scholars Chapter

- Local Financial Institutions

- Family Affiliation

- College-Career Goals

- Geographical Region

- Merit Qualification

- Service

Step 7: Establish a research schedule

There are billions of dollars of available scholarship money, much of which goes unclaimed each year. The organizations awarding scholarships are not going to beat a path to your doorstep. You must do your research to find out where they are, what the requirements are, and when the applications are due.

Place all leads, copies of pages from books highlighting various scholarships, web sites, etc., into your scholarship box and set aside time to do your Internet research. As was outlined in Chapter 1, developing teams of parents, friends, members from your place of worship, and other students to research the many scholarship opportunities will greatly expand your efforts. As you identify scholarships, place them into folders labeled by month, i.e., January, February, etc., representing the deadlines. Complete the packages and send them off by the deadline.

Step 8: Package yourself

Carefully research the large scholarships. Understand the organization's philosophy and its ideal scholarship recipient, and package yourself to be that recipient. Write the essay that the scholarship committee needs to hear, highlight the achievements that they think important, and get letters of recommendations from the type of people whom they value. Make them want to give you the scholarship.

Step 9: Establish a submission schedule

Getting your scholarships requires steady consistent effort. It is not as simple as sending in a couple of scholarship applications and waiting to be discovered! (Plan to submit applications at specific intervals, e.g., weekly, bi-monthly, monthly, every other month, etc.)

Step 10: Identify the available local, state, and federal financial-aid sources

Service-Cancelable Loans

Explore the opportunities for service-cancelable loans to assist in financing your college education. These loans may allow you to earn a salary while repaying your education loan after graduating from college or they may be forgiven entirely if you work for a certain number of years in an area related to your education and recognized as an area of critical need in your state (e.g., education, health care, social services, etc.).

These types of loans may be available based on fields of study, military service, law enforcement, or teaching.

Speak to your counselor or contact your state department of education to identify the available service-cancelable loans.

You should be able to get information on the following federal financial-aid programs from your counselor or at the Federal Student Aid web site at *www.studentaid.ed.gov/*.

Programs administered by the U.S. Department of Education:

- Federal Pell Grant

- Federal Supplemental Educational Opportunity Grant (SEOG)

- Federal Work-Study (FWS)

- Federal Perkins Loan

- Federal PLUS Loan (Federal Family Education Loan Program (FFELP))

- Federal Direct Consolidation Loan

- Federal Stafford Loan (Federal Family Education Loan Program (FFELP))

Go to your state department of education or state finance commission web site to identify the full range of financial-aid programs available to students in your state. For example, the following state-supported programs are available to Georgia residents:

- Georgia HOPE Scholarships and Grant

- Georgia Tuition Equalization Grant

- Georgia Governor's Scholarship

- North Georgia College & State University ROTC Grant

- Law Enforcement Personnel Dependents Grant

- Georgia Public Safety Memorial Grant

Step 11: Apply, apply, apply

Applying for scholarships is a numbers game. It is like asking someone to dance at a party. No matter how many times you are turned down, if you persist, someone is going to dance with you. Do not apply for a few big ones; instead, apply for as many as you can, as often as you can.

Step 12: Do not pay entry fees

There are too many scholarships to waste your time and money paying entry fees for a chance to win back your money. Do not allow yourself to become a victim of a scholarship scam. If the scholarship offer sounds too good to be true, it probably is. If you have to send in an application fee to apply, you are probably the victim of a scam!

Step 13: Share your information

The best way to inspire people to share their information with you is to approach them first with information. Many families are going through the research process just like you. By sharing information, you will multiply your opportunities manifold.

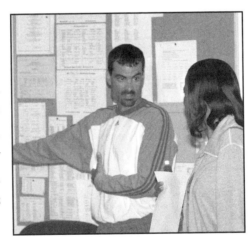

Step 14: Keep that winning essay

Despite researching and referring to all the essay-writing books, you do not know that you have written a winning essay until the check is in the mail. When you write that winning essay, keep using it. It is as good as gold and you should rework it as needed and use it over and over again.

Step 15: Develop a relationship with your counselor

Counselors deal with a lot of students, many of whom unfortunately are ungrateful. Become friends with your

counselor and let him or her know that you want to apply for scholarships and that you appreciate any information that he or she can share with you. Once you get the information, do not be like the majority of students. Use it! If you successfully win a *scholarship*, go back to your counselor and personally let him or her know how much you won and how much you appreciate his or her help. Share your successes so that your counselor knows that you are a student who values his or her time and information. This sharing will help you to develop a relationship with your counselor and you will become more than a number.

Chapter 13

The 1998-1999 application season was the most competitive in U.S. history, with the best colleges reporting extremely low admit rates. Just to name a few, Harvard and Princeton admitted 11 percent of their applicants; Columbia, 14 percent; Stanford, 15 percent; Amherst, 19 percent; and Swarthmore, 21 percent. Those excluded from these small percentages of admitted students include many highly qualified applicants who believed they were likely or certain to do well in the college application process because their numbers and scores looked just like those of the fortunate few who got in.

— *[How to Get in to the Top Colleges]*

Your Application Package

Your application package represents the final steps in preparing for and getting accepted into the college of your choice. There is a scripture in the Holy Bible in the Book of Galatians [Chapter 6, verses 4-7]:

But let every man prove his own work, and then shall he have rejoicing in himself alone, and not in another. For every man shall bear his own burden ... for whatsoever a man soweth, that shall he also reap."

As you put together your application package you will see what you have sown in the areas of:

- academics, standardized test scores, academic awards;

- extracurricular activities and community service;

- personal qualities; and

- intangibles.

Notes:

What you have sown will determine the strength of your application package, which will influence the college admissions cycle that you choose to use. Some of the groups in which you may find yourself include:

- *Academic Superstar:* Your grades, course work, and standardized test scores have elevated you to the level of "Academic Superstar." You may have received a number of merit-based scholarships and find yourself a recruited student who has many college options. Hopefully, one or more of your options are schools that you have noted on your top-ten list.

- *Recruited-athlete:* Your success within one or more varsity sports has qualified you as a recruited-athlete. You may have already received offers via the National Letter of Intent program and now find yourself going through the difficult task of evaluating schools and offers. Hopefully, you have received scholarship offers from some of the schools on your top-ten list or are in a position to use offer letters from other schools to negotiate a financial-aid package with the schools on your list.

- *Strong Candidate:* The success that you have achieved within one or more of the areas (i.e., academics, extracurricular activities, etc.) makes you a strong candidate for admissions. While your acceptance is not guaranteed, you may feel that you are a strong enough candidate who is likely to receive enough acceptance letters that you will be able to compare financial-aid packages prior to committing to a particular college.

- *Legacy Student:* Regardless of whether you are an academic superstar, recruited-athlete, or strong candidate you have made up your mind and are committed to apply under the guidelines as a legacy applicant.

- *Weak Candidate:* After reviewing your application package, you realize that you are not a stand-out student in any area. However, if you are serious about going to college, then you, more than any other student, will have to do some research. Identify schools where you meet their minimum requirements, particularly schools with open admissions policies, and you must take the time to put together a quality application package and meet all of their posted deadlines. NO EXCEPTIONS!

Admissions Cycles

The admissions cycle that you choose to submit your application should reflect your situation, i.e., academic superstar, legacy student, weak candidate, etc. Sit down with your parents, mentor, or high school counselor to identify the admissions cycle that is best for you. Once you have made your decision, focus all your attention on creating quality application packages and meeting each college's posted deadlines.

Early Decision: This program is offered by approximately 270 colleges and is utilized by students who are absolutely certain of their first-choice school by the beginning of their senior year. Many colleges have higher admit rates for Early Decision applications (see table on the following page). For Legacy consideration, many schools will require that students apply through their Early Decision program. **A student can apply, "Early Decision" to only one school.** Under this program a student applies to the college under a binding contract early in the fall (the deadline is usually November 1 or 15) and is notified of the college's decision as early as December. If admitted, the student is obligated to attend the school.

Notes:

Apply under the Early Decision program only if you:

1. Are absolutely certain that, if admitted, you will enroll in the school to which you have applied.

2. Are in a position to accept whatever financial-aid package that is offered.

When applying "Early Decision" you forfeit your opportunity to compare financial-aid offers or enrollment packages from other schools. Studies have shown that Early Decision admission rates are higher than regular decision applications and that the Early Decision program tends to benefit students who are in a position to accept whatever financial-aid package is offered.

US News America's Best Colleges 2009 Early Decision Acceptance Rates		
School	Acceptance Rate	Deadline
Barnard	48%	11/15
Bates	46%	11/15
Bowdoin	30%	11/15
Brown	23%	11/1
Carnegie Mellon	29%	11/1
Claremont McKenna	29%	11/15
Columbia	24%	11/1
Cornell	37%	11/1
Dartmouth	28%	11/1
Davidson	40%	11/15
Duke	38%	11/1
Elon	75%	11/1
Hampshire	71%	11/15
Howard	71%	11/1
Kenyon	55%	11/15
Lehigh	58%	11/15
Northwestern	40%	11/1
Pomona	22%	11/15
Rensselaer	50%	11/1
Rice	34%	11/1
Smith	64%	11/15
Swarthmore	34%	11/15
Syracuse	77%	11/15
Union	77%	11/15
Vassar	38%	11/15
Wake Forest	51%	11/15
Wellesley	51%	11/1
Williams	37%	11/10

Admission rates for early-decision applicants are higher than for regular-decision applicants. For example, in 2002, Johns Hopkins University admitted 59 percent of its early-decision applicants compared to 33 percent of its regular-decision applicants; the University of Pennsylvania admitted 38 percent of the early pool compared to 16 percent of the regular pool (Loftus, 2002, p. 70). Thus, students feel pressed to maximize their chances of getting into a school instead of taking the time to research schools and identify one or more offering a good fit (Gerson, 1998, p. 68).

Administrators at the University of North Carolina at Chapel Hill discontinued their early-decision program in 2002 because an internal analysis showed that the program worked against minority and low-income students. Their study revealed that 82 percent of the early-decision applicants were white compared to 69 percent of the applicants from later applicant pools (Lucido, 2002, p. 28). Also, applicants from the early-decision pool were less likely to apply for need-based aid than applicants in early-action or regular-decision applications (Lucido, 2002, p. 28).

Both Yale and Stanford Universities announced in November of 2002 that they will drop their early-decision programs in 2003, with applications for the 2004-5 academic year. Both universities plan to adopt a nonbinding early-action program that forbids early applicants to their schools from applying early to other colleges (Young, 2002).

If you need financial aid and want to make a commitment to an Early Decision program, then you should consider:

1. Applying to an in-state university where tuition costs are lower or where you are assured that you qualify for a state scholarship program like Georgia's Hope Scholarship.

2. Putting in the necessary effort to acquire enough financial aid through scholarships and grants that you are confident that whatever financial-aid package is offered by the school will not be a financial hardship on you and your family.

Early Decision II: This program has the same restrictions as the Early Decision program but is offered by some schools as a second round of Early Decision that has a later deadline than Early Decision (usually a January deadline).

Early Action: This program works like Early Decision, but is not binding and students are not obligated to attend the school if accepted. Students typically receive a response to their application ahead of regular decision applicants. Students applying via the Early Action program generally submit their application packages in the fall of their senior year, generally between November 1 and November 15. Colleges will usually notify students of their decision by the end of December. If the colleges that you are applying to do not have restrictions on their Early Action programs that limit the number of schools that you can apply to, it is in your best interest to apply to your first-choice schools under their Early Action program to reduce the amount of time that you are awaiting their decisions.

Notes:

Single-Choice Early Action: This program works like a combination of Early Action and Early Decision. Like Early Action, students are not obligated to attend the school if accepted; however, like Early Decision, students may only apply to one school under the Early Action program.

Regular Admissions: The standard admissions evaluation cycle requires submission of your application by a deadline (usually in early to mid-January of the year in which you want to attend college). All applications received by the college are held until the deadline date and all applications are reviewed together. Late applications are reviewed AFTER the review of all applications received by the announced deadline.

Rolling Admissions: This evaluation cycle allows applications to be reviewed and decided upon as they arrive in the admissions office. It is best to get your application in as soon as possible after the announcement of the opening of the admissions cycle.

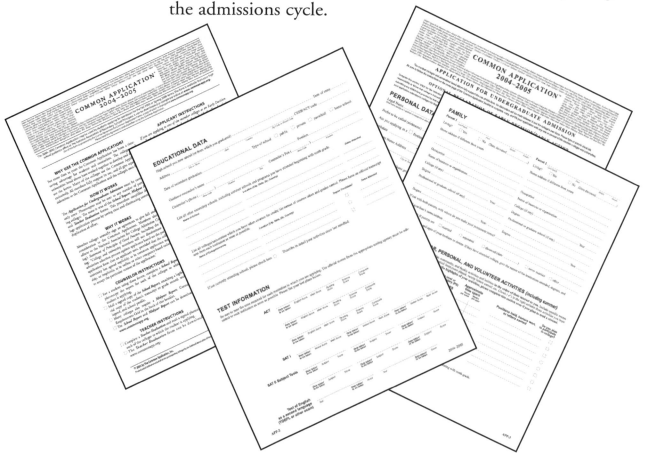

After You Make a Decision

After deciding on the admissions cycle that you are going to submit your application package(s), you must follow the deadlines.

Avoid such common mistakes as:

- contacting counselors too late to meet application deadlines;

- not filing your FAFSA in a timely manner;

- contacting the college admissions office so late that the majority of financial aid has already been committed to other students;

- failing to take the SAT/ACT until the spring of your senior year;

- not filing for Early Admission to your first-choice school;

- not taking the required SAT Subject Tests required by your first-choice schools; or

- submitting incomplete applications or financial-aid forms.

The Common Application

In the article, *"The Common Application,"* Michael Pugh notes:

The Common Application is a standardized undergraduate college application form that is accepted at more than 240 accredited, independent colleges and universities nationwide. Schools that accept the Common Application include Boston University, Cornell College, New York University and Syracuse University. Some of these institutions use the Common Application exclusively.

The Common Application, sponsored by the National Association of Secondary School Principals (NASSAP) looks similar to most college applications, with all the usual fields for name, address, school and test data, as well as questions about your work experience and volunteer activities. For the personal essay, you may choose one of four questions, or propose a question of your own.

How it Works

Create a Common App online account. Create a folder with your username, password, and printout of your application.

You can either complete the Common Application online and submit it directly to the colleges of choice online or download the file and mail it to your desired schools.

> **Download it for free at www.commonapp.org**

The four-page application functions just like a spreadsheet document, allowing you to jump around from field to field, cut and paste text, and save multiple versions of your work. Once the form is complete, just print it out, photocopy it, and send it to any number of participating institutions.

If you wish to save your data, you should use Common App Online. At the welcome page (www.app.commonapp.org), you can register and set up a secure, personal account (free). Using this web-enabled system from any computer with Internet access, you can enter/save data, go in/out of your account, complete your Common App and many college supplements, and either submit electronically or print and mail the hardcopy. Once you've created an account, you can save, alter and revise your application as often as you like before submitting.

Once you establish your common application data file, create a folder with copies of the information that you have entered together with your username and password.

Supplements and Extra Materials

Many colleges and universities require a supplement in addition to the Common Application. Supplements usually contain additional questions and, in some cases, further essay questions. Most colleges that require supplements have them available for download on their web site or directly from the Common Application web site.

If a college or university does not require a supplement, do not be afraid to include extra materials. If you are a musician or artist, include samples of your work with your application. If you would like to highlight additional volunteer or community work, include supplemental information.

Students applying to multiple colleges can avoid the tedious and time-consuming task of filling out multiple college applications. If you are applying to two or more participating schools, the Common Application may be well worth your while.

Follow Directions

A lot of common mistakes can be easily avoided by following directions. All college applications may look the same, but read the directions carefully—they can be quite different.

Keep a sharp lookout for these stumbling blocks:

- Submit the correct number of essays. If the directions state "choose one," select only one of the suggested essay topics.

- If the directions say to "complete all," write an essay for every topic requested.

- If an essay question has more than one section, provide an answer for every part. Make sure that your responses answer the questions—and make clear which response goes with which question.

Notes:

- Compute the grade point average according to the instructions. Different schools use different methods for computing GPAs.

- Be careful not to confuse "country" with "county."

Common Mistakes

There is no way to *avoid* common mistakes; however, if you go through the process of painstakingly checking your application packages and essays, one-by-one, making particular note of the following common mistakes, you can substantially *reduce* your mistakes.

- Incorrect word usage:

  - *if* instead of *of*
  - *an* instead of *and*
  - *no* instead of *know*
  - *from* instead of *form*
  - *to* instead of *too*
  - *though* instead of *through*
  - *chose* instead of *choose*
  - *whose* instead of *who's*

- Listing the current year for your birthday (e.g. 1/1/03 instead of 1/1/88).

- Writing down the incorrect school name (e.g., Fisk instead of Spelman, or Yale instead of Amherst College).

- Using "white out." Do not undermine all your hard work because you were too busy, too anxious, too negligent, too sloppy, or simply too rushed to take the time to submit a complete, thorough, and quality application.

- Not following instructions

- Not clearly stating what you want to study

- Rushing

- Repeating yourself

- Burying outstanding accomplishments in mundane activities

- Writing down an incorrect home address

Sins of Omission

Before you seal the envelope, do a final check to see that you have enclosed all requested or necessary information. After you read and reread, proof and reproof, give your entire application package to someone—parent, counselor, teacher, mentor, coach, or another student to read again.

If you are really forgetful or at times miss the small details, you should identify someone who is picky, meticulous, never misses anything, has a critical eye for detail ... someone who has annoyed you in the past (an English teacher)! This person may now become your closest ally. Use this person to review your application and your application package.

Get together with your friends and schedule an applications packaging day where your packages are prepared, reviewed, and critiqued.

Get computers, printers, and Internet access to ensure that everyone develops a quality application package.

- If you have written your essays on separate sheets of paper, do not forget to include them in the application packet.

- Do not forget to sign your application.

- Do not forget to enclose your check for the application fee or application fee waiver.

- Be sure to list your intended major. If you are not sure, write "undecided." Do not forget what was previously outlined regarding choosing a major that may increase your chances of getting in.

Notes:

- When a college asks for senior year classes, be sure to submit your classes for the entire year, not just first semester.

Give Them What They Ask For

Carefully read all the instructions; sometimes it is easy to misunderstand what you are being asked to provide. If you are not sure what the college is asking for or you are confused by a certain question, talk to your parent, mentor, counselor, teacher, or ask the college. A quick call to the admissions office will save you from making an embarrassing error.

- Permanent address. As previous stated, the address that you use should be one at which the college can contact you during the entire admissions process. If your family moves around a lot, then identify an aunt, grandparent, coach, mentor, teacher, friend, place of worship, or P.O. Box that will provide a permanent mailing address.

- If you are asked what grade level you are entering, write down your year in school for the next academic year.

- When you are asked to list your activities, do not limit yourself to activities in high school (unless that is specified). Include work with community organizations, volunteer efforts or part-time/full-time work.

- For "nickname," include your preferred name, if you have one (e.g., Jim, instead of James, Mike instead of Michael, Sue instead of Susan). Do not write in the names your friends use when they joke around with you (e.g., "Boo Boo," "Big Dog," "Hot Mama," "Little Man" etc.).

- If the application asks for "zip code + 4," enter your entire nine-digit zip code.

If you have followed the strategies outlined in this book, you have gathered and organized all the information that you will need to put together a quality package. Plan to commit an entire day to putting together your college application packages. Depending on the number of schools that you are applying, you may need more than one day.

Take a Test Run

It is good practice to create a draft of each application, cover letter, and essay. This procedure helps to ensure that your final draft is complete and correct. It is never too soon to create these drafts. If you followed the earlier instructions, you should have downloaded or requested an application from each of the schools on your top-ten list. Complete the application and file it away. When you are ready to submit your application in the 11th grade, simply request a new application and use your completed application as your draft.

Before the start of your senior year, take a test run at completing applications, financial-aid forms, your FAFSA, and your scholarship and admissions essays. Once you begin your senior year, there are going to be so many dates, deadlines, college fairs, senior meetings, and important classes and events that you are likely to be pressed

Notes:

for time and anxious as you await letters from the colleges to which you have applied. Reducing your stress level will require that you get as much as possible done prior to the opening of school. If you are still working from your top-ten list of schools or if you have narrowed your list to the top two or three, you should do the following before your first day of class:

1. Set up an Applications Box.

2. Create a hanging file folder for each college to which you are planning to apply.

3. Create an applications package for each college.

4. Outside each application package, make a list of all forms or papers that you have not included, i.e., transcript, teacher recommendations, etc.

> • *Application Packages*
> • *List of Outstanding Items*
> • *Acceptance Letters*
> • *Financial-aid Packages*
> • *FAFSA*
> • *PIN*
> • *SAR*
> • *Scholarships*
> • *Grants*

5. Make a copy of ALL the papers that you have enclosed in each package.

6. Ensure that you have organized all your important information, i.e., recommendation letters, résumés, transcripts, AP exam scores, financial-aid data, SAR, FAFSA, etc.

7. Set up a correspondence folder for each college. Use these folders to file correspondence that you receive such as acceptance letters, financial-aid packages, requests for additional information, etc.

Package Your Application for Your Counselor

Different high schools have different policies and procedures regarding how they would like students to prepare their college application packages. Check with your counselor for the specific guidelines for your high school. Following is a checklist that would satisfy most high school counselors.

❑ Completed application (if you completed the Common Application, include any requested supplemental forms).

❑ Completed financial-aid application.

❑ Application fee (or fee waiver).

❑ Slides of your work if you are an artist or a photographer.

❑ CD or DVD if you are an athlete, a musician, a dancer, or in theater.

❑ Résumé or listing of your activities (as outlined in the worksheet section of this book).

❑ Student essay (if one is required).

❑ Teacher recommendations (or recommendation requests if required).

❑ Stamped, self-addressed postcard listing all enclosed materials for admissions to check off and return to you.

❑ Transcript request form (and appropriate fee).

❑ With the exception of the transcript request form and fee, enclose all your information in a large envelope with the correct postage (at least two first-class stamps).

❑ Attach the transcript request and fee to the outside of the envelope.

❑ Take your information to your counselor.

Get an Application Fee Waiver

There are many ways to save the application fees, which can amount to hundreds of dollars if a student is applying to several colleges:

- *Demonstrate financial need.*

- *Submit the application through a college fair where many schools waive the application fee.*

- *Begin contacting the college. Oftentimes colleges will send prospective students fee waivers.*

- *Ask for one!*

Notes:

Be aware of your deadlines and turn this package in to your counselor at least 3 weeks before it is due.

What Your Counselor Does

Once you have prepared your application package for your counselor, he or she will typically complete your package by including:

1. High school transcript: The high school transcript is the official record of your classes and grades over three years—grades from the senior year fall semester are also evaluated once they arrive in the admissions office.

2. High school profile: The high school profile contains a description of your high school and its students, as well as information about the courses offered at your high school and its grading system.

3. Standardized test scores: The standardized test scores will reflect your SAT and ACT results. Advanced Placement (AP), International Baccalaureate (IB), SAT Subject Tests, and high school graduation exams may also be included.

4. Counselor and teacher recommendations.

Once the Application is in the Mail

Once you have prepared your application package and given it to your counselor, the wait begins for the majority of colleges and universities. However, some schools will contact you to schedule an interview. As was the case with your essay, this is your opportunity to make a convincing case for your admission.

The Process

It is likely that you will not have to go through an interview. Only the most competitive schools tend to conduct interviews. However, you may apply to a school that will host informational meetings or on-campus visits. You should approach the interview as you did your essay; meeting college personnel face to face is your opportunity to further present

yourself and to personalize what is contained within your application package.

The College Interview

If you have done your best job at preparing and packaging yourself, you have met all of the required deadlines, and have successfully navigated the application process, you may be rewarded with an invitation to be interviewed by one of your first-choice colleges. You may receive an invitation for an on-campus interview by the admissions officers or you may be invited to a local interview with an alumni in your area. The interview is your opportunity to further personalize the "person" behind the application.

Your interview may be a direct result of your essay. While your essay provided personal insight into who you are, the admissions interview will provide insight into what you know about the college to which you are applying and further personalizes why you would be a good student for that particular college.

Preparation

As was the case in preparing your essay, your academic preparation, extracurricular activity involvement, community service, awards, recognition, and research regarding the school's philosophies, beliefs, traditions, and programs have the information that you need to prepare for the interview. Prepare for the interview or informational meeting as you would if presenting a research paper or developing a class project.

Your final preparations should include:

• *Review Your Research:* Refresh yourself with the important information that you gathered that led you to consider admission into this particular college. Highlight some of the areas that you would like to further discuss or bring to the attention of the interviewer to let him or her know that you are knowledgeable of the school's beliefs, traditions, and programs.

• *Review Your Application Package:* Read the essay that you submitted with your application and refresh yourself with your stats.

• *Create Some Questions:* Assuming that you have followed the strategies outlined in this book and that you are a good candidate for admission, you should be prepared to ask questions so that you reaffirm that this is a school that you want to attend. Your questions should pertain to information that wasn't provided in your research, through one of the admissions meetings, or through a campus visit. *How are roommates assigned? How are conflicts between roommates handled? Is there a storage area available during the summer months or if I go abroad for an exchange program? Is there a school policy for athletes making up exams if away from campus due to a game or event? Prior to enrollment, is there a mandatory student orientation that would require travel to and from the campus? Is there preferred admission status given to undergraduates who choose to continue in a Master's or Ph.D. program? How difficult is it to become a TA or to become involved in performing research? If my EFC remains constant, can I expect my financial-aid package to remain relatively constant? What is the ratio of full-time to part-time faculty for the school and what is the ratio for my major? How easy is it to get the courses I want at the times I want to take them? Are upperclassmen given priority at registration?*

- *Prepare Answers to Some Basic Questions:* Put yourself in the position of the interviewer and ask yourself, "What type of questions would I ask someone applying to my college?" Do some role-playing with your parents or friends and answer such questions as: *Why do you want to attend this college? What do you expect to gain from college? What do you plan to major in and why? What type of alumni do you see yourself becoming in the future? Do you plan to continue your studies after receiving your undergraduate degree? Why do you believe that you are a more desirable candidate for admissions that other candidates? What is it about our school that makes us your top choice? What do you believe that you can contribute to our school community?*

- *Prepare Yourself to Have a Conversation:* The interview is an opportunity for you to share your dreams and your passions with someone in a position to help you. Share your goals and your aspirations and why this particular university is important to you. What do you want the university to offer you and what can you offer the university?

- Role play and video tape your mock interview.

Remember that this is a conversation, and that the interviewer wants to know about you. Be yourself and be honest in your answers.

- *Provide more than a "yes" or "no" answer.* Keep your answers as conversational as possible. Try to find specifics that back up your answers so you will be able to enter the conversation.

- *Be spontaneous.* Though you should practice answering some basic questions, answer honestly, naturally and spontaneously in the interview. Do not memorize your answers, or you will sound as if you are reading from a script.

- *Be positive.* Highlight the good things from your academic past and put a positive "spin" on your background. Remember that problems can be viewed as challenges.

The Interview

When the big day comes, it is important to set yourself up for success. Dress appropriately by choosing a more conservative outfit, with a minimum of accessories, make-up, jewelry and cologne. If you are into hip-hop fashions, this is not the day to make your fashion statement! I suggest that young men remove earrings, that young men and young women remove tongue rings, piercings, and cover up any tattoos. This is the advice I would give my own son and thus, this is the advice I am giving you. Do not get hung up on your fashion expression and do not give someone a reason to dislike you. Make whatever fashion or political statements AFTER you have been admitted. The exception, of course, would be those schools that are looking for eccentric students to ensure a diverse school community. If you choose this course (i.e., earrings, tongue piercings, tattoos, etc.), then make sure you present yourself as a great student beyond the fashion statement!

Make sure you know exactly where your interview is being held. Call in advance and ask for directions if you are unsure, and schedule enough time to get there. Plan to arrive at least 15 minutes early. Rather than risk arriving late, arrive on campus early enough to go exactly to the room where the interview is going to be held so that you are absolutely sure of where you are really going. Then walk around and get a feel for the campus. This experience may stimulate more questions that you can raise during the interview.

Once you get in the interview room, introduce yourself and greet the interviewer(s) with a firm handshake and smile. There are a number of steps to making a strong introduction and leaving a lasting impression:

1. Make eye contact.

2. Extend your hand.

3. Allow the other person to seat their hand into yours (i.e., palm to palm).

4. Squeeze the person's hand and extend a greeting, i.e., "Good afternoon."

5. Follow your greeting with an introduction in the form of your first and last name, "My name is Mychal-David Wynn."

6. Focus on the interviewer's eyes or lips and listen as he or she give his or her name. "Hello, Mychal, my name is Mr. Jones."

7. Repeat the name to yourself several times to lock it into your memory, "Mr. Jones, Mr. Jones, Mr. Jones."

8. Stand until asked to sit.

9. Sit and consciously maintain good posture with your head up, chest out, and back with a natural arch.

For those of you who find this all to be just a little silly, I have an activity for you.

1. Set up a video camera.

2. Have your counselor or parents invite 4 adults whom you have never met into a room.

3. While the video camera is taping, enter the room and meet each of the adults.

4. Leave the room.

5. Return to the room and greet each of the adults by name and have a seat.

Most students will find that they make the following common mistakes:

1. They do not extend a firm handshake to each person.

2. They forget to state their first and last name.

3. They forget one of the adult's names.

4. They sit before being directed to sit.

5. They have poor posture after sitting.

The saying in sports is, "How you practice is how you play." Take the time to prepare yourself for a great interview.

Following the Interview

Immediately following the interview, take time to make some notes of what was said, jokes that were made, information that was shared, or something that will refresh the interviewers' memory of your interview. As quickly as possible following the interview, write a thank you note to each of the interviewers and incorporate something unique pertaining to your interview. Hopefully you received a business card from each of the interviewers. Take the time to ensure that you correctly spell each interviewer's name.

Following are some typical thank you notes:

Dr. Polyne,

Thank you for the opportunity to meet with you and discuss the programs at Amherst College. I sincerely appreciated the opportunity of speaking with Dr. Womberly of the art department. The broad range of programs would afford me an opportunity to fully explore visual arts media. I am particularly interested in the five-school consortium and the opportunities to experience professors and programs at the other four schools.

Again, thank you for answering my questions and sharing information about Amherst College.

Dr. Carreker,

Thank you for the opportunity to meet with you and discuss the programs and campus community at Fisk. While I thought that I had done extensive research and knew everything there was to know about Fisk, I was surprised to learn of the rich tradition through the association with Vanderbilt. The articulation agreement between the two schools would provide a wonderful opportunity for me to continue my studies through the Fisk-Vanderbilt dual degree MBA program.

Dr. Jones,

Thank you for taking the opportunity to answer all of my questions. As you are aware, I have done a lot of research to find the college and college community that I believe is right for me and one where I believe that I can make a valuable contribution. While I knew that Emory had great programs, the information that you shared helped me to understand just how great the programs are!

Responses to Your Application

After completing your application and sitting through the interview, your wait begins. Ultimately, you will experience one of four possibilities:

1. **Admit:** You are offered a place in the incoming class.

2. **Deny:** You are not being offered a place in the incoming class.

3. **Wait list:** You are not being offered a place in the incoming class at the present time, but there is still a possibility of being admitted in the future if there is a space in the class after all admitted applicants notify the school of their decisions.

4. **Defer:** You are put on hold. A final decision is delayed until more information is evaluated or until the admissions committee can better compare you against other applicants. Deferred admissions occur during Early Admission, Rolling Admissions, or Early Action admissions cycles.

5. **Conditional:** You have been accepted contingent upon your fulfilling some condition such as submitting additional information, passing a physical for a recruited-athlete, taking and passing additional classes, or receipt and confirmation of your high school transcript, standardized test scores, etc.

Chapter 14

Colleges admit people rather than numbers. Stanford says it succinctly: "In essence, we are looking for high-energy students who will pursue our academic program with vigor and still have the time and interest to contribute actively to Stanford's residential community." This is a lot different from saying that it wants students with good transcripts and SAT scores. Schools look for leaders—students who take initiative and work well in teams. Schools look for visionaries—students who are determined to make an impact on the community around them, who have ideas about what they want to do with their lives. Schools look for humanitarians—students who show empathy and compassion for others and contribute their own energy toward furthering the lives for other people. Schools look for persistent go-getters—students who have overcome substantial odds in reaching their accomplishments.

— [How to Get into the Top Colleges]

Senior Year

Your senior year will contain many important dates and deadlines. It is imperative that you organize yourself. You must know where your information is, you must keep track of important dates and deadlines, and stay focused. The first three years of high school have prepared you for and led you to this point. You should have performed your research, done your college visits, and prepared your essays. You should already have arranged your list of top-ten schools into numerical order. The only thing that should cause you to change your mind at this point is an offer package from a school that was not on your list—an offer that is so good that you must give the school and the package serious consideration.

Notes:

Organize your information so that everything that you need is readily available as you complete and submit your paperwork in accordance with the following deadlines. Check off each box as you go and stay focused.

July/August

This is the stretch run. Senior year is analogous to the two-minute warning in football. There are only two minutes left in the game. At this point, you are either ahead on the scoreboard or experiencing a sense of urgency as you attempt to get back in the game. You either have a tight grip on the game or feel the game slipping away.

❑ Complete a preliminary FAFSA and CSS profile. Identify the information that your parents must still acquire, i.e., W2 forms, estimated income, bank statements, etc. Set up a calendar to gather together all of the necessary information by December 31.

❑ Review your SAT/ACT scores and decide whether or not to take either or both again. If so, register for the fall exams.

❑ Review the information that you have gathered from your top-ten list of schools. Make sure that you have completed a draft application for each school and make any final request for information, e.g., brochures, financial-aid forms, etc.

❑ Carefully review each of your desired schools' SAT Subject Test requirements and register for any needed SAT Subject Tests.

❑ Organize your scholarship essays.

❑ Count your money. How much financial aid have you gathered thus far? Continue identifying financial-aid and scholarship opportunities and continue submitting essays and applications.

❑ Organize your college admission essays for each school that you are applying to.

❑ Review your transcript. How many credits and core requirements will you need to pass during your senior year? If you are planning to enroll as a student-athlete, compare your transcript against the NCAA clearinghouse guidelines and eligibility requirements.

❑ If you are a student-athlete and you have not done so, register with the NCAA Clearinghouse.

❑ Meet with your counselor to confirm that you have taken the necessary courses thus far and that your senior-year schedule will meet the graduation requirements in your high school and be accepted into the colleges to which you are applying.

❑ Confirm that you have passed all of the required exit exams and schedule test dates for those exams that you have not passed.

❑ Review with your counselor such issues as guidelines for transcripts, recommendations, how long to allow for counselor recommendations, etc. Get any needed request forms and attach to each of your application folders.

❑ Get a wall or desk calendar and write down all the dates and deadlines relating to admissions (i.e., Early Action, Regular, Rolling, etc.) and financial aid (i.e., application deadlines, FAFSA filing, merit scholarships, etc.), so that you do not miss any dates or deadlines.

September

❑ Early September is the registration deadline for the October SAT.

❑ Schedule college interviews.

❑ Request your final letters of recommendation from teachers, advisors, employers, coaches, counselors, etc.

October

❑ Submit Early Decision or Early Action applications.

❑ Request transcripts for each of your application packages.

Notes:

❑ Review your preliminary FAFSA and CSS Profile for early admissions consideration.

November

❑ Ensure that your SAT, SAT Subject Tests, or ACT scores are sent to your college choices.

❑ Complete an expected family contribution (EFC) calculation to ensure that you have your portion of your family's expected contribution.

❑ Update your résumé, bio, or admissions package with your new extracurricular activities, awards, community service, etc.

❑ Begin practicing your college interviews.

December

❑ If you applied under the Early Decision guidelines you should be receiving a response from your Early Decision school. If you are accepted, move forward with setting up your calendar to meet all requested deadlines and requirements for your financial-aid package. If you were not accepted, continue with your plan for further consideration at this school and for submitting your application packages to your other choices.

❑ Complete your final college applications and prepare your FAFSA forms. Make sure that you and your parents/guardian file a copy of your final pay stubs, 1099s, and W2 forms in your applications box and complete your income calculations.

❑ Confirm your important senior-year dates, i.e., ordering your cap and gown, graduation practice, senior rings, etc.

January

❑ Submit your FAFSA as soon as possible after January 1.

❑ Complete all college financial-aid forms.

❑ Send required mid-year reports to colleges.

❑ Verify that all your applications have been received.

❑ Request your mid-year transcript and place a copy into your file.

February

❑ Approximately four weeks after submitting your FAFSA, you should receive your SAR. Review it for accuracy and immediately correct any errors. Write your DRN down onto your college worksheets and file a copy in each applications folder (this way it will be nearly impossible for it to get lost).

March

❑ You still have one more chance to take the SAT! This month is the final deadline for late registration.

❑ Start planning for a summer job or internship so that you can make money for your first year of college.

April

❑ Most *regular admissions* decisions and financial-aid packages will arrive this month.

❑ Review your financial-aid packages and pay attention to response deadlines and requests for additional information.

❑ If you are wait listed by any college, contact the admissions office to reaffirm your desire to attend.

Notes:

May

❑ Final AP exams and SAT Subject Tests. Have your scores sent to the school where you plan to enroll.

❑ Send thank you notes to teachers, counselors, coaches, and others who wrote recommendation letters or provided financial assistance, and to scholarship programs to both thank and advise them of your final college choice.

❑ Notify (in writing) the schools that you have decided not to attend.

❑ Ensure that you have received all necessary forms from the school that you plan to attend (i.e., financial aid, housing, health insurance, etc.).

June

❑ Have your final transcript sent to your college.

❑ Get a head start by setting up your bank accounts, wire transfer requirements, etc., near your college.

❑ Set up your first-year budget.

July/August

❑ Notify the financial-aid office of your college about any scholarships that you have been offered.

Start packing.

What if you are not accepted into your first-choice?

The reality is, thousands of students will receive letters from their first-choice schools denying them admission. If you are one of these students then you will have to continue your planning. Do not allow a denial letter to discourage you from the pursuit of your dreams.

If you are committed to your first-choice school then become proactive and continue planning to be admitted through the school's transfer program.

1. Write a letter to the admissions officer to reiterate that the school is your first choice.

2. Ask the admissions officer about the school's transfer policy.

3. Accept admissions to one of the schools that you have been admitted to which has the type of school community, major, and classes comparable to your first-choice school.

4. Schedule your classes based on the transfer course requirements at your first-choice school.

5. Enter college and make a positive contribution to the school that you enter while you continue to prepare yourself to be admitted as a transfer-student to your first-choice school.

You may find yourself among those students who are not admitted into their first-choice college, but who discover themselves treasuring the experience at the college where they ultimately enroll.

Be The Captain Of Your Ship

Be the Captain of your ship
and follow your dreams wherever they lead
allow the winds of faith to fill your sail
and be patient as you set your speed

Witness the brilliance of the rising Sun
whose rays reach across your bow
warming your spirit as they guide you forward
reassuring your faith somehow

And during the days when the sky has darkened
transforming a quiet to a stormy sea
remain steadfast and determined
to continue sailing to where you want to be

Although others may turn their ships around
afraid to ever again leave shore
simply drop your anchor until the storm has passed
then hoist your sail once more

There is beauty to be found in all the world
as faith guides your ship to sea
there is joy to be found in companionship
and in solitude you'll find serenity

To be the Captain of your ship
requires you to chart your way
to believe in yourself and in your dreams
and to maintain your course each day

When you sail your ship toward the horizon
the only guarantee of what you'll find
is that you'll never hunger for what might have been
through your courage you'll gain peace of mind

— Mychal Wynn

Glossary

As you begin and continue through the college-planning process, you will find references to many unfamiliar terms in regards to college admissions, financial aid, standardized tests, and course work. The intent of this Glossary is to provide a comprehensive listing of the terminology pertaining to the college admissions process.

3-2 Liberal Arts and Career Combination: A program in which a student completes three years of study in a liberal arts field followed by two years of professional technical study (i.e., engineering, forestry, architecture, etc.), at the end of which the student is awarded the Bachelor of Arts by the first institution and Bachelor of Science degree by the second.

568 Group: The 568 Group is made up of 28 of the top colleges in the United States, including Amherst College, the University of Chicago, Columbia, Duke, Georgetown, Rice, Stanford, and Yale universities. (Four of the Ivies are not participating: Brown, Dartmouth, Harvard, and Princeton.) The group, named after a law that waives antitrust provisions to allow the members to meet, wants to lessen the confusing variation in financial-aid offers by requiring financial-aid officers to use the same method for determining a student's financial need.

AA (Associate of Arts): A degree which is granted to a student who has completed a two-year program (64-66 credits) in liberal arts and is equivalent to the first two years of study for a bachelor's degree.

AAS (Associate of Applied Science): A degree that is granted to students who have completed a technology or vocational program. It is generally considered a terminal degree as it prepares students for immediate employment upon graduation. In some cases, the credits earned while completing an AAS can be transferred to a bachelor's degree, but only when specified by the school or program in question.

Academic Year: A period of time that schools use to measure a quantity of study. Academic years vary from school to school and even from educational program to educational program within the same school.

Academic Index: A formula used by schools to index rank/grades and test scores to quickly compare applications.

Acceptance Form: This form documents the student's receipt of an award letter. The form usually includes a space to indicate acceptance of offered financial aid, declination of all or part of the package and some means for requesting an appeal to modify the award. Acceptance letters and award letters are frequently combined into a single document.

ACT (American College Testing Exam): The ACT Assessment is a curriculum-based college admissions test. This means that the multiple-choice questions on the ACT are a measure of what you have learned in your high school classes rather than aptitude or I.Q. The ACT tests the four subject areas of: English, Mathematics, Reading, and Science Reasoning with an optional writing test. ACT results are accepted by most U.S. colleges.

- **English:** 75-question, 45-minute test that measures your understanding of the conventions of standard written English (punctuation, grammar and usage, and sentence structure) and of rhetorical skills (strategy, organization, and style).
- **Mathematics:** 60-question, 60-minute test designed to assess the mathematical skills students have typically acquired in courses taken up to the beginning of 12th grade. Use of calculators is permitted.

- **Reading:** 40-question, 35-minute test that measures your reading comprehension.
- **Science:** 40-question, 35-minute test that measures the interpretation, analysis, evaluation, reasoning, and problem-solving skills required in the natural sciences.

A perfect score is 36.

Admit: You got in!

Admit-Deny: Some schools will admit marginal students, but not award them any financial aid. Very few schools use admit-deny, because studies have shown that lack of sufficient financial aid is a key factor in the performance of marginal students.

All-American: A high school athlete who is one of the best in the country and is usually recruited.

All-county/All-state: A high school athlete who is one of the best in the county or state.

Alma mater: Latin for "soul mother." This is the term used to refer to the college from which a person graduated.

Alumnus: Alumnus (in Latin a masculine noun) refers to a male graduate or former student; the plural is alumni. An alumna (in Latin a feminine noun) refers to a female graduate or former student; the plural is alumnae. Traditionally, the masculine plural alumni has been used for groups composed of both sexes and is still widely so used: the alumni of Indiana University. Sometimes, to avoid any suggestion of sexism, both terms are used for mixed groups: the alumni/alumnae of Indiana University or the alumni and alumnae of Indiana University. While not quite equivalent in meaning, the terms graduate and graduates avoid the complexities of the Latin forms and eliminate any need for using a masculine plural form to refer to both sexes.

AP (Advanced Placement): The AP program is managed by the College Board. The AP program consists of over 30 courses that lead up to an examination, given in May of each year, that can, depending on a student's score, result in college credit. AP courses are generally looked upon favorably by college admissions officers as evidence of a challenging high school program. AP exam scores range from 0 to 5. Scores above 3 are considered passing and may be eligible for college credit; however, individual colleges have their own procedures and requirements for awarding credit for AP exams. Some colleges will award credit based on the AP exam score; other colleges do not offer credit, but may award advanced standing based on the scores and number of AP exams taken.

AP Scholar: Recipients of the AP Scholar Award are notified in the fall following the May exam.

AP Scholar: Grades of 3 or higher on 3 or more AP Exams on full-year courses.

AP Scholar with Honor: Average grade of 3.25 on all AP exams taken, and grades of 3 or higher on 4 or more of these exams on full-year courses.

AP Scholar with Distinction: Average grade of at least 3.5 on all AP Exams taken, and grades of 3 or higher on 5 or more of these exams on full-year courses.

AP State Scholar: One female and one male student in each U.S. state and the District of Columbia with the highest average grade (at least 3.5) on all AP Exams taken, and grades of 3 or higher on the greatest number of exams. The minimum requirement is a grade of 3 or higher on 3 exams on full-year courses.

National AP Scholar: Students in the United States who receive an average grade of at least 4 on all AP Exams taken, and grades of 4 or higher on 8 or more of these exams on full-year courses.

Department of Defense for Education Activity (DoDEA) Scholar: One female and one male student attending DoDEA schools with the highest average grade on the greatest number of AP Exams. The minimum requirement is a grade of 3 or higher on 3 exams on full-year courses.

AP International Scholar: One male and one female student attending an American international school (that is not a DoDEA school) outside the U.S. and Canada with the highest average grade on the greatest number of AP Exams. The minimum requirement is a grade of 3 or higher on 3 exams on full-year courses.

Articulation Agreements: Agreements between colleges offering two-year programs that allow for students to continue their studies at a four-year university.

AS (Associate of Science): A degree which is granted to a student who has completed a two-year program (64-66 credits) in the sciences and is equivalent to the first two years of study for a bachelor's degree.

ASVAB (Armed Services Vocational Aptitude Test Battery): Armed Services Vocational Aptitude Test Battery is specifically designed to identify individual aptitude in five career areas. Branches of military service use these results to determine eligibility for entrance and job training placement. This battery of tests is given at each high school and is open without cost to any senior.

Award Letter: The form that notifies the student that financial aid is being offered. The award letter usually provides information about the types and amounts of aid offered, as well as specific program information, student responsibilities and the conditions that govern the award. The Award Letter often includes an Acceptance Form.

Award Year: The time beginning on July 1 of one year and extending to June 30 of the next year.

BA (Bachelor of Arts): A degree that is granted to a student who has completed a four-year program (120-128 credits) in the liberal arts.

Base Year: The U.S. Federal tax year used for analyzing student financial need. **The base year is the calendar year preceding the award year.**

BS (Bachelor of Science): A degree that is granted to a student who has completed a four-year program (120-128 credits) in the sciences.

Campus-Based Programs: The term commonly applied to those U.S. Department of Education federal student aid programs administered directly by institutions of postsecondary education. Includes: Federal Perkins Loan, Federal Supplemental Educational Opportunity Grant (FSEOG) and Federal Work-Study (FWS) programs.

Candidate's Reply Date: May 1 has been designated by the College Board as the date by which a student must make a commitment to the college he or she will attend in the fall. Many schools will notify a student of admission before April 15 (the last day the colleges must inform students about their applications).

Career Office: The office that provides student assistance ranging from résumé tips to interview techniques to finding an internship, it's the place to go for anything related to finding a job.

Carnegie Unit: The unit was developed in the United States in 1906 as a measure of the amount of time a student has studied a subject. Most U.S. high school classes earn the equivalent of 1 Carnegie unit per semester.

CCA (Collegiate Commissioners Association): The Collegiate Commissioners Association administers the National Letter of Intent program. There are specific National Letter of Intent signing dates established each year. Contact the NLI office at 205.458.3000 or check the NLI web site at *www. national-letter.org.*

CEEB (College Entrance Examination Board): Administers the SAT and SAT Subject Tests examinations.

Class Rank: A student's position in his or her graduating class. Most ranks are expressed as a fraction; for example, your rank may be 5/400, which would mean you graduated 5th in a class of 400. In some states, class rank may be the single deciding factor for admissions into the state university system.

CLEP (College-Level Examination Program): CLEP is the College-Level Examination Program that provides students with the opportunity to demonstrate college-level achievement through a program of exams in undergraduate college courses. There are 2,900 colleges that grant credit or advanced standing for CLEP exams. Each college publishes its qualifying criteria and number of credits awarded for CLEP exams. The qualifying criteria and credits awarded will vary by college.

COA (Cost of Attendance): The cost of attendance represents tuition, fees, room and board, books and supplies, travel and incidental expenses. The COA is compared to a student's EFC to determine the student's need for aid:

$$COA - EFC = student's\ financial\ need$$

College: Though the term "college" is commonly used to describe many types of postsecondary education, it is also used to describe a particular kind or subset of educational institution. "College" can be used to distinguish solely undergraduate institutions from those that also maintain graduate programs. Within a given school, its "colleges" may be its areas of study, like the "College of Arts and Sciences" or the "College of Architecture."

College Board: The College Board is a not-for-profit organization that administers many standardized tests including the PSAT, SAT, SAT Subject Tests, and AP exams. You will register with the College Board when you take any of these tests. Additionally, the College Board offers official test prep materials, a scholarship search, a personal inventory tool, and educational loans. You can find out more information about the college board at *www.collegeboard.com.*

Commencement: Also known as graduation. A ceremony during which colleges award certificates and degrees to graduating students.

Commercial Loans: Commercial loans, also known as private or alternative loans, are available through several financial services providers. To qualify, you must pass a credit check, and the interest rate will be higher than that of a Direct or FFEL Stafford or Perkins loan. For these reasons, it is wise to investigate such low-interest, federally-sponsored options before applying for a commercial loan. In addition, beware of scholarship scams that are simply commercial loans in disguise.

Common Application: Sponsored by the National Association of Secondary School Principals (NASSAP), the Common Application is accepted by over 240 colleges. If you are applying to two or more of the colleges/universities that use the Common Application, it may be worth your while to use it. You fill out one application and submit it to all the schools you're interested in, with the appropriate application fees for each school. Some schools have a supplementary form that has to be filled out as well. If you're applying online, check to make sure each college has received a complete application. You can find out more information and apply online at *www.common.app.org*.

Community College: Also known as a "junior" or "two-year" college. These schools provide college courses for recent high school graduates and adults in their communities. Community colleges generally have fewer admissions requirements than four-year institutions and courses typically cost less than comparable courses at four-year schools. Most community colleges award two-year associates degrees, though some are now awarding bachelor's degrees. Many students use community college as a springboard to a four-year college or university. Some community colleges have established relationships with four-year universities called "Matriculation Agreements" that allow students easy transfer of credits and preferred admissions status.

Commuter College: A college where less than half of the students live on campus.

Commuter Student: A student who does not live on campus; typically "commuter" refers to a student living at home with his or her parents, but can also mean any student who lives off-campus.

Concentration: A concentration is a grouping of courses in a certain area like sports management or global economics. Concentrations are generally offered as supplements to majors or minors and as such require fewer courses than either. When investigating schools, it can be helpful to look over their lists of majors, minors and concentrations in order to make sure that a good number of courses in your areas of interest are offered.

Conditional Acceptance: An admissions status that is conditional upon a student fulfilling certain requirements either prior, or subsequent to, gaining college admission. Such requirements may include taking and passing additional classes prior to college enrollment, demonstrating English proficiency, or maintaining a certain minimum number of classes and GPA during the first year of college classes.

Consortium: A group of colleges or universities, usually in geographic proximity to each other, which share programs, libraries, facilities, and social events. Knowing that a college is a member of a consortium will provide you with the information on many opportunities available to the students.

Contact Period: Recruiters of student-athletes may make in-person or off-campus contacts and evaluations.

Co-op: Cooperative education (co-op) integrates classroom study with paid, supervised work experiences. These jobs are part- or full-time and may lead to academic credit.

Cooperative Education: In a cooperative education program, students spend time engaged in employment related to their major field of study in addition to their regular classroom experience. In some programs, students may attend classes full-time for six months and then work full-time in their area of study for six months.

Credit (or Credit Hour): The unit of measurement some institutions give for fulfilling course requirements.

CSS (College Scholarship Service): The division of the College Board which is responsible for the PROFILE form and the needs analysis which determines the family's contribution toward payment of a student's education.

CSS Profile (College Scholarship Service Financial Aid Profile): The CSS asks more about assets and investments than the FAFSA. The CSS profile generally calculates a higher EFC than the FAFSA. About 800 colleges require incoming freshman to complete the CSS Profile. These colleges use the information on the CSS Profile to help the director of financial aid determine how much of a discount from the cost of tuition, room, and board a student should receive.

CTBS (Comprehensive Tests of Basic Skills): In some school districts students in second, fourth, fifth, sixth, seventh, and eighth grades take the CTBS each spring. The CTBS is a norm-referenced test, which assesses individual student achievement in the areas of reading, language, mathematics, science, and social studies. Because it is a norm-referenced test, individual student achievement is compared with that of other students nationally who are in the same grade. Schools use the results from this test, in combination with other classroom assessments, to identify strengths and weaknesses of individual students in each of the areas tested.

Dead Period: Recruiters of student-athletes may write letters or make telephone calls; however, they cannot make in-person contact or evaluations on or off campus or permit official or unofficial visits.

Decile: A division of 10ths used to rank students; the top decile is the top 10 percent, and the second decile is a student who ranks in the second 10 percent of his class.

Default: Failure to repay a loan according to the terms agreed to when you signed a promissory note.

Deferral: A decision regarding an early decision or early action student about whom an admission decision will be made during the regular decision period. If you're deferred in December, the college will typically notify you in April/May of a decision.

Deferred: A decision regarding your admission is being postponed. You may be required to take additional courses, provide additional information, or be given other reasons that the college will state in their letter to you.

Demonstrated Need: The formula that takes the total annual cost of attending college and subtracts the student's EFC to arrive at the amount the student will need to pay for college.

Deny: You were not accepted into this college at this time.

Division I (I-A and I-AA): Division I schools have at least seven sports for men, and seven for women, with two team sports for each gender.

- Division I schools must play 100 percent of the minimum number of contests against Division I opponents (there is an exception for football and basketball).

- Division I basketball teams have to play all but two games against Division I teams and must play 1/3 of all their contests in the home arena.

- Division I-A football programs must meet minimum attendance requirements.

- Division I-AA teams do not have minimum attendance requirements.

Division II: Division II schools have at least four sports for men and four for women, with two team sports for each gender, and each playing season represented by each gender. Football and basketball teams must play at least 50 percent of their games against Division II, I-A, or I-AA opponents.

Division III: Division III schools have to sponsor at least five sports for men and five for women, with two team sports for each gender, and each playing season represented by each gender. ***Division III schools cannot award athletic scholarships.***

Division III Exception: Currently the NCAA qualifying requirements do not apply to Division III colleges. Student eligibility for financial aid, practice, and competition is governed by institutional, conference and other NCAA regulations.

Double Major: Allows a student to complete two college major fields of study simultaneously.

DRN (Data Release Number): A four-digit number, located in the lower left corner of the first page of the SAR. Students need this number to apply to additional schools.

Dual Enrollment: Programs established between high schools with local colleges that allow students to earn college credit while still in high school.

Early Action: An Early Action program has earlier deadlines and earlier notification dates than the regular admissions process. Unlike the Early Decision program, the Early Action program does not require that a student commit to attending the school if admitted.

Early Action (Single-Choice): This program works like a combination of Early Action and Early Decision. Like Early Action, students are not obligated to attend the school if accepted, however, like Early Decision, students may only apply to one school under the Single-Choice Early Action program.

Early Admission: Procedure used by colleges that allows gifted high school juniors to skip their senior year and enroll instead in college. The term "Early Admission" is sometimes used to refer collectively to Early Action and Early Decision programs.

Early Decision: Some colleges offer the option of an early decision to students who meet all entrance requirements, are certain of the college they wish to attend and are likely to be accepted by that college. Students participate in the Early Decision plan by indicating their desire to participate on their college application. The decision regarding admission is made by mid-December of the student's 12th year in high school, as opposed to the regular admissions notification of mid-April. A drawback of the Early Decision program is that students will have to commit to a school before they find out about the financial-aid package.

A student can apply Early Decision to only one school.

Early Decision II: This policy is offered by some schools as a second round of Early Decision, usually with a January deadline.

EFC (Expected Family Contribution): The federal government uses the data you supply on the FAFSA to determine your estimated family contribution. This is the amount your family can afford to pay for college tuition. The EFC serves as a baseline to help the college estimate how much you can pay, how much more you'll need, and how much financial aid you are eligible to receive. There are two methods used to determine your EFC (i.e., federal and institutional).

$$CPO - EFC = Financial\ Need$$

Electronic Applications: An alternative to traditional paper applications, electronic applications can take several forms. Some schools allow you to print from their web site or a CD-ROM, application forms which you can fill in by hand and send to the admissions office. Other schools support online applications that you can fill out and submit over the Internet. If you decide to apply electronically, you will not have to wait to receive materials in the mail and you may even save some postage. Best of all, applying electronically will get your application in the hands of admissions officers that much sooner.

EOCT (End-of-Course-Test): A test that is administered to assess students' subject-area knowledge.

EOG (End-of-Grade): A test that is administered to assess students' knowledge within a specific subject area or across a broad range of subjects.

Equivalency Sports: All sports other than "Head Count" sports. Generally, this means that one full grant-in-aid (full ride) can be divided among more than one student-athlete. Note that all Division II sports are considered equivalency sports.

Evaluation Period: Recruiters of student-athletes can only assess academic qualifications and playing abilities. No in-person or off-campus recruiting contacts are permitted.

Exit Exam: Some states require that high school students pass one or more exit exams prior to students' being granted their high school diploma.

FAE (Financial Aid Estimator): About a month after receiving the SAR report, U.S. students will receive a financial-aid offer in the mail from the schools applied to. Many Division II and III colleges use an FAE to provide preliminary information from which they can estimate the amount of financial aid needed to attend their school.

FAFSA (Free Application for Federal Student Aid): The Free Application for Federal Student Aid (FAFSA) is used to apply for financial aid, including grants, loans, and work-study. In addition, it is used by most states and schools to award non-federal student financial aid. The form is a snapshot of a family's financial situation including income, debt, assets, etc., for both the parents and the student. Families must complete the FAFSA every year that the student attends college. Many colleges award institutional grants (discounts from the announced tuition, room and board) and other financial aid based on the information generated by the FAFSA. When information from the FAFSA is used as a baseline for awarding financial aid, this formula is called **federal methodology.** When an institution uses its own unique formula for determining student need and consequently which students will receive tuition discounts, this is called **institutional methodology.** FAFSA information is available at *www.fafsa.ed.gov/* or by calling 1.800.4.FED.AID.

FAO (Financial Aid Officer): The college's financial aid officer applies the school's own methods in determining each award and can also factor in extenuating circumstances such as a recent job loss. The Financial Aid Officer will review the SAR and eventually interview the student. The FAO is the person at the college who, ultimately, makes the final decisions regarding a student's financial-aid package.

Federal Methodology: Federal Methodology is used by the government and public institutions.

Federal Student Aid Programs: Programs administered by the U.S. Department of Education:

- Federal Pell Grant

- Federal Supplemental Educational Opportunity Grant (SEOG)

- Federal Work-Study (FWS)

- Federal Perkins Loan

- Federal PLUS Loan (Federal Family Education Loan Program (FFELP))

- Federal Direct Consolidation Loan

- Federal Stafford Loan (Federal Family Education Loan Program (FFELP))

FCAT (Florida Comprehensive Assessment Test): The primary purpose of the FCAT is to assess student achievement of the high-order cognitive skills represented in the Sunshine State Standards (SSS) in Reading, Writing, Mathematics, and Science. The SSS portion of FCAT is a criterion-referenced test. A secondary purpose is to compare the performance of Florida students to the Reading and Mathematics performance of students across the nation using a norm-referenced test (NRT). All students in Grades 3-10 take the FCAT Reading and Mathematics in the spring of each year. All students in Grades 4, 8, and 10 take FCAT Writing and FCAT Science is administered to all students in Grades 5, 8, and 10.

Fellowships: Fellowships and scholarships are available to students in most disciplines. They are sponsored by colleges and a broad range of organizations and institutions. Fellowships offered by organizations are often allocated in monthly stipends and can usually be used at any university. Fellowships are more common at the graduate level, but some undergraduate fellowships do exist. Additionally, there may be grant and fellowship money available for specific research projects or study abroad. Contact your major department, financial-aid office, or career center for more information.

FFEL: Federal Family Education Loan (FFEL) Program Stafford Loans are low-interest education loans made by private lenders to students and parents. These loans may be either subsidized or unsubsidized and have several repayment options.

Financial Aid: The term "financial aid" is used to describe the combination of loans, scholarships, grants, and work-study that will help a student pay for college.

Freshman Fifteen: The extra weight gain—about 15 pounds—associated with freshman year.

FSAIC (Federal Student Aid Information Center): Federal department for questions about federal student aid call 800.433.3243.

FSEOG (or SEOG): Federal Supplemental Educational Opportunity Grants (FSEOG) are government-sponsored, college-administered loans awarded to exceptionally needy students. Eligibility for FSEOGs is determined by the federal government and the program gives priority to students receiving federal Pell Grants. FSEOGs are awarded by each school from available federal funds. There is no guarantee that each school will have enough funding to award an FSEOG to every eligible student.

GED: General Education Development Certificate is awarded after a student passes a specific, approved high school equivalency test.

GPA: Grade point average represents the numerical average of a student's course grades. Calculation may be based on numerical points assigned to individual grades, i.e., A=4, B=3, C=2, D=1, F=0 or the calculation may be based on the actual numerical points earned within each course, i.e., 94.3, 87.5, 77.7, etc.

Grant Aid: The most sought after type of financial aid, grant aid does not have to be paid back. You may receive grant aid on the basis of either need or merit, and it may come from your school or the federal government. Federal grants include the need-based Pell and Federal Supplemental Educational Opportunity (FSEOG) grants.

Greek System: The common governing body for fraternities and sororities. These organizations vary in their role, size, mission, and traditions from college to college. First and foremost, they act as a social outlet from the rigors of intensive study. These organizations have espoused high ideals of friendship and service since the founding of Phi Beta Kappa in 1776.

Half Time: At schools measuring progress in credit hours and semesters, trimesters, or quarters, "half time" is at least six semester hours or quarter hours per term for an undergraduate program. A student must be attending school at least half time to be eligible for certain types of financial aid.

HBCUs (Historically Black Colleges and Universities): 98 colleges and universities as defined by the amended Higher Education Act of 1965 as any historically black college or university that was established prior to 1964, whose principal mission was, and is, the education of black Americans, and that is accredited by a nationally recognized accrediting agency or association determined by the Secretary [of Education] to be a reliable authority as to the quality of training offered or is, according to such an agency or association, making reasonable progress toward accreditation. For a listing of HBCUs go to the U.S. Department of Education web site at *www.ed.gov/about/inits/list/whhbcu/edlite-list.html.*

Head Count Limits: Represents the maximum number of athletic scholarships per Division I sport. For example:

- I-A Football: 85
- I-AA Football: 63
- Men's Basketball: 13
- Ice Hockey: 30
- Women's Basketball: 15
- Women's Gymnastics: 12
- Women's Tennis: 8
- Women's Volleyball: 12

Head Count Sports: Used for some Division I sports. Any athlete who receives institutional financial aid, no matter the amount, is counted as one. Head count limit sports exist in Division I only.

High School Schedules:

Traditional Schedule: A traditional 6-8 period schedule is the traditional Carnegie-unit-oriented schedule. Students usually have six to eight class periods during the school day that last for the entire school year and result in the awarding of one Carnegie unit. Elective classes may rotate for 9- or 18-week sessions, which earn .25 or .5 Carnegie units for each session. Schools that have traditional 6-8 period schedules usually have 45-55 minute class periods.

Block Schedule: The block schedule has fewer classes than a traditional 6-8 period schedule. Usually class times are longer and the schedule is accelerated to cover more material. Customarily, each ninety-minute period meets for ninety days in a semester to cover one academic year's worth of content credits (Carnegie units).

Intensive Block: In this format, students attend two core classes at a time. These core classes can be coupled with up to three other year-long elective classes. Students complete the core classes in 60 days and then move on to another two. School years are organized into trimesters.

4 x 4 Block: In this, the most common block schedule, the school day is divided into four 90-minute blocks. The school year is divided into two semesters, with four of what used to be year-long courses completed each semester. This format enables students to attend four classes per day, each lasting anywhere from 85-100 minutes. Students complete in one semester what would have taken them a full year in traditional schedules.

Alternating Plan (also known as the A/B plan): Like the 4 x 4 block schedule, the basic A/B plan organizes the school day into four 90-minute periods, but "A" days and "B" days have different classes, for a total of eight classes each semester. On an A/B schedule classes usually last for the entire year and earn one Carnegie unit.

75-75-30 Plan: With the 75-75-30 plan, the school year is divided into two 75-day terms followed by a 30-day term. Students take three courses during fall term and again during winter term. The spring term is frequently devoted to enrichment activities.

Copernican Plan: There are several variations of the Copernican plan. Students may attend blocked classes for 30, 45, 65 or 90 days, usually in the mornings. The afternoons are devoted to seminars and to the kinds of electives students typically want to take all year long.

Modified Block: These are usually variations of either the 4 x 4 or A/B plans. For example, a school might operate a A/B block schedule Monday through Thursday, and then have all eight classes meet for short periods on Friday. Or, they might have two 90-minute blocks every morning and three 60-minute blocks every afternoon. This is sort of a "build your own block schedule" format. For example, schools may have students attend school based on a 4 x 4 block on Monday through Thursday, and a regular eight-period schedule on Friday. Or, they might have two blocked classes in a day, combined with three regular periods.

Parallel Block: The parallel block is used primarily in elementary schools, whereas the previous four formats are used primarily in secondary schools. The Parallel block takes a class of students and divides them into two groups. One group of children stay with their classroom teacher for instruction in an academically demanding subject such as math or language arts, while the other group attends physical education or music, or visits the computer lab; after a prescribed length of time the two groups swap.

Hook: Refers to something contained in an admissions essay that engages the reader. Usually the "hook," is a unique personal trait or experience. For example, a student who has overcome a physical handicap, survived a high-poverty–high-crime community, participated in a disaster relief effort, or has visited another country as part of a humanitarian mission may refer to these experiences as a starting point for their college essays. A student's hook will be something about the student that's unique and interesting.

Hope Credit: A nonrefundable federal income tax credit equal to all of the first $1,000 "out-of-pocket" payments for qualified tuition and related expenses and 50 percent of the second $1,000, for a maximum $1,500 per student, per year. The Hope credit applies to the first two years of postsecondary education. You may not claim both the Hope Credit and the Lifetime Learning Credit for the same student.

242

Hope Scholarship: Available to Georgia residents who earn at least an 80 numeric average (college prep track) or 85 numeric average (vocational tech track) in the CORE curriculum (Language Arts, Math, Science, Social Studies & Foreign Language). HOPE assistance includes full-time tuition, approved mandatory fees, and a ($100-$150) book allowance, when attending a public college/university. At a private university, the HOPE scholarship is $3,000 per academic year. In addition, the student may qualify for the Georgia tuition Equalization Grant of $1,100. HOPE does not cover room and board and can only be used at a Georgia institution. HOPE is renewable if the student maintains a 3.0 GPA and attends full-time. More information is available at *www.gsfc.org*.

Humanities: Major grouping of subjects of study, e.g., Art History, English Literature, Languages, History, Music, Philosophy, and Religious Studies.

IB (International Baccalaureate): IB courses focus on critical thinking and writing and were designed to provide an international credential for university entrance. Like APs, IB courses can result in college credit and are considered more rigorous than standard courses. Some international high schools award IB diplomas upon the completion of a certain sequence of IB courses. IB tests are scored on a scale of 1-7 with 7 being best.

Institutional Methodology: Institutional Methodology is an alternate method typically used by a private college or university to determine a students' eligibility for scholarships and grants under their direct control.

Institutional Methodology requires completing a CSS Profile form, which is processed by the College Board. The tax year before a student enrolls in college is the year that will be analyzed to determine a student's aid eligibility. This is called the base income year, and it's a crucial period because it sets the tone for the types of financial-aid packages that a student can expect throughout the college years (though you will have to reapply every year). Institutional Methodology almost always increases the student's EFC. The Institutional Methodology tends to include additional assets like home equity that aren't included on the FAFSA. When these additional assets are added, the student's EFC will increase. The school then takes this new EFC, subtract it from the "Cost of Attendance" (COA) to determine how much assistance the student needs. If the student's Institutional EFC is higher, the amount of assistance is lower, and the student ends up paying more.

International Student: A student who is not a U.S. citizen and does not live in the United States.

Internships: Part-time or full-time opportunities to gain professional work experience while in college. Some interns are paid, while others receive college credit. Either way, the experience is invaluable to a student looking for employment after college.

ITBS (Iowa Tests of Basic Skills): Developed by the University of Iowa, the ITBS is given to students in grades 3-8 and the Iowa Tests of Educational Development (ITED) is given to students in grades 9 and 11. These tests are norm-referenced, standardized tests. Norm-referenced means that the test compares individual student performance with the performance of other students (in the state or national reference group) in the same grade, taking the test at the same time of year. These tests then rank order the students. ITBS/ITED are also standardized, which means that they are administered to all test takers in the same way under the same conditions. The national average score is 50, and is based upon a national sample selected from 1995.

ITED (Iowa Tests of Educational Development): *See ITBS.*

Ivy League: The athletic conference that boasts eight of the country's foremost academic universities:

1. Brown
2. Columbia
3. Cornell
4. Dartmouth
5. Harvard
6. Penn
7. Princeton
8. Yale

Admissions into an Ivy League school is among the most competitive in the United States.

Joint Enrollment: *See Dual Enrollment.*

Lab Sciences: High school science courses that supplement textbook study with hands-on experimentation. Examples include biology, chemistry, and physics. Other courses, such as economics, may be considered scientific disciplines, but do not qualify as lab sciences. Consult your guidance counselor or your prospective college's admissions office for further details.

Legatee: A student whose parent graduated from the college's undergraduate school.

Lifetime Learning Credit: The Lifetime Learning Credit may be claimed for the qualified tuition and related expenses of the students in the taxpayer's family who are enrolled in eligible educational institutions. Through 2002, the amount that may be claimed as a credit is equal to 20 percent of the taxpayer's first $5,000 of out-of-pocket qualified tuition and related expenses for all the students in the family for a maximum of $1,000. Individuals with modified adjusted gross incomes of $50,000 or more and joint filers with modified adjusted gross incomes of $100,000 or more are not eligible for the Lifetime Learning Credit.

Liberal Arts: Courses of study providing a broad range of exposure in the arts, natural sciences, social sciences, and humanities.

Magnet School: A public school with a specialized or unique focus.

Major: A concentration of courses (usually around 9 or 10) in a specialized field of study.

Minority: For admissions purposes, a minority is someone who is black, Hispanic, or indigenous. For reporting purposes, colleges typically include those of Asian heritage and sometimes international students.

"Match" School: A college where a student has a 75 percent chance of being accepted.

Merit-Based Aid: In general terms, merit-based aid is any form of financial aid not based on demonstrated financial need. Merit-based aid, which can take the form of grants, scholarships, or loans on favorable terms, is generally granted by each school or its alumni associations and wealthy benefactors. A student may qualify for merit-based aid by meeting certain academic requirements, such as grade point average or test scores, or for aspiring toward certain career goals. Alternatively, a student may qualify through an essay competition. The financial-aid package may include both need- and merit-based aid.

Minor: A concentration of courses in a field of study other than the major.

NACDA (National Association of College Directors of Athletics): The National Association of College Directors lists the names and addresses of all the coaches in the United States. Contact 216.835.1172 for more information.

NAIA (National Association of Intercollegiate Athletics): The NAIA revolutionized national collegiate athletics by becoming the first organization to offer collegiate athletics to both men and women with the establishment of athletic programs for women on August 1, 1980. The championship calendar for women began that year with basketball, cross country, gymnastics, indoor and outdoor track and field, softball, tennis and volleyball. Soccer was added in 1984, and golf was included in 1995.

National Achievement Scholarship: The National Achievement[SM] Scholarship Program is an academic competition established in 1964 to provide recognition for outstanding Black American high school students. Black students may enter both the National Achievement Program and the National Merit® Program by taking the PSAT/NMSQT® and meeting other published requirements for participation. The two annual programs are conducted simultaneously, but operated and funded separately.

A student's standing is determined independently in each program. Black American students can qualify for recognition and be honored as Scholars in both the National Merit® Program and the National Achievement Program, but can receive only one monetary award from NMSC.

National Merit Scholarship: A distinction awarded upon the basis of a U.S. high school junior's score on the NMSQT/PSAT (National Merit Scholar Qualifying Test/Preliminary Scholastic Aptitude Test). Those scoring at or above a certain level are eligible to apply for a limited number of National Merit Scholarships.

The test may be administered for practice during the student's sophomore year, but only the junior year score counts.

NCAA (National Collegiate Athletic Association): Founded in 1906, the NCAA is made up of 977 schools classified in three divisions: Division I: 321 schools; Division II: 260 schools; Division III: 396 schools.

The NCAA sponsors 88 championships in 23 sports, including the highly publicized Final Four in men and women's basketball. Almost 40,600 men and women student-athletes compete annually in NCAA sports. **Fall Sports:** Cross Country; Field Hockey; Football; Soccer; Volleyball; and Water Polo. **Winter Sports:** Basketball; Bowling; Fencing; Gymnastics; Ice Hockey; Rifle; Skiing; Swimming & Diving; Indoor Track and Field; and Wrestling. **Spring Sports:** Baseball; Golf; Lacrosse; Rowing; Softball; Tennis; Outdoor Track & Field; Volleyball; and Water Polo.

NCAA Clearinghouse: U.S. high school student-athletes who want to be eligible to compete as college freshman in athletic competition must register with the NCAA Clearinghouse. The only exception is for those students who have been home-schooled during all of grades 9 through 12.

The best time to register is after the student's junior, but before the student's senior year, when junior year grades appear on the student's transcript.

A student can get the necessary forms from their counselor, by calling the NCAA Clearinghouse at 877.262.1492 or at *www.ncaaclearinghouse.net*.

NACAC (National Association for College Admission Counseling): Founded in 1937, the NACAC is an organization of 8,000 professionals from around the world dedicated to serving students as they make choices about pursuing postsecondary education. NACAC is committed to maintaining high standards that foster ethical and social responsibility among those involved in the transition process. Go to *www. nacac.com* for more information.

Need-based Aid: If the Cost of Attendance (COA) exceeds a student's Expected Family Contribution (EFC), the student will be eligible for need-based aid to cover the difference. A financial-aid package may consist of a combination of grants, scholarships, loans, and work-study. The total amount of a student's financial-aid package will be determined by a combination of demonstrated financial need, federal award maximums, and the school's available funds.

Need-blind Admissions: The ability of an applicant to pay does not affect the college's consideration of his/her application.

Need-conscious Admission: Due to tight money and limited financial aid, some colleges consider a student's "ability to pay" in the admission decision.

Needs Analysis: The process used to evaluate an applicant's financial situation to determine how much student aid he or she needs to help meet postsecondary educational expenses.

NJCAA (National Junior College Athletic Association): The idea for the NJCAA was conceived in 1937 at Fresno, California. A handful of junior college representatives met to organize an association that would promote and supervise a national program of junior college sports and activities consistent with the educational objectives of junior colleges. The NJCAA, which now has 503 member schools in 42 states, is the national governing body of 15 men's and 12 women's sports over three divisions. Approximately 45,300 athletes compete for 50 national championships in 24 regions.

NMSQT (National Merit Scholarship Qualifying Test): When the PSATs taken during a high school student's junior year, the scores are used to qualify for national Merit Scholarships. Students with scores in the top 5 percent nationally, receive Letters of Commendation. Students with scores in the top 1.5 percent are National merit Semifinalists and may compete for scholarships of $2,000 or more.

Online Applications: Online applications are a specific type of electronic application. When students use an online application, they submit personal and academic information to the school over a secure Internet site. A student will, however, probably be required to supplement their online application with hard copies of their transcript, letters of recommendation, etc.

Open Admissions: Students are admitted regardless of academic qualifications. The school may require an additional probationary period during which the student must earn satisfactory grades to ensure continued enrollment.

Orientation: Most schools offer orientation for incoming students to help ease the transition into college. During orientation (which can last a couple of days to over a week) students have the opportunity to participate in a variety of programs and information sessions that allow them to experience a small taste of what their undergraduate years will be like.

Out-of-State Student: This term generally applies to students applying to a public college or university. Tuition rates are lower for state residents; out-of-state students must pay a higher rate of tuition until they have established the legal residency requirements for the state.

Partial Qualifier: Under the NCAA guidelines certain student-athletes qualify as partial qualifiers. They cannot compete in contests or events, but are eligible to practice with a team at its home facility and receive an athletic scholarship during their first year at a Division I school and then have three seasons of qualification for competition.

Pell Grants: Given by the Federal Government, these grants are awarded to those students demonstrating exceptional financial need. Pell grants do not need to be paid back.

Perkins Loans: Awarded by the student's school, these low-interest loans (.5 percent) are given to students (both undergraduate and graduate) that demonstrate exceptional financial need. Repayment of this loan begins nine months after the student graduates, leave school or drop to less than half-time student status.

PG Year: Post-graduate year attended after graduating high school; usually completed at a prep school in order to compete in sports or improve grades.

PLUS (Parent Loans for Undergraduate Students): This is an unsubsidized federal loan for parents or legal guardians of dependent undergraduate students. This loan allows parents to borrow all or some of the difference between financial aid received and the cost of attending the school, including room, board, and other charges. The PLUS is not based on need, so the FAFSA is not required.

Preferential Aid Package: A process by which colleges award better financial-aid packages to more desirable applicants.

Presidential Scholar: The United States Presidential Scholars Program was established in 1964, by Executive Order of the President, to recognize and honor our nation's most distinguished high school students. In 1979, the program was extended to recognize students who demonstrate exceptional talent in the visual, creative, and performing arts.

Each year, 141 high school seniors are named Presidential Scholars. These students are chosen on the basis of academic and artistic success, leadership, and involvement in school and community affairs.

There are two ways to become a Presidential scholar. One hundred twenty-one scholars are chosen on the basis of "broad academic achievement." Twenty students are selected as arts scholars, on the basis of excellence in visual, performing, or creative arts, in addition to scholastic achievement.

Private Counselors: You may consult private counselors as you prepare to select and apply to colleges. They may operate as consultants or as employees of educational service providers such as Kaplan or the Princeton Review. Private counselors can help students assess their personality and academic needs to form a list of desirable college attributes. They can also assist students in figuring out where and to how many schools they should apply to.

PROFILE: *See CSS/Financial Aid PROFILE.*

Promissory Note: The binding legal document that is signed when acquiring a student loan. It is very important to read and save this document because it will be referred to at a later date when the student begins repaying the loan.

PSAT/NMSQT (Preliminary SAT ®/National Merit Scholarship Qualifying Test): PSAT/NMSQT stands for Preliminary SAT/National Merit Scholarship Qualifying Test. It's a standardized test that provides firsthand practice for the SAT: Reasoning Test. It also gives students a chance to enter the National Merit Scholarship Corporation (NMSC) scholarship programs. The PSAT/NMSQT measures: verbal reasoning skills; critical reading skills; math problem-solving skills; and writing skills.

A perfect score is 80.

Quartile/Quintile: A division of fourths or fifths used to rank students; the top quartile is the top 25 percent, and the second quintile is a student who ranks in the second 20 percent of his class.

Quiet Period: Recruiters of student-athletes may make telephone calls, write letters, and make in-person contact only on the college campus.

Rank: *See Class Rank.*

"Reach" School: A college where the applicant has a 25 percent or less chance of acceptance.

Registration: Registering on time is an important part of doing your best on admissions tests. Generally, registration involves filling out a form with your personal information, indicating your testing site preferences, and submitting a fee. Register as early as possible and you'll have a good chance of getting your first-choice test site. Consult the College Board, ACT Web site, or your guidance counselor at least two months before your desired test date to begin the process.

Regular Student: Refers to a student who is enrolled or accepted for enrollment at an institution for the purpose of obtaining a degree, certificate, or other recognized educational credential offered by that institution.

Remediation: Students who are not fully prepared for college academically are often required to complete remedial classes. The courses are designed to bring the student up to the level required for satisfactory college-level performance. Such courses are usually not granted credit towards graduation.

Residential Campus: A college that provides (or requires) on-campus housing for most or all students. Many colleges require all first-year students to live in college housing.

Residential College: Has two meanings: (1) a college at which more than 50 percent of the students live on campus, usually a college at which more than 75 percent of the students live on campus; (2) a residential organization within a larger college, often of 200-600 students. Yale is the father of the "residential college" system, whereby students are assigned to a smaller college within Yale (such as Berkeley) and typically live in that college during their four years at Yale. Helps to make the college experience more personal and diminishes the need for fraternities.

Résumé: A 4-year list of work, extracurricular, and award experiences that will be used for college and scholarship applications.

Rolling Admissions: Students' applications are considered when all required credentials have been submitted. There is either no deadline or a very late deadline; qualified students are accepted until classes are filled. Applicants are notified of admission continuously throughout the enrollment period.

Room and Board: The cost of the dormitory room and meal plan.

ROTC (Reserve Officers' Training Corps): A program that allows students to earn a college degree and an officer's commission at the same time. Upon graduation, the student serves in a branch of the military.

"Safety" School: A college where the student has a 90-100 percent chance of being accepted.

Salutatorian: The second-ranked student in a graduating class.

SAR (Student Aid Report): The SAR is generated by the U.S. Department of Education and is based on the information provided on the FAFSA. In the lower left corner of the first page of the SAR will be a four-digit number. This is the DRN (Data Release Number). Students will need this number to apply to additional schools.

The college's financial-aid office will calculate (federal methodology) the federal and state financial aid available to students from the EFC number and other information of the SAR.

SAT (also called the SAT Reasoning Test): The Scholastic Aptitude Test (SAT) is administered by the College Board. The SAT uses multiple-choice questions to assess reading and mathematical reasoning ability. The SATs usually taken by college-bound high school students during their 11th or 12th grades.

The top score for the SAT is 2400. 800 for Math, 800 for Critical Reading, and 800 for Writing.

SAT Subject Test: The SAT Subject Tests assess knowledge in various high school subject areas. Most colleges require some version of the Math test and a foreign language test. Even colleges that do not require the SAT Subject Tests will usually review the scores as additional info about a student's abilities. Students usually take these tests in the spring of their junior year and the fall of their senior year.

If the test is linked to a specific subject like Chemistry, it is best to take the test as soon as possible upon the completion of the course.

SAT-9 (Stanford Achievement Tests 9th Edition): The Stanford Achievement Test Series, 9th Edition, not to be confused with the Scholastic Aptitude Test (also SAT) is a combination of multiple-choice and open-ended subtests for grades K-12.

Scholarships: A type of financial aid which does not require repayment or employment and is usually awarded to students who demonstrate or show potential for achievement—usually academic—at that institution.

Score Choice: A student may withhold SAT Subject Test scores from colleges. If a student chooses score choice the student must go through the process of "releasing" their scores to colleges.

Selective Admissions: Admissions procedure used by colleges and universities, where additional standards and criteria are required. Usually for specific programs or departments.

SEOG (Student Educational Opportunity Grant): *See FSEOG.*

Single-Choice Early Action: *See Early Action (Single-Choice)*

Social Sciences: Major grouping of similar subjects, e.g. Psychology, Sociology, Political Science, Economics, and Geography.

Squeeze Play: A student uses an offer of admission from one college to force an early offer from another school. Early offers of admission are often accompanied by generous financial aid awards and are usually only given to recruited applicants.

SRF (Student Release Form): A Student Release Form (SRF) must be completed and submitted to the NCAA Clearinghouse to allow access to your high school transcript.

SSR (Secondary School Report): A report from the student's high school that provides such information as student transcript, class rank, discipline information, and other pertinent information about the student and student's high school.

Stafford Loans: These loans, both subsidized (need-based) and unsubsidized (non-need-based), are guaranteed by the federal government and available to students to fund education. Federal Stafford Loans are the most common source of education loan funds. They are available to both graduate and undergraduate students. *See also Direct Loans and FFEL.*

Student-Athlete: A student who plays or is planning to compete in a college-level sport.

Study Abroad: While in college, many students choose to spend time studying in a foreign country. During their stay there, students are immersed in the culture, history, and academic-life of their chosen destination.

Subsidized/Unsubsidized Loans: Subsidized loans are based upon financial need. With these loans, the interest is paid by the government until the repayment period begins and during authorized periods of deferment afterwards. Unsubsidized loans are not need-based, so all students are eligible to receive them. Interest payments begin immediately on unsubsidized loans, although you can waive the payments and the interest will be capitalized.

Syllabus: Course requirements given out by the instructor. Includes detailed information about the course, such as the grading scale, attendance policies, testing, and assignment dates.

TA (Teaching Assistant): Most often a graduate student, who will teach discussion sections of large lecture classes. Used most often at larger universities.

TerraNova CTBS ™: TerraNova is a norm-referenced achievement test that compares students' scores to scores from a "norm group." The norm group for TerraNova is a U.S. national sample of students representing all gender, racial, economic, and geographic groups.

Test Prep: Books, videos, CD-ROMs, and classroom courses designed to assist a student in preparing for such tests as the SAT, SAT Subject Test, ACT, and PSAT. It is wise to do some sort of prep, if only looking over the informational packet about each test to familiarize yourself with the number and type of questions you'll be expected to answer.

TOEFL (Test of English as a Foreign Language): Used as a national test for college admission and placement for students who have English as a second language and whose scores on the SAT might not reflect their potential for higher education because of inexperience with the English language.

Transcript: A student's high school academic record. The student's guidance counselor or school registrar compiles this listing of all courses, grades, and standardized test scores. A college will likely ask for official copies of a student's transcript, which is usually signed across the seal by the appropriate school official and should not be opened.

Transfer: The process of transferring from a community college to a four-year university or from one four-year university to another four-year university. Transferring can be a tricky process, especially when it comes time to figure out how many of a student's previously earned credits will count at the new school. To make the transition as simple as possible, a student should request application materials from prospective schools as early as possible and figure out how credits will be accounted for BEFORE beginning the transfer process.

Transfer Credit: Course credit that is accepted from or by another college or university. Usually college level credits with a grade of "C" or better.

Tuition: The cost of attending college classes.

University: Though it is common to use the term "college" to describe all postsecondary schools, a student may be applying to universities as well as colleges. There can be some important differences: Universities generally support both undergraduate and graduate programs and tend to be larger than colleges. Many universities are comprised of colleges that represent undergraduate and graduate programs, or specialized areas of study.

Valedictorian: The top-ranked student in a graduating class.

Viewbook: A college's sales brochure.

Virtual Tour: An online college tour that can be viewed on some college web sites.

Wait List: Being placed on a wait list indicates that a student has not been denied admissions to a college, but their admissions status is on hold until those students who have been admitted make their decision. If a student has been placed on a waiting list, they will be notified if a place becomes available.

Waiver of View Recommendations: A practice whereby the student waives the right to see the recommendation letters. This is a customary practice so that teachers and counselors feel free to express honesty in their recommendation letters.

Weighted-GPA: Some high school honors, AP (Advanced Placement), AT (Academically Talented), GT (Gifted and Talented), or IB (International Baccalaureate) classes add points to grades to reflect their unusual level of difficulty. If you have taken such courses, your GPA may be considered weighted. Some colleges convert weighted GPAs to standard GPAs for the purposes of comparison.

Westinghouse: A competition for high school students. The finalist award is given to a few students each year who have completed outstanding scientific research; this is perhaps the most notable award a high school student can earn and is highly regarded by all colleges.

Who's Who: A for-profit company that publishes books listing students from throughout the country.

Yield: The percentage of accepted candidates who decide to enroll in a college. Because no college will have 100 percent yield, all selective colleges will send letters of acceptance to more students than they actually can enroll.

References

A Guide to Student Financial Aid in Georgia. (2004-05). Georgia Student Finance Commission. http://www.gsfc.org

ACT. http://www.act.org/aap/

Andrew, Allen. (2001). *College Admissions Trade Secrets.* Lincoln, NE: iUniverse, Inc.

Bauld, H. (2001). *On Writing The College Application Essay: Secrets of a Former Ivy League Admissions Officer.* New York, NY: Harper & Row.

Boyer, Ernest L. (1983). *High School: A Report on Secondary Education in America.* New York, NY: Harper & Row.

Carnegie Foundation for the Advancement of Teaching. (1906). *First Annual Report.* October 15, 1906.

Cassidy, D. (2003). *The Scholarship Book 2003.* New York, NY: Prentice Hall Press.

Cohen, K. *Rock Hard Apps: How to Write a Killer College Application.* (2003). New York, NY: Hyperion Books.

College Board. http://www.collegeboard.org

Conley, David T. (2005). *College Knowledge: What It Really Takes for Students to Succeed and What We Can Do to Get Them Ready.* San Francisco, CA: Jossey-Bass.

Dunn, R., & Dunn, K. (1992). *Teaching Elementary Students Through Their Individual Learning Styles.* Boston, MA: Allyn & Bacon.

Dunn, R., & Dunn, K. (1993). *Teaching Secondary Students Through Their Individual Learning Styles: Practical Approaches for Grades 7-12.* Boston, MA: Allyn & Bacon.

Dunn, R., Dunn, K. & Perrin, J. (1994). *Teaching Young Children Through Their Individual Learning styles.* Boston MA: Allyn & Bacon. 1994.

Dunn, R., & Dunn, K. (1999). *The Complete Guide to the Learning Styles Inservice System.* Boston, MA: Allyn & Bacon.

FastWeb. http://www.fastweb.com

Gardner, Howard. (1983). *Frames of Mind: The Theory of Multiple Intelligences.* New York, NY: Harper and Row.

Get a Jump! What's Next After High School. (2003). Lawrenceville, NJ: Thomson-Peterson.

Getting Ready for College: A Guide to Admissions. Clayton High School. Clayton, MO.

Guide to Historical Black Colleges and Universities. (2004). Published by General Motors Corporation and Johnson Publishing Company, Inc.

Hernandez, Michele A. (1997). A is for Admission: The Insider's Guide to Getting into the Ivy League and other top Colleges. New York, NY: Warner Books.

How to Get Into College: 2001 Edition. (2000). New York, NY: Newsweek.

Hughes, Chuck. (2003). *What it Really Takes to Get into the Ivy League & Other Highly Selective Colleges.* New York, NY: McGraw-Hill.

International Baccalaureate Organization. http://www.ibo.org

Kaplan, Ben. (2002). *How to Go to College Almost for Free.* New York, NY: HarperCollins.

Lagemann, Ellen Condliffe. (1983). *Private Power for the Public Good: A History of the Carnegie Foundation for the Advancement of Teaching.* Middletown, CT: Wesleyan University Press.

LaVeist, Thomas and Will. (2003). *8 Steps to Helping Black Families Pay for College.* New York, NY: The Princeton Review.

Lazear, David. (1991). *Seven Ways of Knowing: Teaching for Multiple Intelligences.* Palatine, IL: IRI/Skylight Publishing.

Loftus, M. (2002, September 23). *Early decision.* U.S. News & World Report, 70.

Lucido, J. (2002). *Eliminating early decision: Forming the snowball and rolling it downhill.* The College Board Review, No. 197, 4-29.

Mazzoni, Wayne. (1998). *The Athletic Recruiting & Scholarship Guide.* New York, NY: Mazz Marketing.

Montauk, R. and Klein, K. (2000). *How to Get into The Top Colleges.* New York, NY: Penquin Putnam.

National Association of College Admission Counseling. http://www.nacac.com

NCAA Guide for the College Bound Student-Athlete. http://www.ncaa.org

NCAA Research Report. *A Longitudinal Analysis of NCAA Division I Graduation-Rates Data. (1996-2001).* NCAA. [http://www.ncaa.org/news/2003/20030901/active/4018n01. html]

Rubensteini, J. and Robinson, A. (2003). *Cracking the PSAT/NMSQT.* New York, NY: The Princeton Review.

Ruggiero, Vincent Ryan. (2001). *Beyond Feelings: A Guide to Critical Thinking.* Mountain View, CA: Mayfield Publishing Company.

SAT. http://www.collegeboard.com

Scholarships, Grants & Prizes, 2004. (2003). Lawrenceville, NJ: Thomson-Peterson.

Schwebel, S. (2001). *Yale Daily News Guide to Summer Programs.* Riverside, NJ: Simon & Schuster.

Student Services, Inc. (1997). *The B* Student's Complete Scholarship Book.* New York, NY: Sourcebooks.

Tanabe, Gen S. and Kelly Y. (2002). *Money-Winning Scholarship Essays and Interviews.* Los Altos, CA: SuperCollege.

TerraNova. http://www.ctb.com/mktg/terranova/tn_intro.jsp

The High School Counselors Handbook. U.S. Department of Education. http://www.fsa4schools. ed.gov/counselors

The Rainbow Study Bible. (1981). Rainbow Studies, Inc.

U.S. News. http://www.usnews.com/usnews/home.htm

U.S. Department of the Interior. (2009). HR Office of Educational Partnerships: *Historically Black Colleges and Universities.* www.doi.gov/hrm/black.html.

U.S. Department of Labor. (2009). Bureau of Labor Statistics. *Education Pays...* http://www.bls.gov/emp/emptab7.htm

Wheeler, Dion. (2000). *A Parent's and Student-Athlete's Guide to Athletic Scholarships.* New York, NY: Contemporary Books.

Wynn, Mychal. (2006). *A High School Plan for Students with College-Bound Dreams: Workbook.* Marietta, GA: Rising Sun Publishing.

Wynn, Mychal. (2004). *A Middle School Plan for Students with College-Bound Dreams.* Marietta, GA: Rising Sun Publishing.

Wynn, Mychal. (1990). *Don't Quit—Inspirational Poetry.* Marietta, GA: Rising Sun Publishing.

Wynn, Mychal. (2001). *Follow Your Dreams: Lessons That I Learned in School.* Marietta, GA: Rising Sun Publishing.

Wynn, Mychal. (2002). *Increasing Student Achievement: A School Improvement Planning Guide.* Marietta, GA: Rising Sun Publishing.

Wynn, Mychal. (2002). *Ten Steps to Helping Your Child Succeed in School.* Marietta, GA: Rising Sun Publishing.

Young, J.R. (2002). *Yale and Stanford End Early-Decision Options and Defy National Group* [Electronic version]. The Chronicle of Higher Education, A58.

Block Scheduling

Buckman, D., King, B., & Ryan, S. (1995). *Block Scheduling: A Means to Improve School Climate.* NASSP Bulletin, 79(571), 9-18.

Canady, R. (1990). *Parallel Block Scheduling: A Better Way to Organize a School.* Principal, 69(3), 34-36.

Canady, R. & Rettig, M. (1995). *Block Scheduling: A Catalyst for Change in High Schools.* Princeton, NJ: Eye on Education, Inc.

Jones, R. (1995). *Wake Up!* The Executive Educator, 17(8), 15-18.

Huff, L. (1995). *Flexible Block Scheduling: It Works For Us!* NASSP Bulletin, 79(571), 19-21.

Reid, W. (1996). *The Administrative Challenges of Block Scheduling.* The School Administrator, 53(8), 26-30.

Rettig, M. & Canady, R. (1996). *All Around the Block: The Benefits and Challenges of a Non-traditional School Schedule.* The School Administrator, 53(8), 8-14.

Schoenstein, R. (1995). *The New School on the Block.* The Executive Educator, 17(8), 18-20.

Shortt, T. & Thayer, Y. (1995). *What Can We Expect to See in the Next Generation of Block Scheduling?* NASSP Bulletin, 79(571), 53-62.

Wyatt, L. (1996). *More Time, More Training: What Staff Development do Teachers Need for Effective Instruction in Block Scheduling?* The School Administrator, 53(8), 16-18.

Publications

Careers & Colleges. http://www.careersandcolleges.com

College Outlook. http://www.townsend-outlook.com

NCAA Guide for the College Bound Student-Athlete. http://www2.ncaa.org/index_students_parents.php

States with High School Exit Exams. August 20, 2003. Center on Public Policy. CNN.com/Education. http://www.cnn.com/2003/EDUCATION/08/13/high.school.exams.ap/

College-related Web Sites

Following is a brief listing of some of the more popular college-related web sites. Once you begin searching for college, scholarship, financial aid, summer programs, and other college-related information you will quickly find that there literally hundreds of sites, thousands of informative college-related web sites, scholarship programs, and billions of dollars in available scholarship moneys available to students like you who are willing to put forth the time to identify them.

Academic Competitions

- U.S. and International math Olympiad
  http://www.unl.edu/amc/index.html

- U.S. and International Chemistry Olympiad
  http://www.chemistry.org

- U.S. and International Physics Olympiad
  http://www.aapt.org

- Research Science institute
  http://www.cee.org/home/index.shtml

- Intel Science Talent Search
  http://www.intel.com/education/sts/index.htm

- Siemens Westinghouse Science and Technology Competition

- MIT MITE^{2}S
  http://www.web.mit.edu/MITES/

- Bronfman Youth Fellowships in Israel
  http://www.bronfman.org

- John Motley Morehead Scholarship Foundation
  http://www.moreheadfoundation.org/

- Jefferson Scholarship Foundation
  http://www.jeffersonscholars.org/default.asp

- Coca-Cola Scholarship Program National Award Winners
  http://www.cocacola.com

- Telluride Association Summer Experience
  http://www.tellurideassociation.org/tasp1.html

- Concord Review
  http://www.tcr.org

- Summer Math Programs
  http://www.hcssim.org
  http://www.ams.org/careers-edu/mathcamps.html

Career Search

http://www.mois.org/moistest.html

http://www.gcic.peachnet.edu/

http://www.usnews.com/usnews/work/articles/ccciss.htm

Essay Writing

http://www.review.com

Financial Aid

http://www.collegeispossible.org

http://www.ed.gov

http://www.educaid.com

http://www.fafsa.ed.gov

http://www.finaid.org

http://www.nasfaa.org

http://www.studentloan.com

http://www.studentaid.ed.gov/

Scholarships

http://www.princetonreview.com/college/finance/articles/scholarships/scholarsearch.asp

http://www.nul.org

http://www.uncf.org

http://www.gmsp.org

http://www.ronbrown.org

http://www.finaid.org

http://www.ed.gov/offices/OSFAP/students

http://www.scholarships.com

http://www.absolutelyscholarships.com

http://www.allaboutcollege.com

http://www.collegeview.com

http://www.kaplan.com

http://www.mapping-your-future.org

http://www.nces.ed.gov/ipeds/cool

http://www.princetonreview.com/

http://www.usg.edu/ga-easy

Scholarship Databases

http://www.collegeanswer.com/index.jsp

http://www.collegeboard.org

http://www.fastaid.com

http://www.fastweb.com

http://www.freschinfo.com

http://www.scholarshipexperts.com

http://www.srnexpress.com

http://www.scholarships101.com/cokeschools/

http://www.scholarships101.com

http://www.freescholarship.com

http://www.ftc.gov/bdp/conline/edcams/scholarship/index.html

http://www.gocollege.com

http://www.gsfc.org

http://www.scholarships.com

http://www.sciencewise.com

http://www.winscholarships.com

http://www.collegenet.com

http://www.collegelink.com

Sports

http://www.asep.com

http://www.athletes.com

http://www.theathleticgroup.com/

http://www.nacda.com

http://www.ncaa.org

http://www.njcaa.org

Test Information

http://www.act.org

http://www.collegeboard.com

http://www.ets.org

http://www.gocollege.com

http://www.princetonreview.com

Tips on How to Apply

http://www.commonapp.org/

http://www.getintocollege.com

http://www.scholasticregistry.com

Web sites for the U.S. Military

http://www.cga.edu

http://www.sunymaritime.edu/core.makka

http://www.nadn.navy.mil

http://www.usafa.af.mil/

http://www.usma.edu

http://www.ngcsu.edu/

http://www.tamu.edu/

http://www.norwich.edu/default.htm

http://www.vt.edu/

http://www.vmi.edu/

http://www.amcsus.org/

http://www.citadel.edu/

Other useful web sites

http://www.collegeboard.com

http://www.act.org

http://www.review.com

http://www.collegeview.com

http://www.collegenet.com

http://www.commonapp.org

http://www.embark.com

http://www.petersons.com

http://www.nacac.com

http://www.kaptest.com

http://www.blackexcel.org

http://www.pureadvice.com

http://www.uncf.org

http://www.hillel.org

http://www.ed.gov/studentaid

http://www.fastaid.com

http://www.finaid.org

http://www.fastweb.com

http://www.fafsa.ed.gov/

http://www.ftc.gov/bcp/conline/edcams/scholarship/index.html

http://www.salliemae.com

http://www.aicad.org

http://www.aacn.nche.edu/Education/index.htm

http://www.Isac.org

http://www.ncaa.org

http://www.naia.org

If you have information, stories, references, or resources that you would like to share please send your information to the following address. Due to the large volume of mail we cannot return any photographs or other information that you send, but we will try to incorporate relevant ideas and resources in future additions.

Also, if your school, school district, place of worship, organization, or agency is interested in purchasing large quantities of this book please contact our offices for possible volume discounts:

Rising Sun Publishing
P.O. Box 70906
Marietta, GA 30007-0906
800.524.2813/770.518.0369
FAX: 770.587.0862
E-mail: info@rspublishing.com
Web site: http://www.rspublishing.com

APPENDIX

COLLEGE LITERACY QUIZ
ANSWER KEY

College Literacy Quiz Answer Key

1. What are AP and IB courses?

    Advanced Placement and International Baccalaureate.

2. When are AP exams given and what scores typically qualify for college credit?

    May; Scores of 3 - 5.

3. Who administers the AP and IB Programs?

    AP: College Board; IB: International Baccalaureate Organization.

4. What does the 'weight,' of such classes mean?

    Additional points added to a student's GPA.

5. Is the Ivy League an athletic or academic grouping of colleges?

    Athletic Conference.

6. How many colleges make up the Ivy League?

    Eight; Brown, Columbia, Cornell, Dartmouth, Harvard, Penn, Princeton, and Yale

7. What does HBCU stand for?

    Historically Black Colleges and Universities.

8. How many HBCUs are there?

    90 4-year and 13 2-year colleges and universities (source: U.S. Department of Education [http://www.ed.gov/about/inits/list/whhbcu/edlite-list.html]).

9. What is the difference between the SAT, SAT Subject Tests, and the ACT and what is the top score for each exam?

    SAT tests reasoning (top scores are 800 for each section—Math, Critical Reading, and Writing— resulting in a combined top score of 2400); SAT Subject Tests are for individual subjects (top scores are 800); ACT tests a student's subject knowledge (top score is 36).

10. How many times can you take the SAT and ACT?

    Unlimited.

11. Which type of high school classes will best prepare you for success on the Critical Reading and Writing Sections of the SAT?

    English, language arts, history, philosophy.

12. What advantage, if any, is there to taking the SAT or ACT more than once?

    You can combine your highest SAT scores from different tests (i.e., math, critical reading, writing) and you can increase your ACT score.

13. What is the PSAT and in which grade (i.e., 9th, 10th, 11th, or 12th) do the scores qualify students as National Merit and National Achievement Scholars?

    Preliminary SAT; 11th-grade scores.

14. What does GPA mean?

    Grade Point Average.

15. What is a weighted GPA?

    GPA plus any additional points from honors, AP, IB or other advanced classes.

16. With what organization does a college-bound athlete have to register?

    NCAA Clearinghouse.

17. What is the significance of taking classes for high school credit while in middle school?

    Counts towards your high school credit requirements and allows a student to take the next level of classes (i.e., Spanish II, Algebra II, etc.).

18. What is joint enrollment?

    Enrollment in both high school and college.

19. What is the significance of taking advanced math classes in middle school?

    Access to a higher level of high school math (i.e., Algebra II, Geometry, Pre-Calculus, Calculus).

20. What is the most important academic skill that colleges want incoming students to demonstrate?

    Communication.

21. Does a student from a top private school have a significantly better chance of being admitted to college over a student from an average public high school?

    No. Students are usually compared against other students from similar backgrounds and schools.

22. What are complementary sports and how can they increase your college admissions opportunities?

    Sports that utilize or develop a similar set of skills, e.g., football–lacrosse, football–track and field, baseball–basketball, etc.

23. Will being a top academic achiever and having high SAT/ACT scores guarantee that you will be accepted into the college of your choice?

    No. Academic achievement and SAT/ACT scores are only part of the admissions criteria.

24. Will average grades and average SAT/ACT scores guarantee that you will not be accepted into the college of your choice?

    No. Academic achievement and SAT/ACT scores are only part of the admissions criteria.

25. Who is a legacy student?

    A student whose parents graduated from the college's undergraduate program.

26. What is FAFSA, why is it important, and when should you complete it?

    Free Application for Federal Student Aid; determines a student's financial need; and should be completed as soon as possible after January 1 of the year that you will be enrolling in college. Must also be completed each year that you are attending college and applying for financial aid.

27. What is EFC?

    Expected Family Contribution.

28. What is Need-based—Need-blind admissions?

    Admissions does not take into account student financial need, however, the student's financial-aid package is based on student need.

29. What is an articulation agreement?

    An agreement between schools, typically a two-year college that allows ease of transfer into a four-year university.

30. How many colleges can a student apply to under the Early Decision program?

    One.

Index

A High School Plan, i, iii-iv, x, xiii, 290
A Middle School Plan, 34, 76, 104, 154, 290
AA, 231
AAS, 231
AAU, 53, 137, 143, 147, 163-164
AB, 71
Abbey Road Overseas Programs, 166
Academic
   Bowl, 134
   Clubs, 88
   Connections, 166
   Honors, 89
   Index, 231
   Quality of Your High School, 62
   Superstar, 200-201
   Support, vi, 83
   Year, 81, 91, 203, 210, 231, 240-241
Academically Talented, ix, 170, 250
Academics, vi, xi, 4, 23, 29-31, 156, 158, 166,
   173, 199-200
Acceptance Form, 231, 233
Acceptance Letters, 200, 212, 231
Achievement
   Scholar, 33, 98-99, 111, 123
   Scholar Designees, 98-99
   Scholarship Awards, 97-99
ACT
   Assessment, 122, 231
   Prep Programs, 26
   Registration, 25, 123
Admissions
   Committees Look For, 58
   Cycles, 201, 222
Admit, 18, 81, 106, 199, 201, 222-223, 232
Admit One, 106
Admit You, 18, 222, 232
Admit-Deny, 232
Advanced Placement, 65, 67, 69, 71, 214, 232,
   250
African-American, 37, 45, 159
Agnes Scott, 202
Air Force, 24, 38, 139
Air Force Academy, 38, 139
Algebra
   I, ix, 47, 49, 53, 55, 87, 117, 121
   II, ix, 49, 55, 60, 87-88, 117, 121
   III, ix
All-American, 232
All-county, 232
All-state, 232

Alma mater, 5, 45, 232
Alternating Plan, 240
American College Testing Exam, 122, 231
American Collegiate Adventures, 166
American Psychological Association, 183
Amherst College, v, viii, 39, 44-45, 67, 127, 139,
   199, 202, 208, 221, 231
AP
   Calculus, ix, 64
   Computer Science, 61
   Exam, 4, 7, 65-70, 118, 212, 232
   Grade Qualification, 69
   Grade Reports, 69
   International Scholar, 70, 232
   Language, 49, 117
   Literature, 49, 58, 110-111, 117, 124
   Prep, 65
   Psychology, 44, 58
   Scholar, 69-70, 232
   Scholar Award, 69, 232
   Scholars, 68, 90
   State Scholar, 70, 232
   Statistics, ix, 87-88
   U. S. History, 55, 58, 88, 110, 124
APA, 183
Application Fee Waiver, 43, 209, 213
Applications Box, 212, 226
Applied Geometry, 49, 117
Armed Services Vocational Aptitude Test Battery,
   233
Army, 24
Art
   Center College of Design, viii, 44
   Club, 134
   History, 71, 241
   Honor Society, 134
Articulation Agreements, 233
Associate of
   Applied Science, 231
   Arts, 231
   Science, 233
ASVAB, 233
   216, 245
Athletic Group, 143
Athletic Recruiting, 142
Athletic Scholarships, 136, 139, 142-143, 236,
   240
Athletics, 18, 30, 36, 52-53, 129-130, 136, 138,
   140, 144-145, 243
Athletics Beyond High School, 138
Auburn, 139
Automotive Mechanics, xi, 145
Award Letter, 231, 233

Award Year, 233

BA, 233
Bachelor of Arts, 231, 233
Bachelor of Science, vii, 231, 233
Badminton, 57
Base Year, 233
BC Calculus, 68
Be The Captain of Your Ship, 230
Bentley College, 167
Berea College, 38
Berkeley, 247
Best Colleges, 20, 34, 39, 199, 202
Bethune-Cookman, 139
Big Ten, 37
Biology, 48-49, 61, 71, 117, 134, 242
Birthday Ninja, 135
Black American, 96-98, 243
Block Schedule, 240-241
Book of Galatians, 199
Boston University, 173, 205
Bowdoin College, 39
Bowie State University, 127
Brian Youth Leadership, 134
Bridgewater College, 127
Bright Future Scholars Awards, 101
Bromwell, 142
Brown, v, 36, 139, 202, 231, 242
BS, 233
Business Administration, 38
Business Policy, 86
BYU, 139

Caltech, 18, 39
Calculus, vii, ix, 55, 64, 68, 71, 87, 113
California Institute of Technology, 39
Camp Bentley, 167
Camps, 10, 23, 26, 28, 108, 142, 148, 161, 163-165, 174
Campus Dirt, 34
Campus Tours, 34, 41
Campus Visits, 41
Campus-Based Programs, 233
Cannes, 166
Career Combination, 231
Career Interests, 162
Career Office, 233
Carleton College, 39
Carnegie, 41, 202, 233, 240
Carnegie Mellon, 41, 202
Carnegie Unit, 233, 240
CCA, 233

CD-Rom, 122, 237
CD-ROMs, 249
CEEB, 233
Chemistry, 48-49, 55, 61, 68, 71, 82, 88, 113, 117, 242, 248
Chicago Public School, 173
China, 12, 14
Chinese, 168
Chowan College, 127
Citadel, 139
Claremont McKenna College, 39
Class Officer, 135
Class Rank, 4, 28, 62, 80, 82, 114, 234, 246, 248
Class Representative, 135
Clearinghouse, 3, 25, 27, 52-53, 105, 109, 140, 224-225, 244, 248
Clemson University, 127
CLEP, 126, 234
Co-curricular Activities, 158
Co-op, 38, 235
COA, 68, 234, 242, 244
COA - EFC, 234
Coast Guard, 38
Colgate, 202
College Admission Counseling, 42, 244
College Admissions, 6, 8, 26-27, 30-32, 54, 57-58, 62, 79, 89, 105, 119, 125, 129-130, 137, 145, 178, 200, 205, 231-232
College Admissions Trade Secrets, 57, 89
College
    Affiliations, 35-36
    Application Essay, 185
    Athletic Programs, 142
    Board, 34, 65, 70, 102, 106, 120, 126, 232-235, 242, 246-247
    Credit, 7, 65, 67, 69, 72-73, 75-76, 166, 169-170, 172, 188, 232, 237, 241-242
    English, 49, 110, 117
    Entrance Examination Board, 233
    Fairs, 26, 33, 37, 42-44, 115, 142, 212
    Guide, x, 34
    Interview, 18, 28, 144, 215
    Literacy Quiz, vi, 6-7
    Literacy Quiz Answer Key, vi
    of Architecture, 234
    of Arts, 234
    Plan, ix, 3, 23, 67, 85, 144, 178
    Planning, vii, x, 104, 114
    Prep Classes, 60
    Preparatory, 48-49, 61
    Preparatory Diploma, 49, 61
    Programs, 26

Prowler, 34
Scholarship Application Essay, 175
Scholarship Guide, 142
Scholarship Service, 235
Scholarship Service Financial Aid Profile, 235
Students, 5, 9, 18, 27, 37, 104, 166, 237
Tours, 37, 41
Visits, 33, 41, 223
College-Bound Athletes, 52-53, 140
College-Career Goals, 194
College-Level Examination Program, 126, 234
College-Planning, 43, 89, 114, 231
College-related Web Sites, vi
College-sponsored Merit Scholarship Awards, 94
CollegeSurfing, 41
Collegiate Choice, 41
Collegiate Commissioners Association, 233
Color Guard, 134
Columbia, 39
Columbia College of Chicago, 167
Commencement, 234
Commercial Loans, 234
Common
    App, 206, 234
    App Online, 206
    Application, 193, 205-207, 213, 234
    Mistakes, 205, 207-208, 220
Community College, 106, 234, 249
Community Service, 1, 4, 19, 21, 58, 100, 108,
    110, 115, 129-130, 132, 134-136, 148, 163,
    181, 199, 216, 226
Commuter College, 235
Commuter Student, 235
Competitive Schools, 46, 158, 215
Complimentary Sports, 8, 142
Composite, 61, 75, 90, 122, 127
Composite Score Selectivity Total Score, 127
Comprehensive Tests of Basic Skills, ix, 235
Computer Science, 38, 61, 71
Computer Technicians, x, 145
Concordia Language Villages, 168
Conditional Acceptance, vii, 235
Contact Period, 235
Contact Schools, 35
Conversion Table, 122
Coop, 38, 235
Cooper Union, 38
Cooperative Education, 38, 235
Copernican Plan, 241
Cornell, 36, 118, 168, 202, 205, 242
Cornell College, 205
Cornell University - Summer Programs, 168

Corporate-sponsored Achievement Scholarship
    Awards, 99
Corporate-sponsored Merit Scholarship Awards,
    94
Cost of Attendance, 39, 234, 242, 244
Course Requirements, 47-48, 73, 80, 229, 235,
    249
Course Work, vi, 4, 28, 30-31, 54, 59, 65, 78,
    147, 156, 200, 231
CPC, 75
CPO - EFC, 237
Credit Hour, 235
Critical Reading, 7, 120, 124-125, 246-247
CSS, 224, 226, 235, 242, 246
CSS Profile, 224, 226, 235, 242
CTBS, ix, 235, 249

Dartmouth, viii, 19, 36, 39, 44, 104, 139, 202,
    231, 242
Data Release Number, 236, 247
Davidson College, 39
De La Salle Catholic High School, vii
Dead Period, 236
Deadline, 75, 115, 192, 195, 201-204, 225, 227,
    237, 247
Dean of Students, 41
DECA, 134
Decile, 236
Deep Springs College, 38
Deferred, vii, x, 50, 222, 236
Delaware State, 139
Demonstrated Need, 236
Deny, 21, 222, 236
Department of Defense, 70, 232
Diploma Program, 72
Diplomas Denied, 50
Direct Loans, 248
Discipline, 19, 155-156, 248
Distinction, 61, 70, 232, 244
Distinguished Scholar Award, 102
Diversity, 34, 41, 159, 162
Division
    I, 52, 140-141, 143, 236, 240, 244-245
    I-A, 83-84, 136, 236
    I-AA, 236
    II, 52, 140, 236-238, 244
    III, 140, 236, 244
    III Exception, 236
DoDEA, 70, 232
Dorms, 41
Double Major, 236
Drill Team, 134

DRN, 227, 236, 247
Drugs, 21, 85, 156
DSL, 192
Du Sable High School, vii
Dual Enrollment, 63, 237, 242
Duke, 18, 27, 39, 61, 127, 139, 168, 202, 231
Duke University, 27, 39, 61, 127, 168

Early
    Action, 203-204, 222, 225, 236-237, 248
    Admission, 205, 222, 237
    Decision Acceptance Rates, 202
    Decision II, 203, 237
East Carolina University, 127
Economics, 48, 62, 71, 80, 107, 113, 166, 235, 242, 248
Education Policy, 47
Education Statistics, 35, 37
EFC, 3, 8, 130, 217, 226, 234-237, 242, 244, 247
Elective, 55, 105, 107, 114, 240
Electives, 48-49, 58-59, 105, 107, 109, 112, 117, 163, 173, 241
Electronic Applications, 237
Eligibility, 52-53, 119, 140, 143, 193, 224, 233, 236, 239, 242
Emerson, 16
Emmanuel, 202
Emory, 30, 202, 221
End-of-Course-Test, 118, 237
End-of-Grade, 50-51, 63, 237
English Literature, 109, 241
Enrichment Programs, 164-165
Environmental Science, 71
EOCT, 118, 237
EOG, 51, 237
Equalization Grant, 196, 241
Equivalency Sports, 237
Estimated Probability of Competing, 138
European History, 68, 71
Evaluation Period, 238
Exit Exams, vi, 31, 47, 50, 63, 65, 106, 118, 182, 225, 238
Expected Family Contribution, 3, 130, 226, 237, 244
Extended Learning Opportunities, 108
Extracurricular Activities, vi, 1, 4, 10, 19, 28, 42, 57, 59, 76, 88, 109-110, 113, 128-131, 134, 155, 158, 192, 199-200, 226
Extremely Well Qualified, 69

FAE, 238
Fairmont State College, 127

FAMU, 18
FAO, 238
FCAT, 238
FED, 135, 238
Federal
    Direct Consolidation Loan, 196, 238
    Family Education Loan, 196, 238-239
    Family Education Loan Program, 196, 238
    Government, 193, 237, 239, 245, 248
    Methodology, 238, 247
    Pell Grant, 196, 238
    Perkins Loan, 196, 233, 238
    PLUS Loan, 196, 238
    Stafford Loan, 196, 238
    Student Aid, 193, 196, 233, 238-239
    Student Aid Information Center, 193, 239
    Student Aid Programs, 233, 238
    Supplemental Educational Opportunity, 196, 233, 238-239
    Supplemental Educational Opportunity Grant, 196, 233, 238
    Supplemental Educational Opportunity Grants, 239
    Work-Study, 196, 233, 238
FFEL, 234, 239, 248
FFEL Stafford, 234
FFELP, 196, 238
Financial Aid Estimator, 238
Financial Aid Officer, 238
Financial Aid PROFILE, 235, 246
Financial Need, 70, 130, 213, 231, 233-234, 237, 243-245, 249
Financial-Aid, 23, 25, 40-41, 43, 98, 102, 111, 116, 130, 188, 193, 196, 200, 202-203, 205, 211-213, 217, 224, 226-228, 231, 237-239, 242-244, 246-247
Financial-Aid Information, 23, 116, 193
Financial-Aid Packages, 200, 212, 227, 242, 246
Fine Arts, 44, 49, 167
First-Choice University, 175
Fisk, 18, 44-45, 208, 221
Fisk University, 44
Fisk-Vanderbilt, 221
Florida Comprehensive Assessment Test, 238
Florida State University, 127
Follow Your Dreams, x, 10, 24, 290
Football, x, 16, 22, 27, 36, 45, 50, 61, 83-84, 119, 138, 141-142, 145-146, 163, 224, 236, 240
Foreign Language, 48-49, 53, 60, 71-72, 83, 88, 109, 117, 134, 241, 248-249
Forensics, 58, 113
Formatting Your Essay, 183

Four-year Average, 139
Free Application, 193, 238
French, 15, 71, 109, 166, 168
Freshman Fifteen, 239
Frostburg University, 127
FSAIC, 239
FSEOG, 233, 239, 248
Fulton County Schools, 48
Funding Your Education, 193

GED, 239
General Education Development Certificate, 239
Geographical, 5, 158-159, 161, 194
Geography, 68, 71, 103, 248
Geometry, ix, 49, 55, 87, 117, 121, 173
George Mason University, 127
Georgetown, 127, 139, 231
Georgetown University, 127
Georgia
    Board of Education, 49
    Governor, 100, 196
    High School Graduation Test, 51
    HOPE Scholarships, 196
    Perimeter College, 75
    Public Safety, 196
    Scholars Awards, 101
    State, 75
    Student Finance Commission, 193
    Tech, 75, 139
    Tuition Equalization Grant, 196, 241
German, 71, 109, 168
GHSGT, 51
Give Them What They Ask For, 210
Glossary, vi, 231
Googling, 51
GPAs, 64, 208, 250
Grade Point Average, 50, 64, 78-79, 81, 208, 239,
    243
Graduation Tests, 50-52, 118
Grant Aid, 239
Grants, xi, 36, 130, 203, 212, 238-239, 242-245
Greek System, 239
GT, 250
Gymnastics, 240, 243

Half Time, 239
Hampshire, 45, 173, 202
Hampshire College, 45
Hampton University, 127
Harvard, 18, 36, 39, 44, 67-68, 127, 143, 159,
    169, 188, 199, 231, 242
Harvard Summer School Secondary School

Program, 169
Harvard University, 39, 67, 127, 143, 169
Haverford College, 39
HBCUs, 7, 18, 37, 44, 239-240
Head Count, 237, 240
Head Count Limits, 240
Head Count Sports, 237, 240
Health, 41, 49, 107, 109, 113, 117, 147, 228
Health Services, 41
Heroes, 180
Heroines, 180
High
    School Course Offerings, 106, 109
    School Graduation Requirements, vi, 2-4,
        25, 31, 47, 51, 60, 80
    School Journalism Institute, 169
    School Plan, i, iii-iv, ix-x, xiii, 5, 18, 21, 27, 30,
        85, 290
    School Profile, 4, 31, 214
    School Schedules, 240
    School Senior, 138, 163
    School Students, 1, 31-32, 65, 77, 89, 91, 96,
        99-102, 105, 141, 155, 166-174, 238, 243,
        246-247, 250
    School workshop, 171
Higher Education Act, 239
Highly Selective, 54, 118, 127, 129
Hispanic, 243
Historically Black Colleges, 37-38, 239
Holy Bible, 199
Holy Cross, 202
Honor Roll, 90
Honors, vi, 1, 4, 31, 56, 58, 60-67, 78-79, 82, 85,
    88-91, 100-101, 103, 107, 110-111, 113-115,
    121, 124, 163, 250
Honors
    Academy, 101
    Algebra II, 60
    Classes, 56, 58, 64-65, 67
    Pre-Calculus, 61
    Program, 100
    Spanish IV, 60
Hook, 89, 118, 241
Hoosier Scholar Awards, 101
Hope, 45, 183, 188, 196, 203, 241
Hope
    Credit, 241
    Scholarship, 188, 203, 241
House Bill, 81
Humanities, 101, 166, 168, 241, 243

I. Q., 5, 122, 231

I-A, 83-84, 123, 136, 140, 236, 240
I-A Football, 84, 236, 240
I-AA, 236, 240
I-AA Football, 240
IA, 83-84, 123, 136, 140, 236, 240
IB
    Diploma, 72-73
    Exams, 72-73
    Programs, 7, 72
IBO, 72, 106
Ice Hockey, 240
Identify Your Team, 24
Important
    Relationships, 21
    Resources, 106
    Themes, 178-179
Indiana University, 169
Indiana University - High School Journalism
    Institute, 169
Institutional EFC, 242
Institutional Methodology, 238, 242
Intangibles, vi, 157-158, 161, 180, 199
Intensive Block, 240
International Baccalaureate, 48, 72, 106, 214, 241,
    250
International Baccalaureate Organization, 72, 106
International Student, 242
Internships, 23, 26, 108, 164-165, 242
Interpersonal Skills, 158
Interview, 4, 18, 28, 35, 134, 144, 161, 214-220,
    222, 233, 238
Iowa Tests of Basic Skills, ix, 242
Iowa Tests of Educational Development, 242
Italian, 168
Italy, 166
ITBS, ix, 242
ITED, 242
Ivies, 231
Ivy League, viii, 7, 18-19, 36, 44, 118, 129, 242
Ivy League Agreement, 36

Jackson State, 45
Japanese, 168
Java, 13
Jobs, x, 108, 147, 162, 191, 235
Johns Hopkins University, 202
Joint Enrollment, 8, 73-76, 80, 106, 115, 242

Kennedy-King Junior College, vii
Kentucky, 38, 139
Killer College Application, 185
KISS, 182

Lab Sciences, 60, 109, 242
Lane College, 45
Language Arts
    Core, 49, 117
    Selective, 49, 117
Law Enforcement, 41, 145, 161, 196
Law Enforcement Personnel Dependents Grant,
    196
Law School, 45
LEAD, 32, 73, 130, 170, 176, 232, 235
Leadership, 19, 26, 30, 45, 63, 85, 94, 99, 131-
    134, 144, 148, 151, 153-154, 167, 170, 179-
    180, 184, 246
Leadership
    Education, 170
    Institute, 167
Learning Styles, 34
Legacy, 8, 28, 33, 133, 158, 160-161, 180, 200-
    201
Legacy
    Status, 158, 160
    Student, 8, 33, 161, 200-201
Legatee, 242
Letters of Commendation, 93, 245
Liberal Admissions, 127
Liberal Arts, 39, 231, 233, 243
Liberal Arts Colleges, 39
Life List, 11-12, 44
Lifetime Learning Credit, 241, 243
Louisiana State, 139
Loyola Marymount, 139

Magnet School, 243
Marines, 24
Masons, 147, 181, 194
Massachusetts Comprehensive Assessment System,
    50
Massachusetts Institute of Technology, 39
Master Degrees, 45
Match, 16, 86, 137, 142, 243
Matriculation Agreements, 235
MBA, 221
MCAS, 50
McCormick Place, 43
Mentoring, 26, 57, 135, 145
Merchant Marine, 38
Merit
    Qualification, 194
    Scholar, 91, 94, 244
    Scholar Designees, 94
    Scholarship, 91-95, 102, 244-246
    Scholarship Awards, 93-95

Scholarships, 94, 188, 225, 244-245
Merit-based, 200, 243
Merit-Based Aid, 243
Meyerhoff Scholars Program, 45
Miami University of Ohio - Junior Scholars
    Program, 170
Michigan, 37, 139
Michigan State, 37
Middle School Plan, 34, 76, 104, 154, 290
Middle Years Program, 72
Middlebury College, 39
Milwaukee Institute of Art, 44
Minimum GPA, 75, 166
Minor, 243
Minority, 202, 243
MIT, 18, 39, 89
Modified Block, 241
MonopolyTM, 67
Morehouse College, 44, 159
Morgan State University, 127
Mt. Holyoke, 202
Mu Alpha Theta, 135
Multiple Intelligences, 34, 154
Music
    Honor Society, 135
    Theory, 71
Musicians, 145
My Stat Sheet, 28

NACAC, 42, 244
NACDA, 243
NAIA, 243
NASSAP, 206, 234
National
    Achievement Program, 96-97, 243
    Achievement Scholar, 33, 111, 123
    Achievement Scholar Recognition, 111
    Achievement Scholars, 7, 96
    Achievement Scholarship, 91, 102, 123, 243
    Achievement Scholarship Program, 91
    AP Scholar, 70, 232
    Association of College Directors, 243
    Association of College Directors of Athletics,
    243
    Association of Intercollegiate Athletics, 243
    Association of Secondary School Principals,
    206, 234
    Awards, 91
    Beta, 135
    College Fairs Program, 42
    Collegiate Athletic Association, 244
    Commission, 38

FFA, 135
Forensic League, 135
Geographic Magazine, 15
Junior College Athletic Association, 245
Letter of Intent, 200, 233
Merit Program, 91, 95-96, 243
Merit Scholar, 91, 244
Merit Scholar Qualifying Test, 244
Merit Scholarship, 91-92, 95, 102, 244-246
Merit Scholarship Corporation, 91, 246
Merit Scholarship Program, 91-92, 95
Merit Scholarship Qualifying Test, 245-246
Merit Scholarships, 94, 244-245
Universities, 39
Young Leaders Conference, 135
Youth Science Camp, 171
Naval Academy, 38
Navy, 24
NBA, 28, 30, 138
NCAA
    Clearinghouse, 3, 25, 27, 52-53, 105, 109,
        140, 224-225, 244, 248
    Division I-A Student-Athlete Graduation Rates,
        84
    Freshman, 138
    Guide, 52-53, 140
    Initial-Eligibility Clearinghouse, 53, 140
    Senior, 138
    Student, 139
Need-based, 8, 130, 202, 239, 244, 248-249
Need-based Aid, 202, 244
Need-blind, 8, 244
Need-blind Admissions, 8, 244
Need-conscious Admission, 244
Needs Analysis, 235, 244
Nelly, 191
New York University, 205
Newsweek, x, 1
NFL, 28, 138
NHL, 28
Night School, 80, 106-107, 114-115
NJCAA, 245
NLI, 233
NMSC, 91-97, 243, 246
NMSQT, 91-93, 95-97, 114, 123, 243-246
NMSQT Selection Index, 92
NMSQT Student Bulletin, 95, 97
Nordic skiing, 141
Norfolk State University, 127
Norm-referenced, 235, 238, 242, 249
North Georgia College, 196
North Springs High School, v, 61, 74

Northeastern University, vii, 38, 40
Northeastern University College of Engineering, vii
Northwestern, 37, 139, 202
Notre Dame, 139
NRT, 238
NYU, 129

Office of Admissions, 160
Ohio, 37, 47, 139, 170
Ohio State, 37, 139
Online Applications, 237, 245
Online Classes, 106-107
Open Admissions, 127, 201, 245
Organizational Affiliation, 194
Out-of-State Student, 245
Ozarks, 38

P. E., 57, 107
Package Your Application, 213
Painting I, 60
Painting III, 61
Parallel Block, 241
Parent Loans, 245
Part-time, 210, 217, 242
Partial Qualifier, 245
Pell Grants, 239, 245
Penn, 36-37, 139, 160, 171-174, 242
Penn State, 37, 139, 171-172
Perkins Loans, 245
Personal Attributes, 184
Personal Qualities, vi, 4, 118, 149-150, 199
Personality Types, 34
Phi Beta Kappa, 239
Photograph, 13
Photography, 135-136, 194
Physical Education, 48-49, 113, 117, 241
Physical Science, 48-49, 53, 60, 82, 117
Physics, vii, 48-49, 64, 71, 88, 113, 117, 242
Plan Your Schedule, vi, 104
PLUS, 49, 78, 118, 196, 238, 245
Political Science, 248
Politicians, 145
Politics, 18, 71
Pomona College, 39
Portfolio, 3, 43, 65, 71
Possibly Qualified, 69
Post-graduate, 245
Postsecondary Programs, 73
Power of Your Subconscious Mind, 150
Pre-Algebra, ix
Pre-Calculus, ix, 55, 61, 87-88

Pre-College Program, 168, 171
Preferential Aid Package, 246
Preliminary
    SAT, 246
    Scholastic Achievement Test, 123
    Scholastic Aptitude Test, 244
Presidential Scholar, 33, 99, 246
Presidential Scholars, 99-100, 246
Primary Years Program, 72
Princeton Review, x, 39, 120, 246
Princeton University, 39
Private Counselors, 246
PROFILE, 3-4, 31, 62, 68, 83, 91, 123, 142, 214, 224, 226, 235, 242, 246
Promissory Note, 236, 246
Psychology, 44, 48, 58, 61-62, 68, 71, 177, 248

Quality Product, 185
Quartile, 246
Quiet Period, 246
Quintile, 246

R. O. T. C., 135
Rank, 4, 28, 62, 78, 80-82, 101, 114, 162, 231, 234, 236, 242, 246, 248
Reach, 46, 150, 246
Reach Schools, 46
Read Your Essay Aloud, 186
Recreational Games, 57, 60
Recruited-athlete, 26, 33, 131, 174, 200, 222
Recruiters, 33, 235-236, 238, 246
Regular Admissions, 204, 227, 237
Regular Student, 247
Remediation, 247
Reply Date, 233
Research Available Programs, 103
Reserve Officers, 247
Residential Campus, 247
Residential College, 247
Responses, 92, 207, 222
Résumé, 103, 213, 226, 233, 247
Rhode Island School of Design Pre-College Program, 171
RISD, 171
Robert C. Byrd Honors Scholarship, 91
Rock Hard Apps, 30, 160, 185
Rolling Admissions, 204, 222, 247
Roster Positions, 138
ROTC, 196, 247
Rutgers, 139

Safety Schools, 46

Salisbury University, 127

Salutatorian, 90, 247

SAR, 193, 212, 227, 236, 238, 247

SAT

    Program, 124-125

    Subject Tests Program, 126

    Subject Tests, 61, 63, 68, 111, 125, 205, 228, 248

    Reasoning Test, 118, 124, 247

SAT-9, 248

SATs, 19, 124

Savannah College of Art, viii, 44

SBIs, 170

Scholarship Book, 188

Scholarship Guide, 142

Scholastic Aptitude Test, 124, 244, 248

School District Curriculum Handbook, 106

School

    Guides, 34

    Profile, 4, 31, 62, 214

Science

    Club, 76, 135

    Honor Society, 135

    Magnet Seal, 61

    Reasoning, 231

Secondary School Report, 248

Selective Admissions, 248

Semifinalists, 93, 97-98, 245

Semifinalist, 92-93, 97-98, 245

SEOG, 196, 238-239, 248

Service-Cancelable Loans, 196

Shakespeare, 16

Shriners, 194

Siemens Westinghouse Competition, 102

Sigma Alpha Tau, 90

Single-Choice, 204, 237, 248

Single-Choice Early Action, 204, 237, 248

Sins of Omission, 209

Sleeping Bag Weekend, 41

Social Sciences, 243, 248

Social Studies, 48-49, 51, 53, 58, 60, 71-72, 75, 107, 109, 117, 166, 168, 235, 241

Socioeconomic, 4, 159-161

Sociology, 248

Solid Senior Year, 79

Sororities, 41, 239

Soul of American Tours, 41

Spanish, 15, 60, 71, 88, 109, 166, 168

Spanish III, 88

Special

    Interest Programs, 26

    Requirements, 52

Scholarship, 95

Scholarship Candidates, 95

Scholarships, 93, 95, 115

Specialized Majors, 62

Spelman College, 18, 127, 208

Sport Group Differences, 84

Sports Scholarships, 142

Spring Break, 110-111

Spring Semester, 74, 80

Squeeze Play, 248

SRF, 248

SSP, 169, 172

SSR, 248

SSS, 100-101, 238

Stafford Loans, 239, 248

Standard Aptitude Test, 247

Standardized Testing, vi, ix, 100, 118

Stanford Achievement Test Series, 248

Stanford University, 39, 203

State Department of Education, 47, 51, 100-102, 106, 196

State Scholar Programs, 101

State University ROTC Grant, 196

STDs, 21

Strengths, 28, 34, 52, 83, 110, 179, 235

Strong Candidate, x, 3, 200

Student

    Aid Report, 193, 247

    Athlete, 142

    Council, 30, 135

    Educational Opportunity Grant, 248

    Entry Requirements, 92, 96

    Government, 110, 130-131, 135, 144

    Planner, 106

    Release Form, 248

    Union, 41

Student-Athlete, 3, 53, 84, 105, 119, 139-140, 143, 224-225, 237, 248

Student-Athlete Graduation Rates, 84, 139

Student-Athletes, 52-53, 80, 83-84, 138, 140, 235-236, 238, 244-246

Student-Athletes Drafted, 138

Student-Athletes Men, 138

Studio Art, 68, 71

Study Abroad, 239, 248

Study Groups, 21, 85-86

Study Skills, 34, 56, 173

Submit Early Admissions, 225

Subsidized, 239, 248-249

Summer

    Business Institutes, 170

    Camps, 26, 28, 148, 163, 174

Enrichment, 164, 172
Planning, 163
Programs, 166, 168, 172-174
School, 55, 80, 106-107, 114-115, 163-164,
    167, 169
Science Program, 172
Study Program, 172
Sunshine State Standards, 238
Supplements, 206-207, 235
Support Services, 41
Swarthmore, 39, 199, 202
Syllabus, 76, 249
Sylvan Learning Centers, 120
Syracuse University, 205

TA, 217, 249
Talent Identification, 168
TASP, 172
Teach, 9, 15, 78, 136, 162, 249
Teamwork, 179, 184
Telluride Association, 172
Telluride Association Summer Programs, 172
Temple Youth Group, 135
Tennessee State, 45
TerraNova, 249
TerraNova CTBS, 249
Texas Tech, 139
The American University of Paris, 171-172
The College Fair, 42-43
The Common Application, 193, 205-207, 213,
    234
The Ivy League, 7, 18, 36, 118, 129
The Kaplan College Guide, x
The Princeton Review, x, 39, 120, 246
The Siemens Foundation, 102
TOEFL, 249
Top Colleges, 54, 57, 59, 67, 83, 88, 113, 199,
    223, 231
Top Ten Rankings, 39
Top-Ten List, 18, 44, 46-47, 62, 68, 76, 79, 111-
    112, 115, 125, 134, 188, 200, 211-212, 224
Total Graduation Credits, 49, 117
Tours, 26, 34, 37, 41, 174
Towson University, 127
Traditional Schedule, 240
Training Corps, 247
Transcript, 25, 30, 50, 52, 57-58, 192, 212-214,
    222, 224, 227-228, 244-245, 248-249
Transfer Credit, 76, 249
Transferring, 249
Trigonometry, ix
Tuck School of Business, 44

Tufts, 172-173
Tufts
    Summer High School Program, 172
    Summer Study, 173
    Summit, 173
    University, 172
Tuition, ix, xi, 1, 3, 38, 40, 67-68, 137, 159, 172-
    173, 191, 196, 203, 234-235, 237-238, 241,
    243, 245, 249
Tuition-free Schools, 38
Tutors, 19, 21, 24, 26, 28, 51, 64-65, 86-88, 114,
    178

U. S.
    Air Force Academy, 139
    Department of Education, 193, 196, 233, 238,
        240, 247
    Government, 71
    History, 55, 58, 71, 88, 110, 124, 199
    News, x, 34, 39
UC Davis, 167
UC Irvine, 167
UCLA, 139
UMass Amherst, 44-45, 139
UNC, 127, 139
UNC Chapel Hill, 127, 139
Undergraduate Students, 245, 248
United States Presidential Scholars Program, 99,
    246
United States Senate Youth Program, 102
University of
    California, 166-167
    Chicago, 39, 173, 231
    Chicago Young Scholars Program, 173
    Colorado, 171-172
    Connecticut, 139
    Dallas, 173
    Dallas Summer Study, 173
    FL, 202
    Georgia, 139
    Illinois, 40
    Iowa, 242
    Kentucky, 139
    Maryland Baltimore County, 44-45
    Massachusetts, 67, 127
    Miami, 139
    Michigan, 139
    New Hampshire, 173
    New Hampshire Upward Bound Summer
        Program, 173
    North Carolina, 202
    Pennsylvania, 39, 173, 202

Pennsylvania Programs, 173
Southern California, 28
Tennessee Knoxville, 45
Virginia, 127
Wisconsin, 166
University System of Georgia, 49
Unsubsidized Loans, 249
Upward Bound, 173-174
Upward Trend, 79
Urbana-Champaign, 40
US News, 202
USATF, 53, 137, 143, 147, 163-164
USC, 28, 139

Valedictorian, 90, 249
Vanderbilt, 139, 221
Varsity, x, 59, 61, 76, 80-81, 133, 135, 137, 144-145, 147, 200
Verbal Section, 57, 124
Veterinarian, 147
Viewbook, 249
Villa Julie College, 127
Virginia Tech, 202
Virtual Tour, 250
Volleyball, 240, 243
Volunteer, 4, 132, 136, 146, 162, 206-207, 210
Volunteer Hours, 4, 132

Wait List, 222, 250
Waiver of View Recommendations, 250
Wake Forest, 139, 202
Washington College, 127
Washington Post, 50
Weak Candidate, 201
Weaknesses, 28, 34, 52, 58, 83-84, 110, 112, 179, 235
Webb Institute, 38
Weight, 7, 57, 68, 79, 147, 239
Weight Training, 57, 147
Weighted-GPA, 61, 78, 82, 250
Well Qualified, 69
Wellesley College, 39, 202
Wesleyan University, 41
West Point, 38
West Virginia, 100-101, 127
West Virginia Governor Honor, 100
West Virginia University, 127
Westinghouse Competition, 33, 102
What Colleges Don't Tell You and Other Parents Don't Want You to Know, 158
Wheelock, 202

Williams College, 39
WNBA, 28, 138
Work Experience, 4, 38, 132, 206, 242
Workbook, 2-3, 9, 28, 41, 290
World History, 60, 71
Worst Learning Situations, 34
Writing Section, 7, 122, 124

Xavier, 44-45, 139

Yale, viii, 18, 36, 39, 44-45, 67-68, 127, 129, 139, 174, 203, 208, 231, 242, 247
Yale
    COA, 68
    Daily News Guide, 174
Yield, 250
YMCA, 41, 120, 137, 146-147, 194
Your
    Application, vi, 5-6, 21, 30, 42, 79, 89, 111, 132-133, 158, 162, 175, 177, 199-201, 204-209, 211, 213-216, 222, 225-226, 237
    Application Package, vi, 5, 30, 79, 177, 199-201, 205, 209, 214-216
    Essay, vi, 35, 134, 161, 175-177, 179, 181-186, 214-216
    Passions, 10, 18-19, 44, 103, 129, 217

— *Notes* —

— *Notes* —

— Notes —

— *Notes* —

— *Notes* —

— *Notes* —

— *Notes* —

— *Notes* —

— *Notes* —

— *Notes* —

www.rspublishing • (800) 524-2813 • (770) 518-0369 • FAX (770) 587-0862
Payment May Be Made By Money Order • Check • Credit Card • Purchase Order

Item #	Description	Unit Price X	Quantity	= Total
6545	College Planning Notebook (3-ring binder with tabs)	24.95		
6500	College-Bound Backpack	7.95		
6903	A High School Plan...College-Bound Dreams	19.95		
6903	A High School Plan...*Student Workbook*	15.95		
6945	A High School Plan...*Facilitator's Guide*	15.95		
6602	College Planning for High School Students	5.95		
6901	A Middle School Plan...College-Bound Dreams	15.95		
6906	A Middle School Plan...*Student Workbook*	15.95		
6601	College Planning for Middle School Students	5.95		
7201	Ten Steps to Helping Your Child Succeed in School	9.95		
7202	Ten Steps to Helping Your Child...*Workbook*	15.95		
6550	College-Bound Journal	5.95		
5601	The Eagles who Thought They were Chickens: Book	4.95		
5603	Eagles: *Student Activity Book*	5.95		
5602	Eagles: *Teacher's Guide*	9.95		
6510	College-Bound Pen-Highlighter	1.95		
5003	Follow Your Dreams: *Lessons That I Learned in Schl*	7.95		

Charge my: ❑ Visa ❑ Mastercard ❑ Discover ❑ American Express

Account Number _____ Security Code _____

Expiration Date _____ Signature _____

SUBTOTAL $ _____

Shipping (Subtotal x 10%)   _____

Add Handling   3.50

Georgia residents
add 6% Sales Tax   _____

DATE: _____ TOTAL _____

RISING SUN PUBLISHING
P.O. Box 70906
Marietta, GA 30007-0906

RISING SUN
PUBLISHING

☎ Phone toll-free: **1.800.524.2813**
FAX: **1.770.587.0862**
e-mail: orderdesk@rspublishing.com
web site: http://www.rspublishing.com

Name _____

Address _____

_____

City_____ State_____ Zip _____

Day Phone (____) _____ E-mail : _____

❑ *Check if you would like to receive our free monthly E-mail newsletter*